RISK: PHILOSOPHICAL
PERSPECTIVES

From airport security to nuclear power, from safety on trains to public health scares, debates about risk are rarely out of the headlines. How can we determine an acceptable level of risk? Should these decisions be made by experts, or by the people they affect? How should safety and security be balanced against other goods, such as liberty?

Risk: Philosophical Perspectives is the first collection to examine the philosophical dimensions of these pressing practical problems. In this outstanding volume, Tim Lewens gathers an impressive collection of new essays from leading scholars exploring the full range of philosophical implications of risk.

Written in a clear and accessible style, the chapters in this collection cover the key areas of:

- risk and ethics
- risk and rationality
- risk and scientific expertise
- risk and lay knowledge
- the objectivity of risk assessment
- risk and the precautionary principle
- risk and terror.

This book is essential reading for all students and professionals interested in the philosophical dimensions of risk and an invaluable resource for those in related subjects such as politics, sociology and law.

Contributors: Carl F. Cranor, Sven Ove Hansson, Martin Kusch, Tim Lewens, D.H. Mellor, Adam Morton, Stephen Perry, Martin Peterson, Alan Ryan, Per Sandin, Cass R. Sunstein, Jonathan Wolff.

Tim Lewens is Senior Lecturer in the Department of History and Philosophy of Science at the University of Cambridge. He is the author of *Organisms and Artifacts* (2004) and *Darwin* (Routledge, 2006).

RISK:
PHILOSOPHICAL
PERSPECTIVES

Edited by Tim Lewens

Routledge
Taylor & Francis Group

LONDON AND NEW YORK

First published 2007
by Routledge
2 Park Square, Milton Park, Abingdon, Oxon OX14 4RN

Simultaneously published in the USA and Canada
by Routledge
711 Third Avenue, New York, NY 10017, USA

Routledge is an imprint of the Taylor & Francis Group, an informa business

Typeset in Goudy by Taylor & Francis Books

British Library Cataloguing in Publication Data
A catalogue record for this book is available from the British Library

Library of Congress Cataloging in Publication Data
Risk : philosophical perspectives / edited by Tim Lewens.
p. cm.
Includes bibliographical references and index.
1. Risk assessment 2. Risk management. I. Lewens, Tim.
HM1101.R587   2007
302'.12–dc22   2006039490

ISBN10: 0–415–42283–3 (hbk)
ISBN10: 0–415–42284–1 (pbk)
ISBN10: 0–203–96259–1 (ebk)

ISBN13: 978–0–415–42283–3 (hbk)
ISBN13: 978–0–415–42284–0 (pbk)
ISBN13: 978–0–203–96259–6 (ebk)

CONTENTS

CONTENTS

ACKNOWLEDGEMENTS

My greatest debt is, of course, to the philosophers who have contributed to this book. In every case they responded enthusiastically to the suggested briefs, their submissions arrived on time, and the end-results of their labours have been extremely impressive. I also owe a significant debt to Tony Bruce at Routledge for his encouragement and refreshing efficiency in connection with this project. Christina McLeish in the History and Philosophy of Science Department in Cambridge gave me invaluable editorial assistance. Finally, I am grateful to David Slavin, of Pfizer's Business Innovation Unit. He has shown considerable vision in appreciating the importance of the conceptual problems presented by risk, and research grants from Pfizer have been instrumental in enabling the completion of this volume.

Tim Lewens
Cambridge,
August 2006

NOTES ON CONTRIBUTORS

Carl F. Cranor, Professor of Philosophy at the University of California, Riverside, has written widely on philosophic issues concerning risks, science and the law. He has published *Regulating Toxic Substances: a philosophy of science and the law* (Oxford University Press, 1993) and *Toxic Torts: science, law and the possibility of justice* (Cambridge University Press, 2006), as well as co-authoring *The Identification and Regulation of Carcinogens* (US Congress, 1987). He served on California's Proposition 65 Science Advisory Panel as well as its Electric and Magnetic Fields Science Advisory Panel.

Sven Ove Hansson is Professor of Philosophy and Head of the Department of Philosophy and the History of Technology, Royal Institute of Technology, Stockholm. He is the author of numerous books and articles on ethics and the philosophy of risk, including *Setting the Limit: occupational health standards and the limits of science* (Oxford University Press, 1998) and *The Structure of Values and Norms* (Cambridge University Press, 2001).

Martin Kusch is Professor of Philosophy and Sociology of Science at the University of Cambridge. His current main research interests are in philosophy of the social sciences, social epistemology, and the sociology of scientific knowledge. His most recent books are *Knowledge by Agreement* (Oxford University Press, 2002) and *A Sceptical Guide to Meaning and Rules* (Acumen, 2006).

Tim Lewens is Senior Lecturer in the Department of History and Philosophy of Science at the University of Cambridge, where he is also a fellow of Clare College. His research focuses on topics in the philosophy of science, the philosophy of biology and biomedical ethics. He has acted as a consultant to industry on matters related to risk, regulation and innovation. He is the author of two previous books: *Organisms and Artifacts* (MIT Press, 2004) and *Darwin* (Routledge, 2006).

D.H. Mellor is Emeritus Professor of Philosophy in the University of Cambridge and a fellow of the British Academy and of the Australian Academy of the Humanities. He works mostly in metaphysics, his main publications being *The Matter of Chance* (Cambridge University Press, 1971), *Matters of Metaphysics* (Cambridge University Press, 1991), *The Facts of Causation* (Routledge, 1995), *Real Time II* (Routledge, 1998) and *Probability: a philosophical introduction* (Routledge, 2005).

Adam Morton holds a Canada Research Chair in epistemology and decision theory at the University of Alberta. He is the author of *Frames of Mind: constraints on the common-sense conception of the mental* (Oxford University Press, 1980), *Disasters and Dilemmas: strategies for real-life decision-making* (Blackwell, 1990), *The Importance of Being Understood: folk psychology as ethics* (Routledge, 2002) and *On Evil* (Routledge, 2006). He is now working on a book about how we manage our cognitive limitations, and on a textbook teaching logic through databases.

Stephen Perry is the John J. O'Brien Professor of Law and Professor of Philosophy at the University of Pennsylvania, and the Director of the Institute for Law and Philosophy there. Before coming to Penn he was a faculty member at the New York University School of Law and the McGill University Faculty of Law. He teaches and writes in the general areas of jurisprudence, tort theory, the philosophy of responsibility and political philosophy.

Martin Peterson works in the Department of History and Philosophy of Science in Cambridge. He received his PhD in philosophy in 2003 from the Royal Institute of Technology in Stockholm. His main interests are the philosophy of risk, decision theory and ethics.

Alan Ryan is Warden of New College and Professor of Political Theory at the University of Oxford.

Per Sandin received his PhD from the Royal Institute of Technology, Stockholm, Sweden, in 2005. The topic of his dissertation *Better Safe than Sorry* was the precautionary principle. His current research interests include the philosophy of risk, military ethics, and the ethics of crisis management and disaster preparedness.

Cass R. Sunstein is Karl N. Llewellyn Distinguished Service Professor at the University of Chicago, Law School and Department of Political Science, and is the author of many books, including *Risk and Reason* (Cambridge University Press, 2002), *Laws of Fear* (Cambridge University Press, 2005) and *Worst-Case Scenarios* (Harvard University Press, 2007).

Jonathan Wolff is Professor of Philosophy at University College London. He is the author of *Robert Nozick* (Polity Press, 1991), *An Introduction to Political Philosophy* (Oxford University Press, 1996), *Why Read Marx Today* (Oxford University Press, 2002) and, with Avner de-Shalit, *Disadvantage* (Oxford University Press, 2007), as well as papers in contemporary political philosophy.

He works as a consultant on the ethics of risk for the railway industry, and is currently a member of the Academy of Medical Science Working Party on the future of the regulation of drugs. His present research concerns a number of issues connecting philosophical theory and practice, including safety, disability, health and crime.

INTRODUCTION

Risk and philosophy

Tim Lewens

The philosophical dimensions of risk

In May 2005, Tony Blair, the UK Prime Minister, explained his choice of topic to an audience at University College London:

> I want to talk today about a particular problem my experience has led me to identify. It is an issue that seems more of a talking point than an issue of policy; that has many different facets to it; that is little discussed in the way I'm about to discuss it; but which, on the basis of my experience, if it goes wrong, has the capacity to do serious damage to our country.
>
> It is what I call a sensible debate about risk in public policy-making. In my view, we are in danger of having a wholly disproportionate attitude to the risks we should expect to run as a normal part of life. This is putting pressure on policy-making, not just in Government but in regulatory bodies, on local government, public services, in Europe and across parts of the private sector – to act to eliminate risk in a way that is out of all proportion to the potential damage.
>
> (Blair 2005)

Philosophy is a subject often believed to have little relevance to 'real-world issues', but Blair's practical concerns immediately raise questions of a philosophical nature. He is right, of course, that we should purge ourselves of 'wholly disproportionate' attitudes to risk. The problem is to say which attitudes are disproportionate. Blair's comments resonate with a debate which, as I write in June 2006, is once again making regular appearances in UK newspapers. This is the debate over whether to build nuclear power stations. Some say nuclear power can provide cheap, clean energy. This is a priority in an age where concern over the effects of global warming is escalating, while the desire to enjoy the energy-hungry fruits of technological advance shows no sign of diminishing. Others point to the terrible and lasting consequences of the Chernobyl disaster, to fears of terrorist groups gaining control of fissile material and to the potential environmental problems associated with the disposal of nuclear waste. One can imagine allegations of a 'disproportionate' attitude to risk being slung by those on both sides of the debate. Does the pro-nuclear lobby have an unrealistic attitude to the risks of global warming, elevating them to levels that make them prepared to back an unsafe technology that one should only turn to in desperate circumstances? Or does the anti-nuclear lobby have an unrealistic attitude to the risks of nuclear reactors and nuclear waste?

What are we to make of debates like this one? How can we tell whether nuclear power is a risk worth running? Is this the sort of question that can be addressed in precise numerical terms? Should we, for example, make an economic form of calculation? Or is this a kind of philistinism? And if the question is not amenable to quantitative analysis, what other tools might we use to clarify the nature of the options we have and to help us come to a decision? What sorts of people should be involved in the decision-making process? Is the question a purely scientific one, to be answered by appealing to nuclear physicists, or maybe engineers and ecologists? Should other experts – financial experts, perhaps – be involved, too? Or are experts the wrong sorts of people to make such wide-ranging decisions? Does a commitment to democracy require that the people on the Clapham omnibus, or at least their elected representatives, be charged with making the decision? But what do they know about nuclear power? Finally, how should we make a decision if we suspect that no one – the experts included – really knows what the risks might be? These are some of the fundamental questions about risk which this book addresses.

It is usual in introductions to collections of essays like this one for the editor simply to give a précis of each of the contributions which follows. This introduction will not take this form. The philosophy of risk is a sparsely populated field.[1] It is likely to be unfamiliar both to professionals of various sorts who deal with risk-related issues and to mainstream philosophers. Consequently, my aim in this introduction is to lay out some of the major philosophical questions raised by the topic of risk, in an effort to orient the reader to the general terrain on which these debates take place. I will also say a little about where on this terrain the contributions collected here are situated. But the best way to find out what their arguments are is simply to read them.

Comparing consequences

Decision-makers of all kinds frequently face situations where they must choose one of several risky options. These decision-makers might be regulators, government ministers, company executives, consumers, citizens or others. In order to illustrate the range of philosophical issues presented by decisions relating to risk, I will focus to begin with not on the case of nuclear power, but on the case of drug regulation. Drug regulators must decide whether to approve new medicines for marketing. How should these decisions be made? According to the major European regulator, the European Medicines Agency (EMEA), a drug should be approved when it has a 'favourable benefit/risk ratio'.[2] On the face of it, this is a sensible rule to use for making any risk-related decision, from the mundane ('Should I take my umbrella with me to the shops?') to the weighty ('Should a new safety system be installed on trains?'). But if we are serious about determining whether the benefits of a course of action outweigh the costs, then we need to find some way of comparing the consequences of our options (approve the drug or refuse it? take an umbrella or leave it at home?), even when those consequences are of very different kinds. What, for example, is the benefit-to-risk ratio of taking an umbrella with me to the shops? We can only give an answer if we can compare, among other things, the potential cost of carrying a superfluous weight (if it doesn't rain) against the potential benefit of staying dry (if it does). But how can we find a common currency in which to compare consequences of such different sorts?

Consider again the case of drugs. Let us suppose that we know from trial data that a new drug has two effects. It reduces the likelihood of breast cancer progressing and it increases the likelihood that people who take the drug will have a heart attack. Suppose, that is, that we have a clear scientific picture of the positive and negative effects of the drug. In reality, the first thing a regulator is likely to do in response to a profile such as this one is to ask whether there is any further intervention that might allow us to preserve the positive effect of the drug while reducing the negative effect. Perhaps, for example, another medicine is available, which eliminates the new drug's effect on heart attacks, but does nothing to disrupt its therapeutic effect on breast cancer. In such a case it seems wise to approve the new drug, with the proviso that it be taken in conjunction with this second modifying medicine.

Let us suppose, however, that there is no such effective modifier available. Suppose we know the drug's positive and negative effects, and we also know that there is no way to alter those effects. Scientific information of this sort is not sufficient to tell us whether the drug should be approved. We also need to have some criterion that will tell us whether the positive effect the drug has on breast cancer risk outweighs the negative effect it has on heart attack risk. Surprisingly, in the case of medicines regulation, there is no single accepted methodology for answering questions like this.[3] But there are plenty of options available. The most obvious way to assess the situation is to attempt to predict the likely number of lives the drug will save from breast cancer and the likely number of people the drug will cause to die from heart attack. This gives us a way of comparing the drug's good and bad effects in a single currency – human lives. And we might argue that the drug's benefit/risk ratio is 'favourable' if the number of lives saved from breast cancer is greater – or perhaps much greater – than the number of lives lost to heart attack.

There are, of course, several more sophisticated ways of comparing good and bad effects. Suppose that the drug in question typically extends the life of breast cancer sufferers by two years, except in a minority of cases where it brings death from heart attack in three months. It is a stretch to say that one has 'saved a life' when one has delayed death by two years. Even so, delaying death by two years is valuable, and one might think that if the drug produces heart attacks extremely rarely it should still be approved. How many heart attacks must the drug produce for it to be deemed unacceptably risky? Considerations like these might tempt us to consider the number of *years of life* the drug saves, rather than simply the number of *lives* saved.[4] But even this may not be sophisticated enough. What if the drug extends the lives of many people by two years, by doing little more than keeping them alive, without preserving their capacities to enjoy life? Here one might be suspicious of using 'life-years saved' as a measure of the overall worth of the drug. Intuitively, the worse the quality of life of those whose lives are extended, the fewer people need to suffer from heart attacks caused by the drug to tip the benefit/risk ratio away from approval. So in addition to considering how many life-years the drug is likely to save, we also need to consider the issue of the quality of those years. The case of drug regulation illustrates a general problem facing efforts to compare consequences of our decision options: attributes of decision outcomes that are comparatively easy to measure (such as lives saved) may only give a crude picture of the value of those options, while attributes that we would ideally wish to know of (such as quality of life) are hard to measure in a satisfactory way.[5]

Clearly, then, the question of how to determine whether the benefit/risk ratio is favourable for some drug is a difficult one. However, there are reasons to think that compared with many other decisions that policy-makers face regarding risk, drug-safety decisions are in fact rather easy. Drug regulators such as the EMEA or the FDA (the US regulator) are charged with deciding whether a drug is safe and efficacious. They do not need to decide whether the drug is cost-effective – that is, whether the health benefit the drug gives is worth the price.[6] This means that drug regulators are primarily in the business of comparing effects of a similar type. They need to ask only whether the benefits to health of a drug outweigh the costs to health. There is no need for them to factor in the price of the drug on the cost side. The fact that positive and negative effects are of the same broad type makes it easier to find a common currency in which to measure those effects.

It is far more difficult to decide how to weigh risks and benefits of a decision option when the relevant effects of that option are of completely different types. Suppose, for example, an official is considering whether to approve the building of a set of wind-turbines on an area of moorland. On the plus side we might list, among other things, the renewable energy and employment opportunities which the wind-farm provides. On the minus side, the turbines are noisy, their construction will disturb an important habitat, and many local residents regard wind-farms as eyesores. These effects are of wholly different kinds, and this makes it much harder to decide whether the overall 'benefit/risk ratio' of the wind-farm is favourable. How much energy production makes up for the disturbance of a moorland habitat? How offended do local residents need to be by the aesthetic appearance of the farm before the creation of new jobs is outweighed?

Economists have devised various tools for thinking through problems like these. In order to understand the rough rationale behind some of the best-known economic tools for making risk-related decisions, it is easiest to begin with a simple example. Suppose you are a cyclist, and you wish to reduce your risk of injury when cycling. You decide to buy a helmet. You go to the cycle shop, and find that helmets range greatly in price according to how effective they claim to be. You trust these claims, but you decide that the most expensive one, even though it promises the highest level of protection, is not worth the money. You settle for a moderately expensive helmet. The fact that you make this decision shows that you make some sort of calculation – perhaps not a very precise one – about how much money you are willing to pay in return for some benefit. In this case the benefit is a reduction in risk, more specifically a reduction in risk of cranial injury. In general, it seems that the more you are willing to pay, the greater the value you attach to the outcome in question. If, for example, you would pay millions for a slightly better cycle helmet, this suggests you place enormous value on cranial integrity – far more value than if you would turn the better helmet down the moment the price gets above twenty pounds.

Sometimes people who are new to economic models of decision-making are shocked at the apparently callous way in which these models attach a financial value to reducing risks of death or injury, as though one could say how much a human life is worth. Economists respond, quite plausibly, by pointing out that we make decisions of this sort all the time with regard to our own lives, for example when we decide that a better cycle helmet is not worth the price. Jonathan Wolff's contribution to this collection looks at these worries in detail.

One way, and perhaps not the best way, of interpreting the economic decision-making tool known as Risk Cost–Benefit Analysis (RCBA) is as a method which uses money as a common currency for measuring the value of consequences of very different kinds. RCBA does this by asking how much people would be willing to pay to have (or to avoid) those consequences. If I would be willing to pay £10 for a slightly better cycle helmet, but £100,000 to own a Monet, this suggests that in some sense I value owning a Monet far more than I value a small increase in safety on my bike. We can use these monetary figures to calculate a ratio which (perhaps) represents how much better it would be if I were to own a Monet than if I were to receive an upgraded bike helmet – it would be ten thousand times better. And since we can use this tool to compare the value of very different consequences – a reduction in risk of cranial injury compared with the acquisition of a painting – we can also (perhaps) use it to decide whether the overall benefits of building a wind-farm outweigh the overall costs. Some of the costs and benefits of building a wind-farm can be directly expressed in monetary terms. These will include the building costs, the market value of the electricity the wind-farm is likely to produce and so forth. For other costs and benefits we cannot do this. But we might quantify the aesthetic offence caused by the farm simply by asking how much money people would be willing to pay to avoid having to see it. In this way we end up with a figure (expressed in some monetary currency) that represents the total benefit delivered by the wind-farm, and another figure that expresses the total cost. If the first number is bigger than the second, it is better to build the wind-farm than not to build it.

Readers will immediately recognise several potential problems with this way of making decisions. Consider the fact that I would be willing to pay £100,000 to own a Monet. This certainly gives an indication of how much I want a Monet. It is not so clear that it reliably indicates how good it would be for me to receive a Monet. This is because the amount of money I would be willing to pay for a Monet depends in part on how rich I am, and also on how much I know about the state of the art market. But the question of how good it would be for me to have a Monet does not seem to depend on either of these things. (It might depend on how able I am to appreciate art, but it does not depend on my knowledge of how much money similar paintings are selling for.) This leads on to the main point I wish to stress here, which concerns the issue of whether RCBA is an objective methodology for deciding whether the costs of some proposed course of action outweigh its benefits. It might seem as though the answer is 'yes' simply on the grounds of the apparently precise, quantitative aspect of RCBA. But this conclusion is questionable. Suppose I ask someone how much he would be willing to pay to avoid a 10 per cent risk of getting cancer. I am asking him how much cash he estimates he would part with to reduce that risk. Considerable argument would be needed to show that, for any given individual, this measures the true value of this aspect of his health. Someone who is deeply depressed, for example, might even say that he would pay money for an increased risk of cancer. It does not follow from this response that the person's health has negative value. The most that follows is that the respondent *believes* his health has negative value, and we can imagine trying to persuade him that he is wrong about this.

In fact, someone's willingness to pay might not even measure the value which the person in question believes (rightly or wrongly) that his health has. Giving a response to the question 'How much would you pay to avoid a 10 per cent risk of getting cancer?' surely feels a little like plucking a number out of the air, and which number is plucked may depend on all kinds of incidental facts about whether the question is posed in emotive or neutral language, whether the person has recently been scared witless by watching hospital dramas, whether the person thinks that it is primarily the job of the state to pay for healthcare, and so forth.[7] These factors all mean that different people give very different answers to questions of this sort. In the economic analysis of workplace safety, for example, where the question under scrutiny is whether some safety improvement measure is worth the cost of introducing it, the analyst consequently needs to make use of *average* responses to the question of how much one would be willing to pay for some sort of risk reduction. None of these thoughts shows that economic methods of cost/benefit analysis are worthless. If a government is considering spending public money on some project to protect public safety, it is surely worth finding out how much of her own money the average taxpayer would be willing to spend on the same project. Indeed, perhaps a better framework for understanding the importance of RCBA is not as a way of determining what the value of some option is, but rather as a way of estimating how an average person would be likely to allocate resources on risk reduction, if the decision were left up to him rather than a centralised agency. In any case, the fact that RCBA is quantitative and backed by a clear methodology does not show that it represents an objective assessment of the value of, say, building a wind-farm.

The articles in this volume from Wolff and Peterson extend these explorations of quantitative methods of risk assessment. Woolf focuses on how we should interpret the so-called 'Value of Preventing a Fatality' (VPF). This is a figure, expressed in monetary terms, which gives guidance to decision-makers regarding how much money it is worth spending in order to reduce the risk of accidents. As before, this figure is determined by asking a series of people how much they would be willing to pay in return for a reduction in risk of death. Martin Peterson's article looks in detail at the difficulties that arise when we try to choose between options that have consequences of very different sorts. He examines a distinct methodology – 'multi-attribute risk analysis' – which is meant to get around these difficulties.

Beyond consequences

We have just looked at the problem of assessing decision options, when those options have consequences which do not seem comparable in any common currency. A second problem for decision-makers is presented by so-called *distributional* issues. Here the question is not simply what the overall consequences of a course of action are, but how those consequences are spread around the people whom they affect.

RCBA attempts, very roughly speaking, to add up the likely overall good consequences of a decision option and to subtract from that figure the likely overall bad consequences. Whichever option is likely to have the best overall balance sheet is the option we should take. RCBA, at least when stated in this simple way, is committed to the general ethical stance known as *consequentialism*. A consequentialist argues that the overall consequences of an action determine whether it is right or wrong. Utilitarianism, for example, is the best-known form of consequentialism. Utilitarians say that the right action is the one which produces the greatest net quantity of welfare (for classic utilitarianism welfare is understood to mean happiness), regardless of how welfare is distributed.

For a flavour of the problems typically levelled against consequentialism, consider three alternative policy options. One leaves a small group of people much better off, while the majority are a little worse off than before. The second leaves everyone somewhat better off than before. The third leaves a small group of people much worse off than before, and it leaves the majority quite a bit better off. Suppose, as seems possible, that the net effect on population-wide welfare of each of these policies is the same. In this case, 'pure' forms of consequentialism say that ethically speaking these three options are on a par, for they are identical in terms of how much welfare is produced. They differ only in what, for the consequentialist, is the irrelevant question of whether that welfare is spread evenly over the population, or whether it is concentrated in particular sub-groups. Pure consequentialism strains against our intuitions here. Many people think that we should not be neutral between these three options. The second option is *fairer* than the other two, and this seems to be an advantage of that option.[8]

RCBA inherits some of the general problems that face consequentialism. If we advocate taking a course of action when it presents a favourable net balance of risks and benefits, we appear not to take into account how those risks and benefits are distributed. Let us return once again to our wind-farm scenario. One might simply ask (among other things) how many jobs will be created by the farm, and how many people will be offended by the sight of it. But merely totting up good and bad effects in this way seems to miss out an important feature of the decision, namely which people suffer the costs, and which people reap the benefits. Are the people who have to look at the wind-farm each day the same people who benefit from the employment opportunities the farm offers? Or do the jobs primarily go to remote managers, who need rarely visit the site, and who are unlikely to live near to it? As Sven Ove Hansson points out in his contribution, questions not merely about the relative magnitudes of risks and benefits, but also about which individuals those risks and benefits fall on, seem relevant to decisions about risk. Other things being equal, it is preferable for the people who will suffer the bad consequences of some choice to be the same people who will enjoy the good consequences.

I wrote above that decisions regarding drug safety are, if anything, less problematic than many other decisions about risk. Distributional problems are partially avoided in the case of drug safety because here the people who may potentially benefit from some drug are typically the same as those who may suffer from its side-effects. For this reason the decisions faced by drug regulators are in some ways easier than the decisions faced by a committee charged with choosing where to site a wind-farm, or a new nuclear power station, where distributional issues need to be taken into account.

Note that these distributional worries are just one set of issues which appear to have ethical relevance, yet which are hard to capture in standard consequentialist models for decision-making. We can list others. It is plausible, for example, that risks which a person *chooses* to run can legitimately be much higher than risks which are *imposed* by some other agent. A regulator might therefore decide that acceptable risks to health from, say, white-water rafting, should be much higher than acceptable risks to health from drinking tap water. Or consider the question of the status of the people who are exposed to risk: a regulator might insist that the risks to which children are exposed should be lower than the risks to which adults are exposed. Jonathan Wolff points out in his contribution that we might think it legitimate for a rail company to focus more time and money on ensuring safety standards for train passengers than it does on ensuring safety standards for trespassers on the line. Carl Cranor's contribution lays out several more apparent blind-spots of consequentialist models of risk assessment, and responds to them by sketching the basic features of a non-consequentialist theory of acceptable risk.

Adam Morton exposes many other important features of the options open to a decision-maker, which may be obscured by simple consequentialist models. To give just one example of the kind which Morton uses to motivate his arguments: imagine you are offered a free choice between two gambles. The first gives you a 50 per cent chance of losing £10, and a 50 per cent chance of gaining £110. We might assess the consequences of this gamble by multiplying the value of each of the outcomes (lose £10 and gain £110) by their respective chances to give a net expected value. So we have (–£10 x 0.5) + (£110 x 0.5), which gives us a net expected gain of £50. The second gamble gives you a 50 per cent chance of losing £10 million, and a 50 per cent chance of gaining £110 million. If we assess the likely consequences of this gamble in the same way, we find, of course, that this gamble gives us a net expected gain of £50 million. Our way of assessing consequences in terms of net expected value tells us that the consequences of the second gamble are much better (a million times better) than the consequences of the first gamble. If we are supposed to choose the option with the best consequences, we should choose the second gamble. But on reflection it seems perfectly rational to prefer the first gamble, on the grounds that although the net expected value of the second gamble is much higher, there is also a significant possibility of losing far more. If we take the first gamble we have a 50 per cent chance of losing £10. If we take the second gamble we have a 50 per cent chance of losing £10 million. We might be unwilling to run a risk of losing so much, even though we also have a good chance of winning an enormous amount. Morton argues that any method for making decisions needs to be able to represent the relevance of these sorts of considerations.

One might respond to this argument by saying that the problem is not with the consequentialist rule of choosing the option with the highest net expected value, but only with our naïve assumption that the values of the different outcomes of the gambles correspond to the money gained or lost. The debt that follows from a loss of £10 million could be crippling, life-destroying, for many people. Except for the super-rich, losing £10 million is more than a million times worse than the trivial matter of losing £10. Indeed, one might add, this is precisely why those of us who are not rich might rationally refuse the second gamble. So long as we measure the value of outcomes in a way that is sensitive to such issues, the general consequentialist scheme for deciding according to net expected value is not put into doubt. Morton replies that this response will not suffice to undermine his basic claim that in addition to taking account of the net expected value of some option, decision-makers may also need to take into account such features as the size of the likely loss associated with that option. The relevance of Morton's argument to decisions about environmental policy, or military policy, should be clear.

Risk and ignorance

So far in this introduction we have looked at the problems posed for decision-makers by the need to compare consequences of different kinds, and the problems posed by the need to consider factors other than the net consequences of an option, such as the fairness of risk distributions. These problems arise even if we know exactly what the relevant consequences that might issue from some choice are, how likely those consequences are to occur, on whom they will fall, and so forth. Even if we knew exactly how likely it was for a projected nuclear power station to melt down, exactly which species would be damaged in its construction, exactly how many people would be employed and precisely who would get rich on the back of its construction, we would still face weighty problems in coming to a decision over whether to build the power station. Yet clearly we frequently do not know these things, or at least (and this is a slightly different problem), if some minority of experts do know the true risks of nuclear power, there are enough contrary opinions stated in equally authoritative voices to make it difficult for anyone else to know what those risks are. Those who speak against nuclear power sometimes argue that the comparative novelty of the technology means that we do not have access to a long enough track-record to be able to say with any justification what the real risks are. And under circumstances like these, they say, it is best to err on the side of caution.

The general message that it is 'better to be safe than sorry' is usually taken to be codified in European Law in the form of the so-called 'precautionary principle'. This principle explicitly dominates most European regulatory policy and some (e.g. Sunstein 2005) argue that it implicitly features in some US regulatory policy.[9] Per Sandin's article in this collection focuses on the precautionary principle, but it is also discussed by other contributors to the volume, including Alan Ryan and Adam Morton. Perhaps the most basic challenge for the precautionary principle can be illustrated using an example. Consider the case of mobile phones. A few years ago some groups of people began to express concern that mobiles might 'fry your brains'.[10] It might seem obvious that even if we have rather scant evidence in favour of this claim, we should nonetheless act as though it were true, in order to be on the safe side. Perhaps there should be public health campaigns to discourage children from carrying mobiles, for example. But this policy decision may also carry significant risks, and not just to mobile phone companies. Sometimes the fact that children have mobiles enables them to get help in emergency situations. So is the precautionary act to discourage children from carrying mobiles to save the frying of their brains or to encourage them to carry mobiles to save their lives (Lewens 2004)?

Similar dilemmas arise in most cases where we might hope to err on the side of caution (Sunstein 2005). Is the precautionary act to insist on exhaustive safety testing of new drugs before they are licensed in order to reduce the chances that people will suffer adverse side-effects? Or does this policy itself threaten disaster, by unnecessarily delaying access to life-saving medicines? Do we err on the side of caution by refusing to build nuclear power stations? Or is the precautionary act to build a small number as a hedge against the potentially disastrous contribution to global warming from coal- and oil-fired power stations? In all of these cases it is hard to say anything sensible about what we should do unless we know something about, for example, whether mobiles really do fry your brains, how likely children really are to be saved from abduction by using their phones, how many people will suffer adverse reactions from some particular drug, how many people the drug is likely to save, and so forth. The precautionary principle is sometimes touted as a regulatory tool to turn to when our knowledge of risk is poor; however, these examples illustrate that without some knowledge of risk it is hard to tell which regulatory response is most likely to keep us safe. None of these considerations shows that the precautionary principle should be abandoned. The challenge for precaution is to find some coherent advice which decision-makers can adopt in cases where their knowledge is partial and they wish to proceed carefully. By carefully dissecting the diverse issues raised by precaution, Sandin's article begins this more constructive work of developing a defensible understanding of what precaution demands.

Although Hugh Mellor does not discuss the precautionary principle directly in his contribution, his essay is nonetheless directly relevant to debates over precaution, for it concerns the question of how we should act when we are comparatively ignorant of risk-related facts. The question of whether, for example, mobile phones should be discouraged among children, depends on facts about how likely mobiles are to cause brain cancer, how likely they are to save children from abduction, and so forth. Mellor is sceptical of the existence of any sensible decision principle that will tell you what you ought to do if you are completely ignorant of these facts. Consequently, if a regulator is completely ignorant of these things, then the regulator simply does not know whether mobiles should be discouraged among children. One might think that Mellor's argument has little practical relevance, for we often are in situations where we are comparatively ignorant, and we still need to make a decision – even if it is a decision to do nothing. One might think it is unhelpful to be told there is no principle to turn to here. But Mellor points out that total ignorance is quite rare. We know, for example, that mobiles are not instantly deadly to the user, and that lost children have sometimes been found in virtue of their calling home. He also argues that in many cases a knowledge of the rough facts will suffice to make a good decision. Even if we do not know precisely how many people's brains will be fried by mobiles, a ballpark figure will often be good enough. So comparative ignorance need not leave us unable to make sensible decisions. What is more, ignorance can be ameliorated by research. And in those rare cases where we really are wholly ignorant, it may be best to admit that without access to some of the relevant facts, our decision is nothing more than a stab in the dark.

Risk and politics

I turn now to a series of issues that concern what we might call the politics of risk. Risk-related decisions, especially when they concern the regulation of unfamiliar technology, typically have two contrasting aspects. First, decisions about which drugs to approve, whether and where to site nuclear power stations, and so forth, are decisions which affect interested parties of diverse kinds. In the case of drug safety these parties might include disease-sufferers, their families, the health systems that pay for drugs, pharmaceutical companies, research scientists and so forth. A decision to build a new nuclear power station might affect the people who would live near to the power station, construction companies that might build it, employees who might work in it, future generations who will have to deal with nuclear waste, and future generations who will have to deal with global warming. The second aspect of risk-related decisions arises from the fact that their outcomes turn, at least partly, on technical questions of various sorts. In the case of drug-regulation these questions are likely to focus on which diseases the drug can be used to treat, what impact the drug has on those diseases, what adverse reactions it may cause, how likely those reactions are to occur, and what measures might be taken to reduce their incidence or severity.

To the extent that we stress this second aspect of technology, we are likely to favour a *technocratic* model for making decisions about risk. This view says that risk-related decisions should be placed in the hands of scientific experts whose knowledge – knowledge which laypeople do not have – enables them to say what the right decision is. To the extent that we stress the first aspect of technology, we are likely to favour a *participatory* model for making decisions about risk. Participatory models advocate canvassing views from many different groups, including non-experts, when risk-related decisions are made. The reasons offered in support of participation are diverse. They often include a conviction that laypersons are not as ignorant about technical matters as one might intuitively suppose, a belief that oversight from laypersons is a useful check on the bias which may exist among industry-sponsored scientists, a general sense that legitimate decisions in a democracy can only be made by a representative sample of people and so forth.

I have already set up the distinction between technocracy and participation in too simplistic a manner, and explaining some of the ways in which it might need to be refined will also help to set the stage for the essays in this collection which discuss the political aspects of risk. First, no sensible person will argue that decisions about risk can be made on the basis of scientific expertise alone. Consider again the decision about whether to build a wind-farm on an area of moorland. Even if scientific expertise enables us to determine precisely what consequences this decision is likely to have – which species will be threatened, how many people will be employed, how much power will be generated, and so forth – this sort of scientific expertise does not enable us to decide whether the wind-farm should be built, because it does not tell us about the comparative value of these different outcomes. An engineer may be able to say how likely a wind-turbine is to collapse and kill someone, and how much power the turbine will produce, but the engineer does not have expertise when it comes to answering the question of how low the probability of a fatal accident needs to be in order for it to be outweighed by some level of electricity-generating capacity. As we have seen, there are technical methods for answering these questions, but even they make an implicit appeal to non-experts, because they attempt to ascertain the relative values (or disvalues) of various outcomes by asking how much the average person would be willing to pay in order to avoid them.

The advocate of technocracy will not be much troubled by this. He is likely to say that when we wish to know the probabilities of various outcomes which our decisions might lead to, we should ask the experts. But when we wish to attach values to those outcomes, we should ask laypeople. It is worth pointing out here that the technocrat should not assume that the only experts worth consulting when it comes to ascertaining relevant probabilities are scientists and professionals in the field of risk assessment.[11] Consider the question of how likely it is for a wind-turbine to collapse. It is possible that local people have relevant knowledge here, which professional scientists and engineers might lack. A local farmer might have privileged knowledge relating to how winds gust at certain times of the year when scientific investigators have not been present, or perhaps relating to a little-known system of tunnels dug under the proposed building site. Or consider again the case of drug safety. A regulator needs to know, among other things, how efficacious a drug is. This depends, in part, on how likely its users are to be able to stick to the recommended dosing regime. Disease-sufferers who have experience of using the drug will be very well placed to answer these questions. Within this area of knowledge, disease-sufferers are experts.

So the technocrat might argue that scientific experts, aided on occasion by various sorts of non-professional experts who also have relevant knowledge, are the ones to tell us what probabilities to attach to various outcomes. Non-experts are the source of information regarding the values of those outcomes. When the two ingredients are combined a rigorous decision will follow.

This general recipe is roughly in tune with the frequent appeals government makes to the importance of 'sound science' for formulating risk policy. Several theorists have argued that it is a mistake to place too much weight on scientific opinion in this way.[12] They have also argued that the rhetoric of 'sound science' implies, falsely, that the scientific element of risk assessment and management is itself free of contentious or objectionable values.[13] These issues relating to science, risk and value are explored most directly in this volume by Hansson, but they also feature in the chapters by Kusch, Morton, Perry, Sandin and others. In extreme cases theorists have argued that resting risk policy on science can be counter-productive. This seems like an extraordinary assertion. If questions about whether to build nuclear power stations depend on facts about, for example, the chances of reactor meltdown, then surely scientists – the sorts of people who make it their business to acquire a detailed picture of these facts – are precisely the people to turn to for advice. In response, it is sometimes argued that what we might call the *theoretical ethos* of the scientist – the desire to discover the truth – is out of phase with what we might call the *practical ethos* of the regulator – the desire to ensure safety. The influential sociologist Ulrich Beck argues for this claim in a characteristically apocalyptic fashion:

> Scientists insist on the 'quality' of their work and keep their theoretical and methodological standards high in order to assure their careers and material success ... The insistence that connections are not established may look good for a scientist and be praiseworthy in general. When dealing with risks, the contrary is the case for the victims; *they multiply the risks* ... To put it bluntly, insisting on the *purity* of the scientific analysis leads to the pollution and contamination of air, foodstuffs, water, soil, plants, animals and people.
>
> (Beck 1992: 62)

Scientific readers may not like Beck's use of scare quotes around 'quality', or his claim that material success is the main driver behind the fastidious nature of scientific work. Even so, the underlying point he is making is worthy of examination, and returns us to the issue of precaution. Our estimates of the chances of various effects issuing from our actions are fallible. We need to bear in mind that we might be wrong about how much power a nuclear power station will produce or how likely the reactor is to melt down. Beck's claim is that scientists tend to be particularly unwilling to assert that something is the case unless they are sure of it. This is what he means when he writes of 'the insistence that connections are not established'. The theoretical ethos means that scientists wish to reduce their chances of saying something false, even if that means saying rather little.

Beck cannot be right that a general reliance on scientists will always lead us to underestimate real risks. We can grant him, for the sake of argument, that if

the regulator asks a cautious scientist 'Can you assure me that there is a significant risk associated with this technology?', then the scientist will say no,
that the evidence is not conclusive, even if in fact there is a significant risk.
But if the regulator instead asks the same scientist 'Can you assure me that
there is no significant risk associated with this technology?', then the scientist
will also say no, even if in fact the risk is negligible. Depending on what
questions we ask, reliance on scientists, coupled to the theoretical ethos, may
lead either to a lack of concern with significant risks or to an unnecessary
concern with trivial risks (so-called 'phantom risks'). Both outcomes can be
dangerous. What is correct about Beck's claim is that the regulator, unlike the
scientist, needs to consider the practical consequences – perhaps disastrous – of
refusing to act as though some proposition were true until one is sure that the
proposition is true. This does not show that we should do without scientific
expertise when making decisions about risk. However, Sven Ove Hansson
argues that considerations of this sort point to the need to modulate the way
that scientific belief feeds in to regulation.

Risk and psychology

There is an abundance of rich psychological work that has been done on the
question of how people reason about risk (e.g. Slovic 2000). An important set of
philosophical questions concerns the ethical and political consequences that we
might draw from this body of work. Much of it suggests that humans are very bad
at reasoning about risk. To take just one example, it seems that our judgements
of how likely an event of some kind is to occur depend on how easy we find it to
bring prominent examples of past events of the same kind to mind (Slovic *et al.*
2002). This rule of thumb has been called the 'availability heuristic'. National
media coverage of events like rail crashes interacts with the availability heuristic
to make people grossly over-estimate how likely further rail crashes are to occur.
In the aftermath of a rail accident people consequently refuse to travel on trains,
and use their cars instead, which are far more dangerous. Alan Ryan's contribution to this collection argues that terrorism relies for its potency on the existence
of error-prone rules of thumb of this kind. On Ryan's analysis, terrorism is able to
paralyse or impede effective government because terrorist acts are of just the sort
which human risk psychology finds it difficult to respond to in a rational way.

In several earlier publications, Cass Sunstein has drawn on the same tradition of psychological work as a premise for an argument in favour of placing
decisions relating to risk in the hands of experts (e.g. Sunstein 2002, 2005). He
has documented several characteristic mistakes which laypeople make in reasoning about risk. Sunstein acknowledges that scientists also make these mistakes (2005: 86), but he claims that 'when ordinary people disagree with
experts, it is often not because of competing value judgments, but because
ordinary people are more likely to fall prey to probability neglect' (2005: 87).
Primarily in order to ensure that the irrationality of the ordinary man does not

hijack policy formulation, Sunstein advocates using quantitative tools such as RCBA to discipline thought about risk. A regulator might be tempted, for example, to impose speed restrictions on rail lines following a crash. But is this the rational response to take? The added frustration which slow trains cause for rail travellers, coupled with a heightened aversion to using trains, might only increase the overall risk suffered by commuters who desert the trains in favour of roads. Sunstein has argued that the effort to undertake a formal analysis of regulatory options using RCBA can alert us to these potentially counter-productive effects of safety measures.

A little earlier I suggested that a technocratic model of risk regulation would leave decisions about risk in the hands of experts, more specifically scientists. This is not the only way of thinking about technocracy. A scientist may have expertise in a field relevant to some specific risk-based decision – the field of human physiology, or soil science, or conservation genetics. But expertise in one of these areas does not make the scientist an expert in the tools of risk analysis itself, tools like RCBA. While scientific experts will have an important role to play in Sunstein's technocracy, Sunstein perhaps gives even more weight to the work of experts in the general analysis of risk.

Martin Kusch's chapter argues against Sunstein's proposal for technocracy. Kusch is prepared to accept the existence of characteristic flaws in human reasoning about risk. Kusch claims instead that experts suffer from just the same handicaps in thinking about risk as laypeople, with the result that Sunstein's proposed technocracy will not protect us from our psychological weaknesses. Kusch thinks that Sunstein is overly optimistic about expert rationality. This stance clearly puts Kusch at odds with proponents of technocracy, but it also brings him into conflict with two of the leading proponents of the participatory model of regulation, Sheila Jasanoff and Brian Wynne. In many cases, advocates of participation have attempted to argue that laypeople's reasoning about risk is rational. Sometimes they have argued that it involves an 'alternative rationality', which needs to be considered alongside the rationality of scientific experts. Kusch claims, however, that the likes of Jasanoff and Wynne have an implausible optimism regarding the rationality of laypeople.[14] His chapter seeks to explore the political consequences of what one might describe as a global pessimism regarding rationality and risk.

Sunstein's own contribution to this collection continues his past work on the imperfections of human reasoning about risk in a way which expands the ambitions of that work considerably. It is comparatively easy to argue that we make mistakes about, for example, the magnitudes of risks, in virtue of the fact that we use simple heuristics, or rules of thumb, for their estimation. Sometimes I will get an answer that is approximately correct if I base an estimate of the likelihood of some event on the ease with which I can recall an event of the same type occurring. But in other cases this way of reasoning goes badly wrong. What allows us to say that it has gone wrong is the existence of an alternative, superior method for determining probabilities. But Sunstein now argues that we also use moral heuristics when reasoning about risk – rules of thumb that tell us what the morally right course of action is, and which are again prone to go wrong. Assuming such rules exist, understanding their nature is an important task for regulators who wish to improve the quality of their responses to the moral challenges laid down by risky situations.

From an abstract perspective, one might have sympathy with Sunstein's position. We are evolved creatures. One might argue that evolution has not equipped us with an infallible psychology, only one with a tendency to give appropriate answers in the context of the environments in which our psychologies were shaped. The availability heuristic, for example, might work fairly well in an ancestral environment without global media, but it can cause unnecessary panic once rare events are allowed to acquire worldwide salience. Evolution has given us error-prone heuristics for estimating probabilities, so why suppose that things are any different when it comes to the general tools we have for evaluating moral features of situations? Shouldn't we expect these to be error-prone, too? The problem Sunstein's argument faces – a problem to which he has an answer – is that it is not clear what alternative methods we might turn to in order to demonstrate that our moral rules of thumb go wrong. It is one thing to point out that the actual incidence of train crashes is much lower than people who use the 'availability heuristic' expect. It is another thing altogether to show, for example, that people who believe that killing is always wrong are led by this heuristic to claim that some particular acts of killing are wrong when they are in fact right.

Philosophy and risk

Most of the foregoing discussion has attempted to document the ways in which philosophy may be used to clarify important practical questions about risk and to improve our responses to those questions. But we should not expect the lines of communication to work in one direction only. There are also important questions to be asked about how philosophy itself – most obviously ethics – can learn from the practical study of risk. Martin Peterson, for example, argues in his contribution here that reflection on risk exposes significant gaps in our theories of what it takes for a choice between two alternative options to be rational. Sven Ove Hansson suggests that general systematic theories in ethics suffer because they have been formulated with a non-risky, deterministic universe in mind. What is more, he argues that our day-to-day ethical intuitions are, in these respects, more sophisticated than ethical theories, because these intuitions are adapted to a chancy world. Stephen Perry focuses on a series of questions that link risk to more traditional ethical concerns relating to rights and harm. Should we understand the imposition of risk as a form of harm? On the face of it, to expose someone to risk is to increase the probability that they will suffer harm. This is perhaps not, in itself, the same as harming them directly. What is more, it is not clear which notion of probability one has in mind when one talks of exposing someone to risk. Is a risky situation one in which there are genuine, non-zero, *chances* of several alternative outcomes arising? Or is it rather one in which, regardless of the chances, one cannot *know* with certainty which outcome will arise? If we go for the second option it is not clear how exposing someone to risk could even involve harming them indirectly, for it is not clear how, if at all, someone is harmed simply by being in a situation where they do not know for sure what will happen. But if we do not harm people when we expose them to risk, do we nonetheless wrong them in some other way? And what rights do people have regarding how the actions of others expose them to risk?

I should say a few words before closing this introduction to justify the order in which the essays presented here have been placed. I have begun with Sven Ove Hansson's broad-ranging article, which gives a good flavour of some of the general issues raised by risk and ethics. Carl Cranor's piece, which explores the prospects for a non-consequentialist theory of ethics, also addresses a wide range of issues and helps set the scene for later contributions. The next three chapters, by Wolff, Peterson and Morton, all address, in one way or another, the shortcomings of prominent quantitative models of risk assessment. The chapters by Per Sandin and Hugh Mellor take on (in very different ways) the topic of how one should choose between risky options when one is comparatively ignorant of the facts of the case. The next three chapters by Kusch, Sunstein and Ryan all concern the interpretation of various pieces of empirical work in the psychology of risk, and their application to political issues. Finally, Stephen Perry's article brings the collection to a close, with its focus on the relationships between risk, harm and rights.

I hope to have shown in this introduction that risk is an area of study which contains a rich variety of philosophical questions. I also hope to have shown that it is an area in which philosophers have plenty to offer of practical relevance. If the reader is not yet convinced, then the remaining essays in this collection will doubtless be more persuasive.[15]

Notes

1 A selection of books which explicitly approach risk from a philosophical perspective includes Rescher (1983), Shrader-Frechette (1985, 1991, 1993), Cranor (1993), Hansson (1998) and Sunstein (2002).

2 This criterion is regularly cited in the EMEA's summary opinions, available at its website http://www.emea.eu.int (accessed 2 August 2006).

3 See Martin Peterson's contribution to this volume for more on the EMEA's stance on risk.

4 For discussion of lives versus life-years in different regulatory contexts see Sunstein (2004).

5 So-called 'quality-adjusted life years' (QALYs) have been devised to give a picture of the effect of health-related interventions on the quality of life. See Nord (1999) and Broome (2004) for philosophical evaluation of QALYs.

6 In the UK this job is given to the National Institute of Clinical Excellence (NICE). Matters of safety and efficacy are decided by a different agency, the Medicines and Healthcare Products Regulatory Agency (MHRA).

7 For philosophical discussion of willingness to pay measures see Wolff (2002), Broome (2004) and Sunstein (2005).

8 A classic introductory discussion of utilitarianism can be found in Smart and Williams (1973).

9 A large literature has emerged on the precautionary principle in recent years. Two notable anthologies on the topic are Raffensperger and Tickner (1999) and Harremoës et al. (2002).

10 Mobile phones and precaution are explored in detail in Burgess (2003).

11 I take this to be the proper conclusion to draw from Brian Wynne's well-known studies of Cumbrian sheep-farmers (e.g. Wynne 1996).

12 Andy Stirling has analysed the language of 'sound science' in risk policy. See, for example, Stirling (2005).

13 This theme runs through much of the work of Kristin Shrader-Frechette (e.g. Shrader-Frechette 1985).

14 See Kusch's chapter for references to relevant elements of the work of Wynne and Jasanoff.

15 Thanks to Martin Kusch, Hugh Mellor, Martin Peterson and Cass Sunstein for comments on an earlier draft of this introduction.

References

Beck, U. (1992) *Risk Society: towards a new modernity*, London: Sage.

Blair, A. (2005) 'Common-sense culture not compensation culture', speech given to the IPPR at UCL, London, 26 May. Online. Available HTTP: http://www.number-10.gov.uk/output/Page7562.asp (accessed 1 August 2006).

Broome, J. (2004) *Weighing Lives*, Oxford: Oxford University Press.

Burgess, A. (2003) *Cellular Phones, Public Fears and a Culture of Precaution*, Cambridge: Cambridge University Press.

Cranor, C. (1993) *Regulating Toxic Substances: a philosophy of science and the law*, Oxford: Oxford University Press.

Hansson, S.O. (1998) *Setting the Limit: occupational health standards and the limits of science*, Oxford: Oxford University Press.

Harremoës, P., Gee, D., MacGarvin, M., Stirling, A., Keys, J., Wynne, B. and Guedes Vaz, S. (eds) (2002) *The Precautionary Principle in the 20th Century: late lessons from early warnings*, London: Earthscan.

Lewens, T. (2004) 'Sometimes safe and sorry', *Lancet*, 363: 1405–6.

Nord, E. (1999) *Cost–Value Analysis in Health Care: making sense out of QALYs*, Cambridge: Cambridge University Press.

Raffensperger, C. and Tickner, J. (eds) (1999), *Protecting Public Health and the Environment: implementing the precautionary principle*, Washington, DC: Island Press.

Rescher, N. (1983) *Risk: a philosophical introduction*, Washington, DC: University Press of America.

Shrader-Frechette, K. (1985) *Science Policy, Ethics, and Economic Methodology*, Boston, MA: Kluwer.

Shrader-Frechette, K. (1991) *Risk and Rationality: philosophical foundations for populist reforms*, Berkeley, CA: University of California Press.

Shrader-Frechette, K. (1993) *Burying Uncertainty: risk and the case against geological disposal of nuclear waste*, Berkeley, CA: University of California Press.

Slovic, P. (ed.) (2000) *The Perception of Risk*, London: Earthscan.

Slovic, P. *et al.* (2002) 'The affect heuristic', in T. Gilovich, D. Griffin and D. Kahneman (eds), *Heuristics and Biases: the psychology of intuitive judgement*, Cambridge: Cambridge University Press.

Smart, J. and Williams, B. (1973) *Utilitarianism: for and against*, Cambridge: Cambridge University Press.

Stirling, A. (2005) 'Opening up or closing down: analysis, participation and power in the social appraisal of technology', in M. Leach, I. Scoones and B. Wynne (eds), *Science, Citizenship and Globalisation*, London: Zed.

Sunstein, C. (2002) *Risk and Reason: safety, law and the environment*, Cambridge: Cambridge University Press.

Sunstein, C. (2004) 'Lives, life-years, and willingness to pay', *Columbia Law Review*, 104: 205–52.

Sunstein, C. (2005) *Laws of Fear: beyond the precautionary principle*, Cambridge: Cambridge University Press.

Wolff, J. (2002) 'Railway safety and the ethics of the tolerability of risk', WCA Consulting. Online. Available HTTP: http://www.rssb.co.uk/pdf/policy_risk.pdf (accessed 2 August 2006).

Wynne, B. (1996) 'Misunderstood misunderstandings: social identities and public uptake of science', in A. Irwin and B. Wynne (eds), *Misunderstanding Science? The public reconstruction of science and technology*, Cambridge: Cambridge University Press.

1

RISK AND ETHICS

Three approaches

Sven Ove Hansson

How is risk related to value, and in particular to moral value? This has often been discussed by risk researchers and by activists in various risk-related political issues. Increasingly it has also become the subject of philosophical analysis, but admittedly, the philosophical discussion on risk is still at a rather early stage. In this contribution, I will try to show how rich this subject is from the viewpoint of moral philosophy by briefly introducing three major approaches to it.[1] The three approaches are:

1 clarifying the value dependence of risk assessments;
2 analysing risks and risk decisions from an ethical point of view;
3 developing moral theory so that it can deal with issues of risk.

The first of these approaches is the most common one (MacLean 1985; Thomson 1985; Shrader-Frechette 1991; Cranor 1997; Hansson 1998). It has been the starting-point for most researchers who have worked in the area of risk and values, including myself.

Clarifying the value dependence of risk assessments

In order to understand why values are controversial in risk assessment, we need to have a look at the role of risk assessments in the risk decision process. The standard view on this process has developed out of attempts to systematize the work carried out by various national authorities, in particular those responsible for environmental protection and occupational safety. It was codified in an influential 1983 report by the American National Academy of Sciences (NAS) (National Research Council 1983). The report puts a strong emphasis on the division of the decision procedure into two distinct parts to be performed consecutively. The first of these, commonly called risk assessment, is a scientific undertaking. It consists of collecting and assessing the relevant information and, based on this, characterizing the nature and magnitude of the risk. The second procedure is called risk management. Contrary to risk assessment, this is not a scientific undertaking. Its starting-point is the outcome of risk assessment, which it combines with economic and technological information pertaining to various ways of reducing or eliminating the risk in question, and also with political and social information. Based on this, a decision is made on what measures – if any – should be taken to reduce the risk.

An essential difference between risk assessment and risk management, according to this view, is that values only appear in risk management. Ideally, risk assessment is a value-free process. But is it value-free in practice, and can it at all be made value-free?

In order to answer this question we must draw the distinction between being value-free and being free of controversial values. There are many values that are shared by virtually everyone or by everyone who takes part in a particular discourse. Medical science provides good examples of this. When discussing analgesics, we take for granted that it is better if patients have less rather than more pain. There is no need to interrupt a discussion on this topic in order to point out that a statement that one analgesic is better than another depends on this value assumption. Similarly, in economics, it is usually taken for granted that it is better if we all become richer. Economists sometimes lose sight of the fact that this is a value judgment.

An important class of uncontroversial values are the epistemic (scientific) values that rule the conduct of science. In science, and in risk assessment, we value truth, avoidance of error, simplicity and explanatory power. There are good reasons why these can be called values, although they are of course not moral values. Carl Hempel called them epistemic utilities and delineated them as follows:

> [T]he utilities should reflect the value or disvalue which the different outcomes have from the point of view of pure scientific research rather than the practical advantages or disadvantages that might result from the application of an accepted hypothesis, according as the latter is true or false. Let me refer to the kind of utilities thus vaguely characterized as *purely scientific*, or *epistemic, utilities*.
>
> (Hempel 1960: 465)[2]

In a discussion of values in science we have use for the two distinctions just made, namely between epistemic and non-epistemic values, and also between controversial and non-controversial values. The presence of *epistemic values* is obvious, but they are not very relevant for a discussion of what we usually mean by science being value-free or value-laden. Next, we have the *non-controversial non-epistemic* values. In the context of risk they may include values such as those expressed by the statement that it is good if the prevalence of cancer decreases. These values are relevant for the issue of value-ladenness, but they are often overlooked. Finally, we have the *controversial non-epistemic values*. These are the values that are at focus in a discussion of the value-ladenness of science and science-based practices such as risk assessment.

Are there any values from this third group in risk assessment, i.e. are there any controversial non-epistemic values? I will try to show that there are. More precisely, my claim is that non-epistemic values are unavoidable in risk assessment because of a rather interesting process: when scientific information is transferred to risk assessment, those of the epistemic values in science that concern error-avoidance are transformed into non-epistemic and often quite controversial values. Let us have a closer look at values of error-avoidance.

There are two major types of error that you can make in a scientific statement. Either you conclude that there is a phenomenon or an effect that is in fact not there. This is called an error of type I (false positive). Or you miss an existing phenomenon or effect. This is called an error of type II (false negative). In scientific practice, these types of error are treated very differently. Errors of type I are the serious errors in science. To make such an error means to draw an unwarranted conclusion, to believe something that should not be believed. Such errors lead us astray, and if too many of them are committed then scientific progress will be blocked by the pursuit of all sorts of blind alleys.

Errors of type II, on the other hand, are much less serious from a (purely) scientific point of view. To make such an error means that you keep an issue open instead of adopting a correct hypothesis. Of course, not everything can be kept open, and science must progress when there are reasonable grounds for (provisionally) closing an issue. Nevertheless, failing to proceed is in this context a much less serious error than walking in the wrong direction.

This difference in severity between the two types of error can also be expressed in terms of burdens of proof. When determining whether or not a scientific hypothesis should be accepted for the time being, the onus of proof falls to its adherents. Those who claim the existence of an as yet unproven effect – such as a toxic effect of a chemical substance – have the burden of proof.

As long as we stay in the realm of pure science, the values that determine where we put the burden of proof are epistemic values. However, risk assessment does not belong to the realm of pure science. Risk assessment has a decision-guiding purpose. Often the same or very similar questions are asked in a (purely) scientific context and in a risk assessment context. We can for instance ask the question 'Is the fruit of the bog bilberry poisonous?' as a purely scientific question. Then the intra-scientific burden of proof applies in the way that I just described. If the same question is followed by 'My four-year-old has picked a lot of them and wants to eat them now', then the burden of proof is, presumably, distributed differently.

It is important to note that this does not mean that we operate with different criteria of truth in the two contexts. Instead, the difference concerns our criteria for reasonable recommendations for action (Hansson 1997b). There are inconclusive indications that the bog bilberry may be poisonous. Therefore, when acting in intra-scientific contexts, the scientist in our example should not *act as if* it is known to be true that these fruits are poisonous. She should not, for instance, write in a textbook that they are poisonous, or refrain from investigating whether they are toxic with the motivation that they are already known to be so. In contrast, the parent should *act as if* it is known to be true that these fruits are poisonous. She should make sure that the child does not eat them.

This example illustrates a general pattern. It would not seem rational – let alone morally defensible – for a decision-maker to ignore all preliminary indications of a possible danger that do not amount to full scientific proof. We typically wish to protect ourselves against suspected health hazards even if the evidence is much weaker than what is required for scientific proof (Rudner 1953). Therefore, in order to guide the type of decisions that we want to make, risk assessments have to be based on criteria for the burden of proof that differ in many cases from those used for intra-scientific purposes.

However, risk assessors are normally not trained in these philosophical distinctions. We sometimes find scientists unreflectingly applying intra-scientific standards of proof in risk assessment contexts. Since these criteria give absolute priority to the avoidance of type I errors over that of type II errors, the outcome may very well be that risks are taken that few of us would accept when the lives and health of our own families are at stake. By just applying standard scientific criteria out of context, a scientist can transform uncontroversial epistemic values into highly controversial non-epistemic values.[3]

The practice of using the same burden of proof in risk assessments that we use for intra-scientific purposes is often mistaken for a 'value-free' or 'more scientific' risk assessment. Risk assessors who use other criteria are often accused of unnecessarily importing values into risk assessment (Charnley 1999, 2000).[4] But of course there is no value-free burden-of-proof standard for risk assessment. Instead of pretending that there is, we should base the standards of evidence in risk assessment on explicitly chosen, transparent criteria that ensure that the risk assessment provides the information needed in the risk-management decisions that it is intended to support (Hansson 1997a, 1999b; Sandin and Hansson 2002).

The use of statistics in science is tailored to the intra-scientific burden of proof. This is perhaps most clearly seen in the use of significance testing. Statistical significance can be seen as a mathematical expression of the usual burden-of-proof standard in science (Cranor and Nutting 1990). Statistical significance is a statistical measure that tells us essentially how probable the observed phenomena are (or would be) under the assumption that the effect we are looking for does in fact not exist. Observations are regarded as statistically significant if this probability is less than .05. For scientific purposes, the standard procedure is to regard statistically insignificant results as inconclusive. This is a necessary (but not sufficient) precaution against type I errors. However, significance testing does not take type II errors into account. Therefore, it is unfortunate that the dividing line between statistical significance and non-significance has in practice often been unreflectingly used as a dividing line

24

between 'the regulatory body should act as if an effect has been demonstrated' and 'the regulatory body should act as if no effect has been demonstrated' (Krewski *et al.* 1989: 9; cf. Leisenring *et al.* 1992). For this purpose, of course, tests of significance are not suited. Other statistical tests must be added that can help us avoid type II errors (Hansson 1995, 2002).

In addition to values related to the burden of proof, risk assessments may also contain other controversial values. I will give three examples of this.

The first example is comparisons with natural conditions. Radiation levels are frequently compared to the natural background, often with the tacit assumption that exposures lower than the natural background are unproblematic. Conversely, in public debates (but more seldom in risk assessments), risks associated with GMOs or synthetic chemicals are denounced as 'unnatural'. These references to (un)naturalness may be efficient rhetoric, but they are bad argumentation. That something is natural or unnatural does not show it to be good or bad. Furthermore, the words 'natural' and 'unnatural' are highly value-laden and very difficult to define in a consistent way (Hansson 2003a). Appeals to naturalness or unnaturalness are often a way to sneak values unnoticed into risk assessments.

Another common implicit value assumption in risk assessments concerns detectability. It is often assumed that effects that we cannot detect directly are a matter of no concern. Hence, if a risk assessment shows that there are no detectable effects, then it is assumed that nothing more needs to be known about the risk. The Health Physics Society wrote in a position statement:

> [The] estimate of risk should be limited to individuals receiving a dose of 5 rem in one year or a lifetime dose of 10 rem in addition to natural background. Below these doses, risk estimates should not be used; expressions of risk should only be qualitative emphasizing the inability to detect any increased health detriment (i.e., zero health effects is the most likely outcome).
>
> (Health Physics Society 1996)

It is difficult to find a morally acceptable argument why risks that we cannot detect should, for that reason, be acceptable or negligible.[5] Unfortunately, quite large effects can be indetectable. As a rough rule of thumb, epidemiological studies cannot reliably detect excess relative risks that are about 10 per cent or smaller. For the more common types of lethal disease, such as coronary disease and lung cancer, lifetime risks are of the order of magnitude of about 10 per cent. Therefore, even in the most sensitive studies, an increase in lifetime risk of the size 10^{-2} (10 per cent of 10 per cent) may be indetectable (i.e. indistinguishable from random variations). Very few people would regard a fatal risk of 1 in 100 as negligible. Therefore, we cannot in general consider a risk assessment to be finished when we know that there is no detectable risk. Even if a risk cannot be directly detected, there may be other means – such as extrapolations from animal experiments – that can be used to estimate its magnitude (Hansson 1999a).

My third example is relevant in almost all risk assessments. It concerns the way in which values relating to different persons are combined in a risk assessment. In this respect, standard risk analysis follows the principles of classical utilitarianism. All risks are taken to be fully comparable and additively aggregable. The 'total' risk is obtained by adding up all the individual risks. In risk–benefit analysis, benefits are added in the same way, and finally the sum of benefits is compared to the sum of risks in order to determine whether the total effect is positive or negative.

The practice of adding all risks and all benefits has immediate intuitive appeal. However, it is not as unproblematic as it might seem at first sight. Even if we assume that risks and benefits accruing to different persons are fully comparable in the sense that they can be measured in the same (additive) units, it does not follow that they should just be added up in the moral appraisal. The crucial issue here is not whether or not a benefit (or harm) for one person can be said to be greater than a benefit (or harm) for another person. The crucial issue is whether or not an action that brings about the greater benefit (smaller harm) compensates for the non-realization of a smaller benefit (greater harm) accruing to another person. Such interpersonal compensability does not follow automatically from interpersonal comparability (Hansson 2004a). The fact that it is worse for you to lose your thumb than for me to lose my little finger does not in itself make it allowable for you or anybody else to chop off my little finger in order to save your thumb.

An obvious alternative to this utilitarian approach is to treat each individual as a separate moral unit. Then risks and benefits pertaining to one and the same person can be weighed against each other, whereas risks and benefits for different persons are treated as incomparable. This type of risk-weighing can be found in certain applications that are strongly influenced by the individual-centred traditions of clinical medicine. Dietary advice is one example. Due to environmental contamination, health authorities recommend limits in the consumption of fish caught in certain waters. Such recommendations are based on endeavours to balance the negative health effects of the contaminants against the positive effects of fish as a constituent of the diet (Knuth et al. 2003). This balance is struck separately for each individual; thus positive effects for others (such as the fishing industry) are excluded from consideration.

Hence, we have different practices in different areas of risk assessment.[6] In most applications, all risks and benefits are added up; but in some applications individuals are instead treated as separate units of evaluation. The choice between these approaches is another hidden value assumption in risk assessments that needs to be made explicit.

It is important for the quality of risk-decision processes that the hidden value assumptions in risk assessments are uncovered. Major parts of this work require philosophical competence. Implicit value components of complex arguments have to be discovered, and conceptual distinctions relating to values have to be made. In addition, systematic evaluations of risk assessments should be performed in order to determine what factors influence their outcomes (Hansson and Rudén 2006). This is an area in which co-operations between philosophy and other disciplines can be very fruitful.

Analysing risks and risk decisions from an ethical point of view

I will now turn to the second approach to risk and ethics, namely the ethical analysis of risk problems. Let me begin by explaining why ethical analysis is needed here. Is not standard risk analysis, with its calculations of probabilities and probability-weighted outcomes, sufficient for decision-guidance?

Modern risk analysis is largely based on a quantitative methodology that is, from a decision-theoretical point of view, essentially an application of expected utility maximization (or expected disutility minimization). The severity of a risk is measured as the probability-weighted severity of the negative outcome that the risk refers to. Hence, a risk characterized by a probability p of a negative event with severity u has the same impact in the calculations as a negative event whose severity equals pxu and about which we are certain that it will occur. Beginning with the influential *Reactor Safety Study* (WASH-1400, the Rasmussen report) from 1975, risk has often not only been *measured by* but also *identified with* expected disutility (Rechard 1999). In other words, risk is defined as the product of probability and severity.[7]

Probabilistic risk analysis is a highly useful tool that provides risk managers with important information. However, it does not provide decision-makers with all the information that they need in order to make risk-management decisions. In particular, important ethical aspects are not covered in these forms of risk analysis. Risks do not just 'exist' as free-floating entities; they are taken, run or imposed. Risk-taking and risk imposition involve problems of agency and interpersonal relationships that cannot be adequately expressed in a framework that operates exclusively with the probabilities and severities of outcomes. In order to appraise an action of risk-taking or risk imposition from a moral point of view, we also need to know who performs the action and with what intentions. For instance, it makes a moral difference if someone risks her own life or that of somebody else in order to earn a fortune for herself. It also makes a difference if risk-taking is freely chosen by the affected person or imposed against her will. Therefore, traditional quantitative analysis of risk needs to be supplemented with a systematic characterization of the ethical aspects of risk, including issues such as voluntariness, consent, intent and justice.

In recent joint work with Hélène Hermansson, we have proposed a framework for such a systematic analysis of risk (Hermansson and Hansson 2007). Our starting-point is that there are three central roles in social interactions on risks. In every risk-management problem there are people who are potentially exposed to a risk, and there are people who make decisions that affect the risk. Furthermore, since non-trivial risks are seldom taken unless they are associated with some benefit, in practically every risk-management problem there are people who gain from the risk being taken. We propose that relationships between those who have these three roles, namely the risk-exposed, the decision-maker and the beneficiary, are essential for identifying the ethical aspects of a risk management problem. It is important for the ethical analysis to know if two, or perhaps all three of these roles are filled by the same persons, if for instance the risk-exposed are the same (or partly the same) people as the beneficiaries, if the risk-exposed are themselves decision-makers, etc. It is also important to know if one of these groups is in some way dependent on one of the others, for instance if the risk-exposed are economically dependent on the decision-makers. For an example, suppose that a city's traffic planning exposes residents in a particular area to a much higher risk of accidents than those who live in other parts of the city. Our ethical appraisal of this risk-exposure can legitimately be influenced by whether these residents had a say in the decision (i.e. whether they are also decision-makers) and whether the risk-inducing arrangement of traffic has advantages for them or only for people living in other districts (i.e. whether they are also beneficiaries).

We propose that for practical purposes, analysis of the ethics of risk can be based on seven questions concerning the (pairwise) relationships between the three risk roles. In my experience these questions cover most of the salient ethical issues in common types of risk-management problem.

1 To what extent do the risk-exposed benefit from the risk exposure?
2 Is the distribution of risks and benefits fair?
3 Can the distribution of risks and benefits be made less unfair by redistribution or by compensation?
4 To what extent is the risk exposure decided by those who run the risk?
5 Do the risk-exposed have access to all relevant information about the risk?
6 Are there risk-exposed persons who cannot be informed or included in the decision process?
7 Does the decision-maker benefit from other people's risk exposure?

There are many types of moral problem that arise in issues of risk. I will mention one such problem that is both theoretically interesting and practically relevant: the definition and implications of voluntariness. It should be obvious that voluntariness is a vague notion. Any sharp line between voluntary and involuntary exposure to risk has to be drawn rather arbitrarily. Nevertheless, for many practical purposes – not least legal purposes – a division between voluntary and involuntary has to be made. There is nothing unusual in this; the same type of vagueness applies to many other concepts that we use.

However, in addition to this, the distinction between voluntary and involuntary risk-exposure depends largely on social conventions that are taken for granted without much reflection. As one example of this, the risks associated with smoking are regarded as voluntary whereas risks associated with emissions from a nearby factory are regarded as involuntary. For many smokers, to quit smoking is much more difficult than to move to a safer neighbourhood. This example shows that our ascriptions of (in)voluntariness tend to be strongly influenced by what we consider to be a reasonable demand on a person. This is problematic since it means that our appraisals of voluntariness cannot be seen as inferentially prior to our ethical appraisals.

Many risks have complex causal backgrounds that make the appraisal of voluntariness particularly difficult. Often, self-harming actions by the affected person combine with actions by others to produce the harmful outcome. Hence, the drug addict cannot use drugs unless someone provides her with them. Similarly, the smoker can smoke only if companies continue to sell products that kill half of their customers. The case of smoking is particularly instructive. In order to defend their own activities, tobacco companies have sponsored antipaternalist campaigns that focus on the voluntariness of smoking and the right of smokers to smoke (Taylor 1984). The (implicit) inference seems to be that if the smoker has a moral right to harm herself, then the tobacco company has a moral right to provide her with the means to do so. The term *extended antipaternalism* can be used to denote the use of antipaternalist arguments for accepting actions and activities that harm or contribute to harming (consenting) others (Hansson 2005a).

This distribution of responsibilities in cases with mixed causality seems to be a result of social conventions rather than of consistently applied moral principles. Other cases with a similar structure to the tobacco case are treated differently. In particular, the manufacturers and distributors of heroin are commonly held responsible for the effects that their products have on the health and well-being of those who choose to buy and use them. (Cigarettes are legal and heroin illegal, but that does not settle the *moral* issue.)

A hypothetical example can clarify how our appraisals of responsibilities for risk exposure depend on social conventions. Suppose that a major soft-drinks company comes up with a new product that customers will become addicted to. The new soft drink has no serious immediate health effects, but in the long run it will give rise to pulmonary, cardiovascular and various malignant diseases, thereby ultimately shortening the lives of about half of the consumers who become addicted to it. Few would claim that the sale of such a product should be allowed. Yet, its properties are analogous to those of cigarettes. The difference is of course that cigarettes are socially accepted and that it is considered politically impossible to prohibit them.

In summary, our appraisals of the (in)voluntariness of risk exposures are difficult to reconstruct in terms of consistent moral principles. This is a good reason to subject them to careful moral analysis and criticism. Our dealings with risk depend largely on social conventions, some of which we may wish to change after carefully considering alternative approaches.

Developing moral theory so that it can deal with issues of risk

The third approach to ethics and risk is a much more ambitious project than the other two from the point of view of moral theory. Studies of risk put focus on problems that should be central in moral theorizing but have been sadly neglected. They can therefore be instrumental in improving moral theory.

Throughout the history of moral philosophy, moral theorizing has for the most part referred to a deterministic world in which the morally relevant properties of human actions are both well-determined and knowable. A possible defence of this could be that issues of risk (and uncertainty) belong to decision theory rather than to moral theory. In fact, it seems to often be assumed that decision theory takes value assignments for deterministic cases as given, and derives from them instructions for rational behaviour in an uncertain, unpredictable and indeterministic world. Suppose, for instance, that moral considerations have led us to attach well-determined values to two outcomes X and Y. Then decision theory provides us with a value to be attached to mixed options such as 50-per-cent-chance-of-X-and-50-per-cent-chance-of-Y. The crucial assumption is that, given well-determined probabilities and well-determined values of the basic non-probabilistic alternatives X and Y, the values of mixed options can be *derived*. Probabilities and the values of non-probabilistic alternatives are assumed to completely determine the value of probabilistic alternatives. This is the conventional wisdom, so conventional that it is seldom stated explicitly. I believe it to be grossly misleading, and this for two major reasons (Hansson 2001).

First, as I have already indicated, risk-taking and risk exposure often have moral implications in themselves that are not mediated by the consequences of the possible outcomes. Compare, for instance, the act of throwing down a brick on a person from a high building to the act of throwing down a brick from a high building without first making sure that there is nobody beneath who can be hit by the brick. The moral difference between these two acts is not obviously expressible in a probability calculus. We can easily develop the example so that both the probability and the severity of personal injury are the same for the two acts, but in spite of this very few people would regard them as morally equivalent.

Second, we need our intuitions about indeterministic events in the development of our system of morality. I have found no good reason to believe that our intuitions on deterministic objects are always more reliable than our intuitions on indeterministic objects. To the contrary, in many contexts we have more experience from uncertain than from certain objects of value. It does not then seem reasonable to disregard all our intuitions on the former category from our deliberations, and reconstruct value assignments to them that are based only on our intuitions on the latter type of objects.

As I have tried to show elsewhere, our current moral theories are not suitable to deal with issues of risk (Hansson 2003b). One of the problems with utilitarianism in this respect is that, as we have already seen, it tends to support full interpersonal compensatability of risks and benefits. This means that a risk for one person can always be outweighed by a slightly larger benefit for another. Deontological and rights-based theories have the opposite problem: they have difficulties in showing how a person can at all be justified in taking actions that expose others to risks. This was well expressed by Robert Nozick: 'Imposing how slight a probability of a harm that violates someone's rights also violates his rights?' (Nozick 1974: 7; cf. McKerlie 1986).

Making a long story short, I believe that a reasonable solution to the distributive issues raised in contexts of risk can be developed in a system of prima facie rights. Such a system should contain a prima facie right not to be put at risk by others: *everyone has a prima facie moral right not to be exposed to risk of negative impact, such as damage to her health or her property, through the actions of others.*

Since this is a prima facie right, it can be overridden. In practice, it has to be overridden in quite a few cases, since social life would be impossible if we were not allowed to expose each other to certain risks. To mention just one example: as car-drivers we put each other's lives at risk. In order to make the prima facie right to risk avoidance workable, we need a normatively reasonable account of the overriding considerations in view of which these and similar risk impositions can be accepted. This can be obtained by appeal to reciprocal exchanges of risks and benefits. Each of us takes risks in order to obtain benefits for ourselves. It is beneficial for all of us to extend this practice to mutual exchanges of risks and benefits. Hence, if others are allowed to drive a car, exposing me to certain risks, then in exchange I am allowed to drive a car and expose them to the corresponding risks. This (we may suppose) is to the benefit of all of us. In order to deal with the complexities of modern society, we also need to apply this principle to exchanges of different types of risk and benefit. We can then regard exposure of a person to a risk as acceptable if it is part of a social system of risk-taking that works to her advantage (Hansson 2003b).

This approach has the important advantage of recognizing each person's individual rights, but still making mutually beneficial adjustments possible. It does not allow you to stop your neighbour from driving a car, thereby creating a (small) risk for you as a pedestrian, since this method of transportation is also accessible to you, and beneficial to you as well. On the other hand it will prohibit exploitative arrangements in which someone is exposed to risks in order to achieve benefits only for others.

With further developments, this approach can help us to deal with the distributive issues in risk. However, it does not help us to deal with the equally fundamental issue of which risks we should accept. This is a matter that transcends the limit between morality and rational self-interest.

Of course the standard answer to this question is that we should apply expected utility theory. However, that theory has many weaknesses that come out very clearly in issues of risk (Hansson 1993). One important weakness that has been overlooked in the literature is its instability against the actual occurrence of a serious negative event that was included in the calculation. This can be seen by studying the post-accident argumentation after almost any accident. If the expected utility argumentation were followed to the end, then many accidents would be defended as consequences of a maximization of expected utility that is, *in toto*, beneficial. However, this type of reasoning is very rarely heard in practice. Seldom do we hear a company that was responsible for a deadly accident justify the loss of lives by saying that it was the result of a decision which, in terms of its total effects, produced far more good than harm. Instead, two other types of reactions are common. One of these is to regret one's shortcomings and agree that one should have done more to prevent the accident. The other is to claim that somebody else was responsible for the accident.

It should also be noted that accident investigation boards are instructed to answer the questions 'What happened? Why did it happen? How can a similar event be avoided?', not the question 'Was the accident defensible in an expected utility calculation?' Once a serious accident has happened, the application of expected utility maximization appears much less satisfactory than it did before the accident. In this pragmatic sense, expected utility maximization is not a stable strategy.

We need a framework for argumentation that increases our ability to come up with risk decisions that we are capable of defending even if things do not go our way. Such a framework can be obtained by a systematizing a common type of argument in everyday discussions about future possibilities, namely arguments that refer to how one might in the future come to evaluate the possible actions under consideration. These arguments are often stated in terms of predicted regret: 'Do not do that. You may come to regret it.' This is basically a sound type of argument. For our purposes, it has to be developed into a procedure in which future developments are systematically identified, and decision alternatives are evaluated under each of these possible developments. Such *hypothetical retrospection* can be used as a means to achieve more well-considered social decisions in issues of risk. However, it cannot be adequately accounted for in terms of regret-avoidance. Psychologically, regret is often unavoidable for the simple reason that it may arise in response to information that was not available at the time of decision. Therefore, regret-avoidance has to be replaced by more carefully carved-out methods and criteria for hypothetical retrospection (Hansson 2007).

For a simple example, consider a factory owner who has decided to install an expensive fire-alarm system in a building that is used only temporarily. When the building is taken out of use, the fire alarm has yet to be activated. The owner may nevertheless consider the decision to install it to have been right, since at the time of the decision other possible developments had to be considered in which the alarm would have been life-saving. This argument can be used, not only in actual retrospection, but also, in essentially the same way, in hypothetical retrospection before the decision. Alternatively, suppose that there is a fire in the building. The owner may then regret that he did not install a much more expensive but highly efficient sprinkler system. In spite of this regret he may consider the decision to have been correct since when he made it, he had to consider the alternative, much more probable development in which there was no fire, but the cost of the sprinklers would have made other investments impossible. Of course, this argument can be used in hypothetical retrospection just like the previous one. In this way, when we perform hypothetical retrospection from the perspective of a particular branch of future development, we can refer to each of the alternative branches and use it to develop either counter-arguments or supportive arguments. In short, in each branch we can refer to all the others.

Hypothetical retrospection aims at ensuring that, whatever happens, the decision one makes will be morally acceptable (permissible) from the perspective of actual retrospection. Just as we can improve our moral decisions by considering them from the perspective of other concerned individuals, we can also improve them by considering alternative future perspectives.

This proposal goes in the opposite direction to much current moral theory: it adds concreteness instead of abstracting from concrete detail. In my view, our moral intuitions are in the end all that we have to base our moral judgments on, and these intuitions are best suited to deal with concrete realistic situations. The concreteness gained through hypothetical retrospection has the advantage that our moral deliberations will be based on 'the full story' rather than on curtailed versions of it. More specifically, this procedure brings to our attention interpersonal relations that should be essential in a moral appraisal of risk and uncertainty, such as who exposes whom to a risk, who receives the benefits from whose exposure to risk, etc. It is only by staying away from such concreteness that standard utility-maximizing risk analysis can remain on the detached and depersonalized level of statistical lives and free-floating risks and benefits.

And this, by the way, is the major service that studies of risk can do to moral philosophy. Introducing problems of risk is an unusually efficient way to expose moral theory to some of the complexities of real life. There are good reasons to believe that the impact on moral philosophy can be thoroughgoing.

Notes

1 For a more general overview of the philosophy of risk, see Hansson (2004c).
2 On epistemic value, see also Levi (1962), Feleppa (1981) and Harsanyi (1983).

3 In many cases this transformation takes place partly in risk assessment and partly in the risk-management decisions on which it is based.

4 For a rebuttal, see Sandin *et al.* (2002).

5 In Hansson (2004b) I called this the 'ostrich's fallacy', honouring the biological folklore that the ostrich buries its head in the sand, believing that what it cannot see is no problem.

6 This difference corresponds to the dividing-line between the 'old' and 'new' schools of welfare economics. See Hansson (2006a).

7 See Hansson (1993 and 2005b) for critical appraisals of this definition.

References

Charnley, G. (1999) 'President's message', *RISK newsletter*, 19(2): 2.

—— (2000) '1999 annual meeting: past president's message: risk analysis under fire', *RISK newsletter*, 20(1): 3.

Cranor, C.F. (1997) 'The normative nature of risk assessment: features and possibilities', *Risk: Health, Safety & Environment*, 8: 123–36.

—— and Nutting, K. (1990) 'Scientific and legal standards of statistical evidence in toxic tort and discrimination suits', *Law and Philosophy*, 9: 115–56.

Feleppa, R. (1981) 'Epistemic utility and theory acceptance: comments on Hempel', *Synthese*, 46: 413–20.

Hansson, S.O. (1993) 'The false promises of risk analysis', *Ratio*, 6: 16–26.

—— (1995) 'The detection level', *Regulatory Toxicology and Pharmacology*, 22: 103–9.

—— (1997a) 'The limits of precaution', *Foundations of Science*, 2: 293–306.

—— (1997b) 'Can we reverse the burden of proof?', *Toxicology Letters*, 90: 223–8.

—— (1998) *Setting the Limit: occupational health standards and the limits of science*, Oxford: Oxford University Press.

—— (1999a) 'The moral significance of indetectable effects', *Risk*, 10: 101–8.

—— (1999b) 'Adjusting scientific practices to the precautionary principle', *Human and Ecological Risk Assessment*, 5: 909–21.

—— (2001) 'The modes of value', *Philosophical Studies*, 104: 33–46.

—— (2002) 'Replacing the no effect level (NOEL) with bounded effect levels (OBEL and LEBEL)', *Statistics in Medicine*, 21: 3071–8.

—— (2003a) 'Are natural risks less dangerous than technological risks?', *Philosophia Naturalis*, 40: 43–54.

—— (2003b) 'Ethical criteria of risk acceptance', *Erkenntnis*, 59: 291–309.

—— (2004a) 'Weighing risks and benefits', *Topoi*, 23: 145–52.

—— (2004b) 'Fallacies of risk', *Journal of Risk Research*, 7: 353–60.

—— (2004c) 'Philosophical perspectives on risk', *Techne*, 8(1).

—— (2005a) 'Extended antipaternalism', *Journal of Medical Ethics*, 31: 97–100.

—— (2005b) 'Seven myths of risk', *Risk Management*, 7(2): 7–17.

—— (2006) 'Economic (ir)rationality in risk analysis', *Economics and Philosophy*, 22: 231–41.

—— (2007) 'Hypothetical retrospection', *Ethical Theory and Moral Practice*, in press.

—— and Rudén, C. (2006) 'Evaluating the risk decision process', *Toxicology*, 218: 100–11.

Harsanyi, J.C. (1983) 'Bayesian decision theory, subjective and objective probabilities, and acceptance of empirical hypotheses', *Synthese*, 57: 341–65.

Health Physics Society (1996) *Radiation Risk in Perspective*, position statement of the Health Physics Society, adopted January 1996.

Hempel, C.G. (1960) 'Inductive inconsistencies', *Synthese*, 12: 439–69.

Hermansson, H. and Hansson, S.O. (2007) 'A three party model tool for ethical risk analysis', *Risk Management*, in press.

Knuth, B.A., Connelly, N.A., Sheeshka, J., and J. (2003) 'Weighing health benefit and health risk information when consuming sport-caught fish', *Risk Analysis*, 23: 1185–97.

Krewski, D., Goddard, M.J. and Murdoch, D. (1989) 'Statistical considerations in the interpretation of negative carcinogenicity data', *Regulatory Toxicology and Pharmacology*, 9: 5–22.

Leisenring, W. and Ryan, L. (1992) 'Statistical properties of the NOAEL', *Regulatory Toxicology and Pharmacology*, 15: 161–71.

Levi, I. (1962) 'On the seriousness of mistakes', *Philosophy of Science*, 29: 47–65.

McKerlie, D. (1986) 'Rights and risk', *Canadian Journal of Philosophy*, 16: 239–51.

MacLean, D. (ed.) (1985) *Values at Risk*, Totowa, NJ: Rowman and Allanheld.

National Research Council (1983) *Risk Assessment in the Federal Government: managing the process*, Washington, DC: National Academy Press.

Nozick, R. (1974) *Anarchy, State, and Utopia*, New York: Basic Books.

Rechard, R.P. (1999) 'Historical relationship between performance assessment for radioactive waste disposal and other types of risk assessment', *Risk Analysis*, 19: 763–807.

Rudner, R. (1953) 'The scientist qua scientist makes value judgments', *Philosophy of Science*, 20: 1–6.

Sandin, P. and Hansson, S.O. 'The default value approach to the precautionary principle', *Journal of Human and Ecological Risk Assessment (HERA)*, 8: 463–71.

Sandin, P., Peterson, M., Hansson, S.O., Rudén, C. and Juthe, A. (2002) 'Five charges against the precautionary principle', *Journal of Risk Research*, 5: 287–99.

Shrader-Frechette, K. (1991) *Risk and Rationality: philosophical foundations for populist reforms*, Berkeley: University of California Press.

Taylor, P. (1984) *Smoke Ring: the politics of tobacco*, London: Bodley Head.

Thomson, P.B. (1985) 'Risking or being willing: Hamlet and the DC-10', *Journal of Value Inquiry*, 19: 301–10.

2

TOWARD A NON-CONSEQUENTIALIST APPROACH TO ACCEPTABLE RISKS

Carl F. Cranor

Introduction

In making social decisions about what risks should be reduced, which removed and which can be left to the judgment of individuals, legislators and administrators of our institutions must make comparative risk judgments – judgments of which risks are more and which are less important. One approach to these issues explicitly or implicitly appears to assume that decision-makers need only examine the magnitude and probability of risks in order to properly compare them. As Gillette and Krier put it:

> They may disagree about details, such as whether one looks at total expected deaths, deaths per person or per hour of exposure, or loss of life expectancy due to exposure, but generally speaking 'experts appear to see riskiness as synonymous with expected annual mortality and morbidity.' ... When experts write about relative risk, they implicitly or explicitly use body counts as the relevant measure. And, in a way seemingly consistent with the logic of their method, they insist that a death is a death is a death...
>
> (Gillette and Krier 1990: 1072)

It is useful to have an accurate estimate of the likelihood of harm from risks even if one does not regard different risks as equally acceptable. This informs people of their chances of serious injury or death and acts as a corrective to those who might be mistaken about their actual chances of being harmed by exposure, so they can take this information into account in guiding their choices.

However, morbidity and mortality statistics by themselves can be quite misleading guides to the acceptability of risks. They can lead to public policy outcomes at odds with the public's assessment of risks (Slovic 1987, Gillette and Krier 1990) and with more morally defensible courses of action (Cranor 1995).

I have two targets in this chapter. First, I disagree with the account of assessing comparative risk judgments based solely on the magnitude and probability of risks to which people are exposed. Such an account presents an overly simple view of which risks are more and which are less *acceptable*. Second, many writers justify social policies toward risks on the basis of comparatively simple utilitarian or cost–benefit grounds. This too is of concern.

In what follows I briefly summarize a partial account of the acceptability of risks (developed elsewhere) that tends to differ in significant respects from views articulated by those in the technical community (Cranor 1995). These are considerations that seem sufficiently plausible that any defensible ethical view should be able to provide reasons to justify them. Whether non-consequentialist or consequentialist theories in the end better support and defend them is a separate issue. I then sketch some important non-consequentialist considerations for judging the acceptability of risks. This view is largely programmatic because many details must be omitted for space reasons, but I try to provide enough of the view to suggest a different way of thinking about the acceptability of risks in our ordinary lives and different attitudes toward fellow members of the moral community who are put at risk by social policies.

By a non-consequentialist view I mean at a minimum a moral philosophic view that denies what consequentialists, or more specifically what utilitarians, affirm, namely that the morally right course of action is a function directly or indirectly of the non-moral goodness or badness of the consequences of an act (or, in the case of rule-utilitarianism, of following a principle). From a philosophical view, utilitarian theories are quite controversial and have a number of well-known difficulties. Moreover, it is important to have alternative views in the literature for comparison.

In what follows I do not necessarily endorse a non-consequentialist view; that would be premature. Rather, I develop some features of a not implausible account, drawing largely from two views of non-consequentialism. Moreover, the view expressed is narrower than non-consequentialism indicated above. Specifically it is more properly considered a form of contractualism or constructivism. It is constructivism in the sense that principles of right and wrong or what one owes to one another are constructed from a position of moral deliberation – much like the views of Kant or Rawls. It is contractualism in that it draws on the contractualism of Kant, Hill or Scanlon in several respects.

A partial account of the acceptability of risks

Consider first some salient properties of the acceptability of risks that focus largely on issues of personal acceptability (only occasionally noting moral acceptability). These are features of risk exposure which, *ceteris paribus*, tend to bear on their acceptability by a representative or generic person. I rely on persons' commonsensical pre-theoretical notions of acceptability for the risk in question. (A slightly less contentious way of making this point is that these are a variety of conceptual distinctions about risks that must be made in order not to conflate distinct issues as we consider their acceptability.) The same features discussed below may also constitute part of the basis of the moral acceptability of the risk exposure, but that would require further development.

The aspects of the acceptability of risks surveyed are not necessarily complete or even always mutually exclusive, but represent some major facets of circumstances that bear on the generic acceptability of risk exposure. However, identifying these features will enable us to think somewhat more clearly about the acceptability of risks and to avoid some obvious as well as some subtler mistakes. This also suggests what is important and valid in public perceptions of risk as well as indicating the importance of such considerations to the management of toxic substances such as carcinogens (Cranor 1995).

I utilize a standard account of risk: it is the chance, or the probability, of some loss or harm – the chance of mishap.[1] However, risks should be distinguished from their *acceptability*, an assessment from some appropriate normative point of view.

(1) We need a term that is neutral between risks being *imposed* upon one and risks that one has *taken*; the somewhat awkward phrases 'exposure to risks' or 'risk exposure' serve that purpose. Too often these ideas are conflated by commentators suggesting that every risk is 'taken'.[2] (There can be borderline cases between these two categories where it will be difficult to determine.)

(2) There is a distinction between risks that it is *permissible* for individuals to take in their own lives and those that they are *required* to live with as a matter of public policy. When this is not done it confuses normative issues. Thus, for example, risks from recreational activities, such as mountain climbing, scuba diving or extreme skiing, should not be invoked to set the standard for risks the public is required to endure as a result of regulation.[3] Most obviously the probability and magnitude of such risks might well be insufficiently protective for legally regulated risks (Cranor 1995).

(3) Intuitively a distinction between risk exposure from natural phenomena and risk exposure from human activities seems plausible. In both instances, if the risks materialize, human beings suffer injuries, diseases or premature death. Reducing both kinds of risks will reduce human suffering. However, if we compare risks from large natural phenomena such as earthquakes, exploding volcanoes, hurricanes, or tsunamis with humanly created risks, such as toxic exposures or dangerous factories in our midst, the humanly created risks tend to be more controllable or avoidable, at least as a result of decisions by the body politic as a whole. For naturally caused risks two major questions are 'How substantial are the risks?' and 'What should the community do to avoid or reduce them, if it can?' For humanly caused risks additional questions would be 'Should the community permit such risky activities?' and 'How should it allow for or guide the presence of such activities?' A community could specify that human activities be done differently or not at all. Even though this is an important distinction, there are subtleties and fuzzy borderlines. The risks from

natural forces can be modified as a result of human preparation and reaction to them. They might be reduced, as building codes aim to do in earthquake country, or increased, as poor preparation seemed to invite from hurricane Katrina (Center for Progressive Reform 2006). Some commentators appear to ignore potential normative differences between these two broad categories of risks, by, for example, explicitly comparing the annual risk of death from natural hazards with drinking one beer per day (Morrall 1986: 27).

(4) The comparative magnitudes of harms and benefits and the probabilities of each materializing are clearly relevant for both the personal and moral acceptability of risk exposure. For example, if risks are life threatening but any benefits associated with them tend to be quite minor, *ceteris paribus*, the risks are likely to be less acceptable from a personal point of view. Different moral views may treat such pertinent features quite differently.

(5) The relationship of the risks and benefits to a person's life is important to judgments of their acceptability. When risky activities are central to one's personal projects or life plan, as they might be for a lifeguard, mountaineer or African explorer, they will tend to be personally more acceptable than risks that are quite peripheral to one's life plan, e.g. drinking water contaminated with carcinogens. These are dramatic examples, but they call attention to important factors that most of us do and should consider in assessing the acceptability of risks, and they are pertinent to many moral views. Some moral theories provide greater moral space for personal projects than others (below).

(6) The relationship between the person creating or imposing the risk and the person exposed to the risk bears on its personal and moral acceptability. From a personal point of view, if one has created a risk to which one is then exposed, one is more likely to know of it, perhaps to understand it better, and to find it more acceptable than if someone else has imposed it on one (which would be more like an invasion of one's interests). From a moral point of view when one party creates a risk and another bears the costs of it, this raises issues about the distribution of benefits and risks of an activity, as well as issues of externalities (as the economists would put the issue). Such matters would need to be explicitly addressed by a moral view.

(7) There are a variety of kinds and degrees of control over risks that must be considered. Some risks are and some are not subject to significant personal control by the risk bearer. For example, some risks to which people are exposed are risks over which the risk bearer has considerable control, e.g. operating chainsaws or other kinds of equipment that can obviously harm one. By contrast, risks from, for instance, harmful air pollutants are largely beyond one's personal control within a region (although there is the possibility of avoiding such risks by moving, but this could represent a substantial personal cost).

There can be several dimensions of control over risks or their materializing. One might exercise control in becoming exposed to risks. One might choose to study close-up a volcano ripe for explosion, but have no control over whether it explodes, possibly little control over whether one is present when it explodes, and lesser control yet over whether one is harmed when it explodes. In other risky activities (e.g. operating dangerous equipment) one can exercise considerable *continuing* control over whether risks are likely to materialize and even have control to opt out of the activity if it becomes too risky.

The more one has control over exposure to risks and their materializing, the more one can provide some degree of self-protection. Such risks are likely to be judged more acceptable to those involved. From a social or moral point of view, in many circumstances the need for protection can be more justifiably left to the individual at risk compared with risks for which the same conditions do not exist. This might be seen as an aspect of the social division of responsibility (Rawls 1982) for risks, with portions of it left to community control or regulation, while other risks could be more safely left to individual control. (There are, of course, many possibilities here.)

(8) Some risks are quite transparent; they carry their dangers on their faces as it were. Chainsaws leave no doubt that they can do to human arms or legs what they do to trees. Five thousand pound cars on the street manifest their considerable dangers at least to normal adults and children beyond a certain age. Risks such as these are *transparent* because persons can utilize their senses to identify the risks and then in many cases modify behavior to respond to them. However, exposure to various chemical carcinogens, such as trichloroethylene or chloroform in drinking water, or benzene or vinyl chloride in the air, may place one at risk without any sensory input to notify one of the risk or its consequences. The more palpable risks are, in many circumstances the better one can exercise caution, care and control in providing *self-protection*. (Even so, we often explain to other adults some of the major risks from dangerous equipment.) Conversely, when risks are less transparent, *ceteris paribus*, those exposed need better protections, because they have greater difficulty detecting the risks, understanding their consequences, and thus realistically are less able to provide self-protection.[4]

(9) Voluntarily incurred risks tend to be personally and morally more acceptable than involuntarily incurred risks. In order to voluntarily incur a risk, one must properly understand and be aware of the risks one is incurring, be competent to make decisions about the risks, and in some robust sense have consented or agreed (explicitly or implicitly) to them (all important features of medical informed consent). The transparency of risks in environmental or workplace contexts is an important aspect of voluntary exposure, but not the only one (e.g. the risks from an incoming tsunami would be transparent, but not voluntary). Gillette and Krier note that '[k]nowledge coupled with freedom of action facilitates individual choice and efforts to control events bearing on the choice' (Gillette and Krier 1990: 1076). Thus, other important features of voluntary risk exposure include alternatives open to those exposed to a risk, the degree to which one can control exposure to it (already considered) and the extent of personal costs in avoiding the risks. If it is difficult to avoid

exposure to risks, *ceteris paribus*, this argues for greater protection from them, if it is available and feasible. If one cannot avoid humanly produced air pollution, or can avoid it only at great cost and inconvenience (greater sacrifice of one's interests), this argues for better protections from it. Sacrifice is a cost, the greater the sacrifice the greater the cost, and, thus, a reason for reducing the risks in the present course of action (Cranor 1995). At the other extreme when risks are easily avoidable, lesser protections may be justified (but even in this case, there may remain an issue of whether one should be subjected to the risks). Risks that one clearly *chooses*, such as mountaineering, are easily avoidable by refraining from the activity.[5] Deeper considerations support the acceptability of voluntarily incurred risks (when they obtain) because of 'concerns about autonomy and equality and power among individuals in the society, for it is these that lets free choice be morally interesting' (Gillette and Krier 1990: 1077). When risks are genuinely voluntary, correctly reflecting these conditions, it is clear why voluntarily incurred risks would be more acceptable.[6] However, there can be difficulties in distinguishing between voluntary and involuntary risks for this can depend upon background conditions, for example does the city's failure to provide a bridge across an extremely busy street make my crossing it each day an involuntary or voluntarily taken risk?[7]

In judging the acceptability of risks imposed on the society at large, we want to know the different features of the acceptability of the particular risky action, but also facets of the acceptability of major alternatives to it before we can make some judgment of the overall acceptability of the risk. In this sense, social alternatives to using toxic substances are especially important in judging the risks from exposure to toxic substances. Are there other substances which serve the same purposes, but without such toxic risks?

The points reviewed above are, I believe, part of a more plausible approach to how we should think about risks and their acceptability than some prominent technical experts have argued (or suggested) by their remarks (Cranor 1995). One generic conclusion from this view is that in order for risks to be comparable, they should be comparably normatively acceptable. A reasonable rebuttable presumption would be that risks would first need to have comparable *normative* properties *and* then have similar probabilities of materializing into similar harms. It seems much better to compare risks normatively before assessing their probabilities and magnitudes rather than the other way around. Thus, writers who explicitly compare the magnitude and probability of risks and suggest that risks of similar magnitude and probability are comparably acceptable (Morrall 1986; Wilson and Crouch 1987) would be making normative mistakes on this view.

There are other implications. It would be a normative mistake to compare risks of bladder cancer from chlorinating drinking water with risks of cancer from Alar in red apples to keep them fresh longer and provide for a greater shelf life, and with risks from chemical pollutants such as trichloroethylene

(TCE) in drinking water, yet risk comparisons similar to this have been suggested. Chlorination provides life-saving benefits for a group of people in their drinking water, but may pose risk life-taking harms for the same group of people (some risk of bladder cancer from trihalomethanes). Alar, subsequently banned in the US, promised some significant benefits to producers, extremely small benefits to consumers and possibly some cost savings to various parties, but no life-saving benefits in return for life-taking risks (that particularly affect children). Moreover, for Alar the risks and benefits largely go to different parties, thus creating distributive issues, while the risks and benefits of chlorination tend to go to the same group of people. Any risks from chlorination are imposed while those from Alar are in some weak sense chosen (since some apples would have and others would not have Alar in them (if consumers knew this)). Finally, risks of cancer from drinking water contaminated with TCE have no benefits to the consumers of water. It seems that a proper comparison of any life-taking risks from chlorination, Alar and TCE cannot be settled merely by considering the probability and magnitude of harm (Cranor 1995).

Finally, I believe that the views summarized here correspond fairly closely to those found in psychometric studies of social attitudes toward risks. Paul Slovic summarizes some of his research as follows:

> Perhaps the most important message from this research is that there is wisdom as well as error in public attitudes and perceptions. Lay people sometimes lack certain information about hazards. However, *their basic conceptualization of risk is much richer than that of the experts and reflects legitimate concerns that are typically omitted from expert risk assessments.* As a result, risk communication and risk management efforts are destined to fail unless they are structured as a two-way process. *Each side, expert and public, has something valid to contribute. Each side must respect the insights and intelligence of the other.*
>
> (1987: 285; emphasis added)

Thus, it appears that the intuitive philosophical views suggested earlier (Cranor 1995) and sketched here generally tend to converge with the risk perception research done by Slovic. Thus, the public's much broader conceptualization of risks (what I would call the acceptability of risks) has a more substantial foundation, is quite legitimate and is more than 'mere' perceptions of risk. We ignore such considerations at the peril of committing both conceptual and normative mistakes.

Toward a non-consquentialist moral approach to the acceptability of risks

The above account of acceptable risks lacks a more theoretical foundation beyond examples that seem pre-theoretically reasonable. However, I believe that some prominent non-consequentialist views hold some promise for providing an account for these acceptability judgments and for better ways of thinking about justifiable risks than utilitarianism or cost–benefit analysis might. I do not explicitly argue against utilitarian views here, but merely present programmatic outlines of an alternative account. Quite sophisticated utilitarian accounts might provide a foundation for these morally intuitive judgments of the acceptability of risks, but that remains to be seen.

Kantian views as articulated by Tom Hill and Tim Scanlon's contractualism are representative. Common to both (and Rawls's theory of justice as well) is that there are substantial restrictions on how individual members of the moral community may be treated. Moreover, these constraints would obtain, even if some alternative principle or action would produce greater community good. Rawls put the point most sharply: 'Each person possesses an inviolability founded on justice that even the welfare of society as a whole cannot override' (Rawls 1971, 1999: 3). Of course, much has to be worked out to determine the various ways in which persons may not be violated or circumstances in which the welfare of society as a whole is pertinent to how some group of persons should be treated. I cannot address these big questions, but the idea expressed in Rawls' language is an important reminder about ensuring basic protections for persons in bringing about social utility.

Hill in much of his writing endorses the kingdom of ends version of Kant's categorical imperative as a reasonable (if elaborate) deliberative procedure to assist in thinking about moral rules and principles that could guide conduct for a community of persons. This captures some important *attitudes* one might adopt toward fellow members of the moral community and sheds some generic light on approaches to risks. Roughly, the proposal is that persons should accept norms that would be adopted by *rational* legislators who *autonomously* will *universal laws* that treat 'one another as *ends in themselves*, with dignity above price', and reason about such rules while 'abstracting from personal differences' between persons (Hill 1992: 46–7; Kant 2002: 433–36).

There is not space to develop all the ideas represented by the italicized words above, but consider some of the main points.[8] First, members of the kingdom of ends would will 'universal' laws or principles (Kant 2002: 433–4). This includes *inter alia* that one in the kingdom of ends would be willing 'to reciprocate' in social interactions, to avoid 'being a free-rider', and, quite importantly, 'to check one's personal policies by reflecting about what would be reasonable from a broader perspective', especially how others would be treated were persons to act on a proposed principle (Hill 1992: 39). These are quite minimal requirements on conscientious thinking and acting. However, a willingness to consider how others will be treated by a principle proposed for action guidance is an important *Gedankenexperiment* from the moral point of view.

Second, in deliberating about moral issues one would abstract from personal differences between persons (Kant 2002: 433). Among other things, one should not design principles to benefit oneself or particular others, but try to find principles applicable to all, despite differences between persons (Hill 2000a: 47).

Third, proper moral deliberation consists in the *rational* assessment of possible principles (Kant 2002: 433–4). This is different, for example, from assessing principles in accordance with what one would want (or conversely rejecting principles that would treat one as one would not *want* to be treated). Among other things, what is important for these purposes is not what a person would be willing to accept 'with all one's prejudices and idiosyncrasies', but what principles one could recommend based on 'reflection from a broader perspective, where "reasons" are not exclusively person-relative' (Hill 1992: 41). Rational assessment of possible principles and actions are what is important from an appropriate deliberative position, not what one desires or wants.

Fourth, one should regard oneself and others as *autonomous* agents (Kant 2002: 434). There are several aspects to this idea (most of which I need not develop). A quite important one is that each moral agent is a legitimate source of moral input. Kant would have us recognize that all moral agents are legitimate sources of moral considerations, and Hill in his interpretations gives particular emphasis to this (Hill 2000b: 78–9). Among other things, we should regard persons and their interests not only as constraining how we *treat* them (next), but also as those whose views about moral and personal concerns we should take seriously in deciding what to do. In the ideal circumstances of the kingdom of ends, members would consider how principles they might adopt would affect other members and especially those adversely affected by the principle. In non-ideal circumstances this idea might be expressed 'by restricting our conduct to what we ourselves can sincerely endorse *as justifiable to other moral deliberators*, even though we lack assurance of their agreement'. In practical matters, *inter alia*, we should 'seek dialogue with other reasonable moral agents, especially those whose lives we will most affect' by our actions when this can reasonably be done in the circumstances (although it often cannot be) (Hill 1992: 45, 2000b: 79). A concrete example in which citizens' input was explicitly sought on risks occurred in California about a decade ago. The State of California engaged in a Comparative Risk Project to try to determine what environmental and other workplace risks should have highest priority for state action (a project of which I was co-chair). As part of this exercise, several groups of people who would not normally be part of such discussions were subsidized to participate simply in order to ensure that they could articulate their concerns so that decision-makers would hear them. Several participants were representatives of groups that might be and often were adversely affected by state policies. One could think of this as a way of bringing Kantianism down to the earth of policy discussions.

Fifth, and particularly central to the kingdom of ends are fundamental notions expressed in the idea of treating the humanity of persons as an end in itself. One might usefully think of this as 'a cluster of prescriptions about how to *regard* and *treat* human beings' (Hill 1992: 43; emphasis added). One should assess principles and proposed actions based on the idea that 'each person is to be regarded as having a special worth that conscientious agents must always take into account' (Hill 1992: 42). Among other things, this means 'one must appropriately take into account the *whole person*' (Kant 1992: 42; emphasis added).

Recognizing that persons have this special worth would place substantial limitations on how one should treat them because they might be thought to be inviolable in certain ways (Kant 2002: 436). At a minimum, *ceteris paribus*, it would not be morally permissible to harm or violate persons or to endorse principles that would do so.[9] More positively one should give 'special weight to what preserves, promotes, and honours each person's capacity to live as a reasonable, conscientious agent' (Hill 1992: 42).

These prescriptions are an implication of the view that, as Kant puts it, the humanity of persons has an 'unconditioned and incomparable worth' (because of the rational capacities that each has) (Kant 2002: 436). Accordingly, each normal person deserves such treatment and is owed such attitudes without having to morally earn them. (It is less clear how some *homo sapiens* who might be brain damaged or quite substantially lacking in rational capacities should be treated; Kant is simply silent on the subject.) Having unconditioned worth means having a worth or value that is not conditional upon others desiring or wanting it. Having incomparable worth as Kant conceived it means that the worth of the humanity in every person is on a scale of value separate from (and not comparable with) the scales of value of things that have 'market price' (can be bought and sold in the marketplace) or 'attachment price' (things that have value because of one's taste) (Kant 2002: 435).

Thus, his view appears to be that reasonable principles in the first instance should not permit persons with this special worth or value to be injured or killed (or put at serious risk of either) for social goods that have mere market or attachment price. Permitting such trade-offs would trade something of incomparable and unconditioned value (damage to the humanity in persons) for something having mere price in Kant's terms. (Again, examples would need to be considered and details developed on this point, because this view is vague and at the same time could easily be too constraining.) The more important implication is that members of the moral community as a matter of principle should not, *ceteris paribus*, be injured or have their lives jeopardized merely because others would be able to satisfy more desires rather than fewer. Kant (or Hill's Kantian views) would not permit such trade-offs, except perhaps when some very special conditions had been satisfied (a detailed discussion of this must be left to a later time).

Persons in the kingdom of ends should adopt moral principles that they could justify even to those who would be adversely affected if a principle were adopted. That is, one would consider a principle from the kingdom of ends, asking whether everyone affected by it would subscribe to it, even when some would be less favourably treated than others (Hill 2002: 211–12, 214). Central to the attitude of one taking this deliberative position is whether members of the kingdom of ends, subject to the constraints it imposes, would be able to justify acting on a principle even to those adversely affected by it. Moreover, this central Kantian tenet is reinforced by several features of the kingdom of ends: aspects of the universalization principle, the autonomy principle and the principle that the humanity in each should be treated as an end in itself.

T.M. Scanlon suggests a related normative view. His is a less conceptually elaborate view, but has a similar guiding constraint, with his complaint model of justification for principles that govern what each of us 'owes to each other':

> According to contractualism, in order to decide whether it would be wrong to do X in circumstances C, we should consider possible principles governing how one may act in such situations, and ask whether any principle that permitted one to do X in those circumstances could, for that reason, reasonably be rejected. In order to decide whether this is so, we need first to form an idea of the burdens that would be imposed on some people in such a situation if others were permitted to do X [objections to permission]. We then need ... to consider the ways in which others would be burdened by a principle forbidding one to do X in these circumstances [and ask whether one so burdened could reasonably reject such a principle].
>
> (Scanlon 1998: 195)

Scanlon argues that restricting moral concerns to the claims of individuals is 'central to the guiding idea of contractualism' (Scanlon 1998: 229).

Overall Scanlon recommends that in assessing a principle, 'we should consider the weightiness of the burdens it involves, for those on whom they fall, and the importance of the benefits it offers, for those who enjoy them, leaving aside the likelihood of one's actually falling in either of these two classes' (Scanlon 1998: 208). Even if a 'small number of people would be adversely affected by a general permission for agents to act in a certain way, then this gives rise to a potential reason for rejecting that principle' (Scanlon 1998: 205). In deciding on which principle to act, an agent would need to assess the respective burdens imposed on *individuals* affected by competing principles. The agent would need to judge the burdens on those subjected to a principle that permits others to act on it (burdens of permission) against the burdens on those if they were forbidden to act on it (burdens of prohibition). Similar analyses would need to be conducted on plausible alternative principles.

Hill considers the justification of actions in accordance with a principle as something that would typically be considered within the constraints of a Kantian deliberative position. Scanlon does not utilize such stringent constraints on whether persons could 'reasonably reject' principles when they were affected by others acting on them (but there are subtleties to his view), but thinks it important to perform the *Gedankenexperiment* of asking whether persons who were adversely affected by a principle could reasonably reject it.

Non-consequentialist guidance for assessing risks

Even though I have merely sketched some major non-consequentialist themes (and much more needs to be developed), this account offers some guidance about attitudes toward fellow citizens and some justification for the pre-theoretical judgments about risks above.

First, the central insight of both views is that in assessing the acceptability of a principle one should consider its effects on 'the whole person' or on the claims of individuals, not merely a person's desires as part of a collective whole. One way to take this idea is to imaginatively consider discussions with those affected by a principle proposed for adoption and ask sincerely whether it is reasonable that others would agree with actions in accordance with the principle even when they might be somewhat adversely affected by it (and there would need to be provisions for comparing their treatment under one principle with treatment under other plausible principles). Second, beyond that, each is entitled to certain minimal protections, each would need substantial protections against risks (details would need to be developed), and each would need support for projects central to his or her plan of life (Hill 2000a: 49; Kant 2002: 431, 434–5). An heuristic for whether whole persons would be treated properly by social policies would be whether they have reasonable grounds for 'rejecting the principle' on which others would act (Scanlon) or whether they would be justified in principle (subject to the constraints of moral deliberation) to those most adversely affected by it (or, if circumstances permitted, justified to the actual persons affected) (Hill 2000b: 78–9). (Of course, alternative principles to guide possible actions in the circumstance would need to be considered in each case.)

Third, both views reveal an *attitude* toward fellow members of the moral community that typically are different from utilitarianism. Some fairly sophisticated utilitarian views assess rules or principles by asking, not whether they could be justified to individuals adversely affected by them, but by asking whether a future in which the principles were adopted would maximize utility or desire satisfaction. If future consequences based on one principle would be better than alternative futures based on other principles, it is the more defensible utilitarian principle. Some even more sophisticated utilitarians, such as Harsanyi (1982), would ask whether persons in an original position would choose a policy assuming they had an equal chance of being anyone affected by it (with different levels of *average utility* produced for persons in different positions in society). This comes closer to non-consequentialist deliberative positions, but is not the same. There is still a focus on average utility and there seems to be no direct concern to specifically address how *individuals* would be affected or whether they would likely agree with how they would be treated by a particular social policy. Nor are moral agents necessarily seen as legitimate sources of moral input as Kantian or Scanlonian views would.

Consider an example. The risks from coal mining were recently brought to national attention in the US with the deaths of 11 miners in the Sago coal mine in West Virginia. Consider this excerpt from an account of some conditions in a typical mine:

> Even well-run mines are frightening places. The average Appalachian mine is less than five feet high, with some less than three feet. Some miners take straws with their lunches because there is not enough space to tilt a soft-drink can over their heads. The roof often pings and rumbles like ice on a frozen pond.
>
> [Small companies with few mines have] operations [that] are usually nonunion. They use reconditioned equipment and hire unskilled men with few other prospects who often worry that large fines will shut down their mines.
>
> (Harris 2006: 1)

Mines are not great places to work, yet to the extent that a nation relies on coal for electricity and heating (and, of course, it could choose not to), there will be a need for coal and miners to extract it. I do not want to suggest that the conditions of coal mines suggested above would be defensible from a well-argued utilitarian point of view; indeed such a theory would argue for safety improvements up to the point at which utility is maximized for the moral community as a whole. Nonetheless, a common argument for not making industries safer than at present is utilitarian in form: although increasing safety for employees will make them safer and the lives of their families better, it will also increase production costs, which will (minimally or modestly) raise prices for thousands or millions of consumers and possibly put some miners out of work, possibly making the world overall a somewhat worse place than it is at present. Of course, such arguments may be incomplete, may be offered disingenuously and may be an attempt to put a public justification on self-interest. Moreover, it is unlikely that these are serious utilitarian arguments in the sense that advocates propose them as the optimal utilitarian outcome to a problem. However, if the number of miners whose lives would be safer is small enough and those whose costs would be kept low without the increased safety are large enough, there can be a reasonable utilitarian argument for not making improvements in working conditions.

By contrast, the non-consequentialist views draw attention to how *whole persons* are affected by a policy, and whether, given the claims of typical individuals affected, it could be reasonably justified *to them* (Hill 1992: 42; Scanlon 1998: 229). This shift in emphasis is not merely a useful heuristic, but an important feature of moral deliberation about principles that appears much more defensible than even a sophisticated rule-utilitarian might utilize (although I have not argued for this). In the mining example, would those most adversely affected by a principle governing their safety have good grounds for reasonably rejecting the principle (Scanlon) or would a principle that would be endorsed in the kingdom of ends argue for greater improvements for those adversely affected by coal production? It is by asking questions such as these (and even imaginatively considering discussions with affected persons) that we express a different attitude toward fellow citizens and that we acquire a better moral view of how persons should be treated morally.

Beyond recommendations for adopting a different attitude toward fellow members of the moral community, the non-consequentialist views sketched above can accommodate several of the plausible features of acceptable risks identified in the first section.

A Kantian account of acceptable risks would distinguish between risks that are central to one's life plan or personal projects (feature (5) above), and those to which they are required to be exposed as a matter of law. Non-consequentialist views will more easily provide moral space for risks that are central to one's life plan than will many utilitarian accounts, since utilitarianism risks squeezing out personal projects as morally impermissible because persons often could create more utility by engaging in some other activity (Scheffler 1982).

This difference between these versions of non-consequentialism and utilitarianism should not be over-emphasized because sophisticated forms of utilitarianism, such as ideal rule-utilitarianism, Harsanyi's (1982) rule-utilitarianism, or perhaps one of the views Scheffler (1982) articulates could provide appropriate space for the importance of personal projects. Moreover, there could be a surprise for certain kinds of risky personal projects lurking in Kantian accounts that utilize a stringent version of the special worth of the humanity of persons. If climbing mountains were a central feature of one's life plan, from a Kantian point of view there could be some difficulties justifying this activity to oneself as a rational person in the kingdom of ends. For example, climbing mountains puts one's life at risk for aims or ends that might only have value as 'market price' or at most 'attachment price'. In short, a mountaineer might be putting one's life (and one's humanity) at risk for something of incomparably lesser value. Thus, although Kant provides for personal projects, some we might regard as quite permissible might encounter difficulties on his account. (Such issues would be moot on Scanlon's view, since he is only concerned with what we owe to *others*.)

Transparent risks would tend to be more acceptable on Kantian views because of the premium they place on persons being fully aware of risks and their consequences, and on their being able to live out rationally chosen, autonomous lives with awareness of such risks. Moreover, transparent risks would be judged more acceptable on Kantian views (as they are more intuitively plausible) than would latent or invisible risks.

Both Kantian and Scanlonian views would strongly endorse the acceptability of genuinely voluntary risks and an important role for choice in their theories. Kantian non-consequentialism is based on both hypothetical consent and derivatively on considerable consultation with, or actual consent by, those affected by principles. Thus, adopting an attitude of consciously taking account of others' views and choices is central to this class of theories (Hill 2000a, 2000b).[10] Scanlon argues that 'principles that no one could reasonably reject often must be ones that make normative outcomes sensitive to individuals' choices, or at least to their having had the opportunity to choose' (Scanlon 1998: 251).

Next, insofar as there is a reasonable moral distinction between risks threatened by natural phenomena and those resulting from human activities, non-consequentialists can readily provide for this. To what extent would one taking the Kantian deliberative view permit such human activities and how should the risks from them be arranged in order to permit the activities consistent with principles that all persons would be treated as having special worth and that all would reasonably agree to? That is, this non-consequentialism explicitly requires hypothetical collective consideration of permissible and impermissible human activities in the moral community. Moreover, once human activities are known to impose risks on some, would those in the kingdom of ends agree that such risks may be reasonably imposed on some members of the community for the benefit of others? Under what conditions would risks to the lives of persons be justified even to those most at risk? Scanlon would be concerned about what we owe to each other by permitting humanly caused risks in the community, and whether principles permitting such activities could be reasonably rejected by those adversely affected by them.

There is an obvious place in non-consequentialism for the intuitive distinction between risks created by the person who is also put at risk – self-imposed risks as it were – and risks created by one party and imposed on another party, which potentially raises distributive issues. To what extent is it permissible for the risk creator to impose risks and costs on others in the community? Distributive issues are quite important for non-consequentialists, focusing as they do on, *inter alia*, the *relations* between persons in the moral community (Kant) or on what treatment we owe to each other (Scanlon). When risks are internalized within the life of one person, this poses fewer issues of justification than when risks created by one party are imposed on another party. For utilitarians, distributive issues become important only as they affect the overall production of utility. What we might regard as misdistributions of benefits or risks within a community in most cases will affect overall utility, but that is a contingent matter, not a matter of principle as it would be for Kant, Hill or Scanlon.

Finally, these versions of non-consequentialism can easily justify the intuitive trade-off between protecting persons from the life-taking risks of water contaminated by bacteria and viruses by use of chlorination that introduces life-taking risks of its own, but at a lower rate. On non-consequentialist grounds it is quite appropriate to secure life-saving benefits by imposing lower level life-taking risks, when there are no other reasonable alternatives available. But this same rationale would not permit life-taking risks from Alar (or from TCE-contaminated drinking water) simply to permit greater desire satisfaction in the community. The rationale for chlorination on Kantian grounds would be that such actions would enhance representative persons' opportunities for living out longer rational, autonomous lives compared with the alternatives, but this is not obviously available to justify the risks from Alar (or from TCE in drinking water) (Hill 1992: 214). It is plausible to suppose that on Scanlon's theory persons could not reasonably reject a principle that permitted such a tradeoff, when there were no more reasonable alternatives available for sanitizing the water supply. Scanlonians could also quite reasonably reject the risks from Alar or from TCE in drinking water.

Conclusion

This presentation of some properties of intuitively acceptable risks and a programmatic non-consequentialist approach to account for them is only a beginning. Clearly much more needs to be done and these issues will need to be addressed more fully in future papers. Thinking clearly about risks and their acceptability in our lives is too important to be left to technical risk assessors and cost–benefit theorists. Finally, we should be able in principle to justify our social policies even to those individuals who would be adversely affected by them without eviscerating their legitimate and central interests because a technical calculation shows utility would be maximized in the community.

Notes

1 The assessment of *risks*, where the probability distribution of some harm is known, is contrasted with *uncertainty*, where the probabilities of loss or harm are not known. Very often risk assessment is more characterized by the many *uncertainties* in trying to estimate probabilities of harm than by known or narrowly identified *probabilities*.

2 Wilson and Crouch (1987) appear to blur this distinction, beginning their essay, 'Everyday we take risks and avoid others'.

3 The permissible-required distinction is one of moral categories, while risks 'taken' compared with those 'imposed' is more of a linguistic category. These might turn out to be the same upon examination, but I do not wish to assert that as a preliminary point (nor do I settle the issue in this essay).

4 This analysis has an individualistic tone to it in the sense of focusing on individual responsibility for exposure at least to some risks. While this is true for many voluntarily incurred risks, I do not suggest that individuals should bear the burden of avoiding risks that are in the public media – air, water, food and in the workplace.

5 Alternatives to a risky course of action do not take us very far. If our drinking water were polluted with reproductive or other toxicants, many, but not all, people might avoid the risks by purchasing bottled water. However, the norms implicit in the idea

of a *public* water supply would tend to argue for cleaning it up even if there are some readily available alternatives to drinking it.

6 Voluntarily chosen risks are clearly 'taken', but I leave open for now whether every risk one 'takes' is properly judged to be a voluntary risk. I suspect that only by distorting one idea or the other will they clearly be co-extensive.

7 I owe this point to Tim Lewens.

8 Many of the considerations that Kant incorporates into the kingdom of ends are representative of what it is to take the moral point of view. Other considerations (or interpretations of some of the same considerations) play a much more substantive role in supporting intermediate moral principles.

9 Of course in situations in which one cannot avoid harming someone no matter which policy is chosen, a theory would need resources to address the conflict.

10 There may be some Kantians who are less sanguine about the role of actual consent (O'Neill 2002).

References

Cranor, C. (1995) 'The use of comparative risk judgments in risk management', in A.M. Fan, and L.W. Chang (eds) *Toxicology and Risk Assessment: principles, methods, and applications*, New York: Marcel Dekker, Inc.

Center for Progressive Reform (2006) *An Unnatural Disaster: the aftermath of hurricane Katrina*. Online. Available: http://www.progressivereform.org/Unnatural_Disaster_512.pdf (accessed July 10, 2006).

Gillette, C. and Krier, J. (1990) 'Risk, courts and agencies', *University of Pennsylvania Law Review*, 38: 1077–109.

Harris, G. (2006) 'Endemic problem of safety in coal mining', *New York Times*, January 10.

Harsanyi, J.C. (1982) 'Morality and the theory of rational behaviour', in A. Sen and B. Williams (eds), *Utilitarianism and Beyond*, New York: Cambridge University Press.

Hill, T.E., Jr (1992) 'Making exceptions without abandoning the principle; or how a Kantian might think about terrorism', in T.E. Hill, Jr (ed.) *Dignity and Practical Reason*, Ithaca: Cornell University Press, pp. 196–225.

——(ed.) (2000a) 'A Kantian perspective on moral rules', *Respect, Pluralism, and Justice: Kantian perspectives*, Oxford: Oxford University Press, 33–55.

——(ed.) (2000b) 'Basic respect and cultural diversity', *Respect, Pluralism, and Justice: Kantian perspectives*, Oxford: Oxford University Press, 59–86.

——(2005) 'Assessing moral rules: utilitarian and Kantian perspectives', in *Normativity, Philosophical Issues* (a Supplement to *Nous*), 15, edited by Ernest Sosa and Enrique Villanueva.

Kant, I. (2002) *Groundwork for the Metaphysics of Morals*, in T.E. Hill, Jr. and A. Zweig (eds), New York: Oxford University Press.

Morrall, J.F. (1986) 'A review of the record', *Regulation*, November–December, 27.

O'Neill, O. (2002) *Autonomy and Trust in Bioethics*, Cambridge: Cambridge University Press.

Rawls, J. (1971, 1999) *A Theory of Justice*, Cambridge: Belknap Press of Harvard University Press.

——(1982) 'Social unity and primary goods', in A. Sen and B. Williams (eds), *Utilitarianism and Beyond*, Cambridge: Cambridge University Press.

Scanlon, T.M. (1998) *What We Owe to Each Other*, Cambridge, MA: Harvard University Press.

Scheffler, S. (1982) *The Rejection of Consequentialism*, Oxford: Clarendon Press.

Slovic, P. (1987) 'Perception of risks', *Science*, 236: 280–5.

Wilson R., and Crouch, E.A. (1987) 'Risk assessment and comparisons: an introduction', *Science*, 236: 267–70.

3

WHAT IS THE VALUE OF PREVENTING A FATALITY?

Jonathan Wolff

Introduction

The idea of the 'value of preventing a fatality' (VPF), or equivalently the 'value of a statistical life', is a technical term used in safety decision-making. It gets its life from risk cost–benefit analysis (RCBA). Where a safety measure is designed to reduce the risk of death there will always be a question of whether it is worthwhile, whether on economic grounds or some other.[1] As soon as it is admitted that there is a conceptual possibility that a potential safety measure could be too expensive to be worth implementing it is necessary to find a way of giving some meaning to this idea, and, if possible, some criterion to settle such questions.

At this point risk cost–benefit analysis offers a surprisingly simple formula for this purpose. To decide whether, according to RCBA, it is appropriate to introduce the innovation it is necessary to know three things. First, how much will the innovation cost? Second, how many lives, statistically, or in probabilistic terms, can it be expected to save? And, third, what, according to the relevant regulations, is the (monetary) value of preventing a fatality? The first two give the cost of preventing a fatality (CPF) for the project, which is to say how much the project costs for each statistical life saved. If installing a widget is going to save two statistical lives over the widget's lifetime, and costs £1 million, then the CPF is £0.5 million. This can then be compared with the VPF as set out in the regulatory framework governing the area under consideration. For example, the UK, for ordinary workplace risks, currently operates with a VPF of a little over one million pounds (Health and Safety Executive 2001: 36; Department of Transport 2004).[2] The US, I understand, uses a figure of around six million dollars (Sunstein 2002: 165). Once these figures are known it is possible to give an answer to the question of whether the innovation should be introduced: it is necessary only to compare the CPF with the appropriate VPF. Current UK case law suggests that there is a requirement to introduce the safety measure unless the CPF is 'grossly disproportionate' to the VPF. In other words, in the UK if the innovation values saving a statistical life at much more than one million pounds there is no obligation to introduce it. Whether this gross disproportion test still applies is a matter of controversy, but in any case if the innovation costs less than the VPF then the regulations suggest that it should be introduced.

There are many questions that can be asked about whether and when RCBA is an appropriate way of approaching safety decision-making. However, for the purposes of this essay I want to put most of these questions to one side. (For broader discussion see Wolff 2002 and Wolff 2006.) My topic here is the narrow one of simply trying to understand what 'the value of preventing a fatality' really means, and whether it can be morally defensible to operate with different VPFs for different circumstances.

Life-saving and risk reduction

For many people RCBA is an astonishingly cold and heartless way of making decisions about safety, as it appears to put a financial value on life. Defenders of the method deny that it has this implication. The Health and Safety Executive, in their major work on this topic, *Reducing Risk, Protecting People*, say the following:

> VPF is often misunderstood to mean that a value is being placed on a life. This is not the case. It is simply another way of saying what people are prepared to pay to secure a certain averaged risk reduction. A VPF of £1,000,000 corresponds to a reduction in risk of one in a hundred thousand being worth about £10 to an average individual. VPF therefore, is not to be confused with the value society, or the courts, might put on the life of a real person or the compensation appropriate to its loss.
>
> (Health and Safety Executive 2001: 65n)

This is a very interesting distinction. It is clear that purchasing – or declining to purchase – devices or services that make small differences to one's safety, or that of one's family, is an ordinary part of life, taking its place alongside other consumer decisions. Purchasing a smoke alarm, or deciding that it is not worth paying extra for a modification to a car to make it somewhat safer, are decisions traded off against other consumption options.

Consequently we have to understand that the concept of saving of a statistical life is a different idea from the saving of the life of a particular named individual. Cases where we are faced with saving the lives of known individuals, such as miners trapped underground, or sailors in a stricken submarine, are, thankfully, rare and when they happen authorities rarely even raise issues of the cost of rescue. A statistical life is quite different: it is an accounting fiction pieced together from a patchwork of mitigations of very many low probability risks, each of which is equivalent to a perfectly ordinary economic transaction, and pervasive throughout life.

It has also been argued that in addition to the distinction between saving a statistical life and saving the life of an identified person, we need to bring in a third category: saving an anonymous life. This, it has been argued, is also quite different from saving a statistical life (Jones-Lee 1989: 174). Compare the following two situations involving a population of one million. In the first, everyone has an independent one in a million chance of dying from a particular hazard. In the second, one person – a person we cannot identify in advance – faces certain death from some other hazard. It is not unreasonable to say that for each individual in this population of one million there is an equal statistical chance of death in each case. Yet the situations are quite different. In the first any number of deaths from the hazard – from zero to one million – are possible, although one death is the most likely outcome, whereas in the second there can only be one death from the hazard.

However, the distinction between a statistical death and an anonymous death can become problematic, in at least two ways. The first problem is that for a particular individual there is no difference in practice between the two situations: in each case for all I know I am personally faced with a risk of death of one in a million. So although for the policy-maker, or outsider, there is a clear difference, for those affected there is none, when considering only their own plight. Second, if the statistics are reliably based on regular past frequencies, then the distinction comes close to collapse. Consider road deaths in the UK. For some time around 3,500 people have died on the roads each year. How many will die next year? Theoretically it is possible that no one will, or millions will, but it is a very safe bet that the number will be between 3,000 and 4,000, and probably this could be narrowed down quite a bit more with a high degree of confidence. We might, then, think of this situation as closer to one in which we know how many people will die: we just do not know who they are yet. If so the distinction between anonymous deaths and statistical deaths is becoming blurred, even though, strictly these are statistical deaths. In policy terms, then, it becomes unclear how much difference this distinction makes.

However, there is a further important distinction. In some cases, the chances of different individuals dying are not independent. Consider an incident such as a nuclear explosion from a power plant. I do not pretend that the following figures bear any relation to reality, but imagine that the risk assessment suggests that such an incident is likely to happen once every hundred thousand years, and if so it is most likely to kill one hundred thousand people. Once again, statistically, the expectation is one death per year, but it is far from obvious that the same framework of evaluation should apply to what we might call 'catastrophic' events as to cases where risks to lives are independent and thus statistically one can expect a regular stream of smaller numbers of deaths.

We may, then, feel that there is a clear policy distinction to be made between 'steady stream' cases and 'catastrophic' cases and a different approach is needed. And it does seem to be true that we have different intuitions about road safety and nuclear safety. Unfortunately, however, cases rarely differ in only one respect, and it can be a subtle question to work out what is driving intuitions in different cases or even to detect what those intuitions are. Should we be more cautious about major nuclear accidents because they involve so many people, and have an impact beyond loss of life, or less cautious because they are likely to be so rare?

We will briefly return to catastrophic events later in the chapter. At this stage I merely wished to raise some complications as a way of bringing out the central use of the concept of the value of preventing a fatality. As understood by regulators it is really a rather misleading way of talking about the value of reducing the aggregate probabilities – probably independent probabilities – of the risk of death for a group of people, rather than a way of talking about saving the lives of particular individuals whether known of anonymous.

Derivation of VPF figures

As should be clear, the RCBA process needs a value – or possibly a set of values – for the VPF. I mentioned that the UK currently operates with a figure of around one million pounds and the US about six million dollars. This variation could reflect different social priorities and values, different methodologies, or be a matter of pure contingency. Yet the figures on their own are mysterious, and a pressing question is how they are to be derived. In the early days of such calculations, the standard methodology seems to have been to base valuations on lost potential economic contribution. That is to say, human beings were regarded as 'human capital' and thus a source of potential income. The value of preventing a fatality is therefore equivalent, on this view, to the cost of losing that potential income. This, clearly, has some unfortunate effects: on this method anyone who is economically dependent, such as the old and the unemployed could have a value so low it could be negative, and if they are ill and in need of health care it could be significantly so (Mishan 1971).

This idea that the 'value of preventing a fatality' or, equivalently, the 'value of a statistical life' is somehow based on 'society's investment' in that individual, or the opportunity cost of lost production, or some calculation based on both, is still common. Consider the following from Jared Diamond's otherwise excellent recent book *Collapse*:

> The value of 'one statistical life' in the US – i.e. the cost to the US economy resulting from the death of an average American whom society has gone to the expense of rearing and educating but who dies

before a lifetime of contributing to the national economy – is usually estimated at around $5 million.

(Diamond, 2006: 504)

This, however, is to confuse the older methodologies, which typically yield a much lower average figure, with new methodologies which yield figures in the range Diamond mentions, but in which investment or lost production costs figure only, at most, as a minor element. Indeed, the idea that we should think of the value of a statistical life in terms of the investment in that life or its possible contribution to production has long been regarded as unsatisfactory (Hammerton *et al.* 1982: 182). One reason, of course, is the peculiarity of the results it achieves, including negative value, which we have already noted. A deeper reason is that it conflates the distinction insisted upon by the HSE between the reduction of a small risk for a large number of people and the economic consequences of saving of a life. Even someone who is old, and has no productive contribution left to make to the economy, may still be prepared to pay good money to reduce a small risk of their own death, and even if they are not prepared to spend money this way 'we' as a society may consider doing so on their behalf. Reducing their risks of death is a benefit to them, even if doing so potentially increases total social costs in terms, say, of health care.

When we understand the value of preventing a fatality in terms of risk reduction, rather than life-saving, and we also realize that paying to reduce a small risk is a perfectly ordinary commercial transaction, then the possibility of new methodologies of valuation open up. The promise is that valuation of VPF can be conducted in terms of willingness to pay: the payments people do, or would, make in the market. The payments people *do make* yields the methodology of revealed preferences, and those people *would make* yields the methodology of expressed preference. The former looks at actual market behaviour as a guide to valuation, the second uses purely hypothetical 'willingness to pay' methods, normally known as 'contingent valuation'.

Both methods have their attractions and drawbacks. Consider, first, revealed preference methodology. This has the advantage of looking at actual market behaviour: the decisions people have actually made in real markets, spending real money that they could spend on something else. The disadvantage is something it shares with any attempt to deduce people's underlying attitudes from their behaviour: what in philosophy of mind is called 'the holism of the mental' (Davidson 1963). Given that both desire and belief play a role in the explanation of actions, it has been argued that every action is compatible with every desire if the surrounding beliefs are adjusted. A person's drinking hemlock is consistent with that person's desire to die, but also to live a long life, if they believe that hemlock is some sort of vitamin boosting drink. In the present context, people might choose to buy a dangerous product, believing it to be safe. Nothing, though, is revealed about that person's attitude to risk from this decision. Furthermore, it is far from always the case for an action to be performed for the sake of a single desired goal. So, for example, it is very unlikely that the only difference between two complex products – two cars, say – is that one is safer than the other. The fact, then, that I have chosen to purchase a safer car does not show that I am prepared to the pay that premium purely for the risk reduction. It may be, for example, that I also prefer the image associated with one make of car rather than the other.

Consequently valuations based on revealed preferences are highly uncertain, and there is a huge variation in the figures such studies do in fact reveal. Sunstein, for example, sets out a list of valuations based on labour-market studies, which essentially explore the wage premium needed to recruit people into more dangerous jobs. These studies produce a VPF which varies from $0.7 million to $16.3 million, in 1997 dollars (Sunstein 2002: 174). Although averages of many studies may be helpful, it is hard to know when a sufficiently broad or representative range of studies has been conducted. For all these reasons some theorists prefer to follow the method of expressed preferences or contingent valuation. The basic idea behind this methodology is that subjects are asked for their views of how much they would pay for a safety improvement, if one were available.

There are at least two main advantages for this methodology. First, the experimenter can set up questions in such a way to ensure that the subject must focus on the safety element alone in the choice. In a hypothetical example all other parameters can be fixed in a way in which this will rarely, if ever, happen in a real market case. Second, a given subject can, in theory, be asked many questions, and so a great deal more data can be generated.

In practice, however, such benefits are rarely seen. There are several limitations. First, there are framing issues. It is well known that if people say that they would pay a particular amount of money to avoid a risk, in general they will also say that they would need a higher sum of money in compensation if the feared event happened. This requires explanation, as many versions of decision theory predict that a given individual's 'willingness to pay' and 'willingness to accept compensation' should be the same. To get a sense of this imagine the highest price you would pay for a pair of tickets to some highly attractive event: the World Cup Final or a star-studded opera. Imagine you have just paid for the tickets and have them in your hand. Now, what is the lowest price you would sell them for? If there is a non-trivial gap between the two sums – as many people report there is – it shows that there is a difference between your willingness to pay and your willingness to accept compensation, and raises the question of what we should say is your 'price' for these tickets.

Second, given that in contingent valuation no money actually passes hands, it is unclear how seriously we can take the figures offered. There is a legitimate worry that some people are simply plucking numbers out of the air, rather than revealing willingness to pay.

Third, and most seriously of all, human beings appear to be very poor at rational decision-making involving very small probabilities. Subjects can very easily be led to make inconsistent decisions: for example, being willing to pay more if a risk reduction is broken down into two steps rather than one, even if the resulting outcome is the same, or paying the same for a larger reduction and a smaller one. In sum, when subjects are asked to express their preferences concerning paying to avoid risks with small probabilities, very little reliable data is generated. Consider again the HSE example where a VPF of £1,000,000 is said to be equivalent to a payment of £10 to avoid a one in a hundred thousand chance of death. If asked 'How much would you pay to avoid a one in a hundred thousand chance of death?' most people, I think, would not feel that they could give a robust or reliable answer. Furthermore, when asked a number of different questions it seems very unlikely that many people would give a consistent set of answers.[3]

To avoid these problems some experimenters have adopted modified techniques. One type of study, for example, asks subjects about their attitudes to risks of a greater probability. Michael Jones-Lee and associates developed one extremely inventive approach (Carthy et al. 1999). To simplify the description of a rather more complex method, the essence seems to come to the following. The subject is first told about a possible motor accident which will leave them hospitalized for a certain period, but from which they would make a full recovery. They are then asked how much they would pay to avoid such an accident, and how much compensation they would need to be prepared to accept that the accident had not left them worse off overall. These sums are then combined, by means of a standard calculation, to derive a single sum for the value of avoiding that accident. In the next phase of the experiment the subjects are asked, in effect, what risk of death would be less preferred than the accident. That is, if they choose option A they will have the accident so described, but if they choose option B there will be a risk of dying, but otherwise one survives unharmed. The question then is when does the risk of dying become unacceptably high in the sense that one would prefer the certainty of the accident to the risk of death. Once this question is answered it then becomes possible to calculate, for that subject, the value of preventing a fatality. The two inputs are the value of preventing the accident, together with the maximum risk of death one would 'trade' the accident for.

This method does, then, yield a determinate answer for each individual. The range of answers is very diverse, However, rather than discuss the range, which I have done elsewhere (Wolff 2002: 57–69), I want to point out the way in which this methodology, at first sight, blurs the two questions separated by the Health and Safety Executive, and in doing so makes a particular assumption about 'linearity'. Indeed, the point may be obvious. In order to obtain meaningful data about the risks people are prepared to run, or to pay to avoid, subjects have to be asked about risks of fairly high probability. Yet the VPF figure is intended to represent the value of reducing a very large number of low probability risks to many people, which together add up to the saving of a life. This, then, presupposes linearity in attitudes to risk: that, say, I would pay no more or no less than a thousand times as much to reduce a risk that was a thousand times as great, at least if I am rational. Yet this seems problematic.

To see the issue more clearly, consider the highly artificial example of being invited to take part in a game of Russian roulette, for a payment. The gun, however, has a variable number of barrels, and let us also assume that there is no reason to doubt that it is a fair gun in the sense that the probability of any barrel being engaged is equal, whether or not it contains the bullet.

Now, I assume that for any person there is some number of barrels and some amount of money that would be sufficient to entice the person to accept the risk. So, for example, imagine that the gun has two million barrels, and hence one's chance of dying was two million to one. I imagine most people would be prepared to accept a finite sum of money – even a rather small amount – to run this risk, at least if it was presented to them in the right way. At the other extreme, imagine you are being asked to play the game with a gun with only two barrels, and hence there is only a 50 per cent chance of survival. If attitudes to risk were linear then you should be prepared to accept a price for this of one million times the smallest price you would be prepared to accept for the one in two million chance. And, indeed, it may well be. But it seems hard to say that it is irrational for someone who would have taken the small risk for one pound to decline to accept one million pounds for a 50 per cent chance of death. Of course some people may be happy to kill themselves, and even for those with a preference for life an exceptionally high sum could tempt them to risk their own lives so they if they do survive they will have a life of luxury. Nevertheless, it would be very strange to argue that someone is irrational if they refuse to accept this price. For many people, I assume, there is simply no price which would tempt them to take a 50 per cent chance of death.

Consider now something in between. Suppose the gun has twenty barrels. If the price was high enough more people might be tempted to accept the offer. But must this price be exactly a hundred thousand times as much as they accepted for taking a one in two million risk? It may be an axiom of some forms of rational choice theory – although by no means all – that attitudes to risk should be linear in this sense, but it seems to be no part of common sense.

Whether these arguments put the Jones-Lee 'chained' methodology into question depend on whether the risks people are invited to consider in these experiments fall into a non-linear part of the curve. If so, then the studies would put too high a price on safety, assuming that people are prepared to pay proportionally more to avoid risks with very high probabilities. However, the values derived from this work may suggest that, actually, there is little to worry about on this score, although further investigation would be of help.

We need also to consider a suggestion from Richard Posner that linearity also fails at the other end of the scale, when we consider catastrophic risks with very low probabilities (Posner 2004). He may well be right about this, although it is very hard to gain firm evidence. One type of revealed preferences study could conceivably demonstrate a lack of preparedness to pay to reduce risks with very small probabilities. These would be studies of what governments are prepared to pay on their citizens' behalf. Although he does not use it to demonstrate failure of linearity at minuscule probabilities, Posner discusses the example of possible asteroid collision. He quotes a UK task force which estimated that the chances of an asteroid collision that would kill 1.5 billion people is 1 in 250,000 in any year. Using a VPF of $2 million, he calculates that RCBA would justify spending $12 billion a year to prevent an asteroid collision (Posner 2004: 180). At present the US government spends $3.9 million tracking large objects in near space: $800 for each statistical life. If we think it would be inappropriate to spend much more than this, then that appears to imply that either we think the probabilities are not as stated, or that we should use a very low VPF for such a risk, or that, somehow, the methodology of RCBA is not appropriate for risks of this nature. Perhaps we think all three of these things.

Matters, inevitably, are complicated. The risk of a natural disaster is quite different from the risk created by a project undertaken for human gain or benefit. Imagine a new, much more powerful, form of nuclear power. Suppose we are told that such a technology risks killing 1.5 billion people every 250,000 years: the same probability as an asteroid collision. It seems unlikely that we would be so phlegmatic about accepting the risks. Possibly the reason for this is that a nuclear power station is a risk we feel we do not have to take. Furthermore it creates profits which can be used to pay for safety improvements. By contrast, an asteroid collision is a risk that has not been created by human action, and does not generate a stream of revenue which can be used to pay for safety measures. Accordingly we may decide not to divert spending away from other valuable projects, and simply run the risk rather than reducing our present standard of living to avoid something that may actually never happen. We might also judge that the risk for the next 100 years is really too small to worry about, and that future generations will be in a position to defend themselves at lower costs. Because of such complications it seems clear that we might need to take into account a whole range of factors before we can decide what it is our social preferences reveal about our attitudes to risks with small probabilities. Incidentally, this is a powerful illustration of the problem of revealed preference methodology: any actual behaviour could have innumerable explanations.

While it is hard to decide what would count as evidence that our attitudes to risk are non-linear, except in the case of risks of very high probabilities, this is not evidence that they are, in fact, linear. We have to be prepared to consider the possibility that attitudes to risk are non-linear. If they are, in fact, non-linear, and we accept that our regulatory regime should be based on attitudes to risk, then it follows that we would have to accept different VPFs for different types of situation. Those which involve very small probabilities would demand very small VPFs, but where we get close to certain death the VPFs should be high. This, in fact, is one way of understanding what we actually do in 'rescue cases' where a child has fallen down a well, or miners are trapped underground, or sailors in a submarine. As mentioned above, often we seem to be prepared to spend without thought of whether it can be justified by RCBA with a standard VPF.

In effect the Health and Safety Executive itself has accepted non-linearity, by adopting what it calls a 'Tolerability of Risk Framework', distinguishing 'unacceptable', 'tolerable' and 'broadly acceptable' regions of risk (Health and Safety Executive 2001: 42–6). A risk of death is unacceptable if it is above 1 in 1,000 per year for the workforce and 1 in 10,000 per year for the public who have a risk imposed on them, and is 'broadly acceptable' and thus requiring no special reduction measures if it falls below 1 in 1,000,000 per year. This is a type of 'limit' case of non-linearity, in which risks higher than 1 in 10,000 (for the public) are given infinite VPFs and those below 1 in 1,000,000 are given no VPF at all. Although crude, this may be the most appropriate approach for public policy for non-catastrophic risks, although it does have rather startling implications. A hazard to which the whole UK population is exposed might cause 50 deaths each year but would fall below the 1 in 1,000,000 threshold, and so, strictly, would not require any money at all to be spent on further mitigation steps.

The variable value of preventing a fatality

Once it is accepted that, in principle, there can be variable VPFs for different probabilities of death, this raises the question of whether there can be variation for other sorts of reasons. Consider the risks involved in railway safety. The 'headline' accident figures concern the number of passengers who are killed in train accidents. However, this is only a small proportion – probably less than 3 per cent on average – of the number of people who die on the railways. About two-thirds of all deaths on the railways are suicides. Deaths of trespassers – adult and children – constitute the second largest group, with passengers and then workforce, other than in circumstances of train accidents, making up the rest. Although the industry, along with its government funder and regulator, has not officially adopted a variable VPF to cover these different cases, one may conjecture that unofficially it does, in that it is prepared to spend much more to prevent some categories of death than others. Passengers, workforce and child trespassers probably have higher priority, and adult trespassers and suicides lower.

One can understand safety decision-makers being rather nervous about announcing different VPFs for these different categories. One can imagine the response: 'Are you saying that the life of a trespasser is less important than the life of a passenger?' And, of course, no one wants to say that, even though this is how different VPFs for different groups would inevitably be interpreted. Yet it is important to see that variable VPFs do not have this implication when we understand that VPFs are simply a shorthand for accumulation of many small risk reductions. The question is whether it is right to pay more to reduce the risk to one group than it is for another. How can we answer this?

It may be helpful to reflect on more ordinary safety decision-making. It seems plausible that people are prepared to spend more to reduce risks to their children than they are for themselves. One reason is that children are generally in more danger, being less able to take precautions for themselves. But putting that to one side, there is also the fact that parents feel themselves to be in a special position of responsibility with respect to their children. Finally people simply care a great deal about children, and particularly their own. Similar types of reason can operate in the case of railway safety. The industry may rightly feel that it is in a special position of responsibility towards its passengers and its workforce, and much less so to adult trespassers and would-be suicides. This is not to deny all responsibility, but to say that, at the least, responsibility is shared. Child trespassers are in a different category, as they are far less able to exercise the right sort of judgement to take responsibility for themselves.

As soon as it is said that the industry has a greater responsibility to reduce risks to one group than to another, and should pay more to do so, then by the definition of VPF it follows that they are placing a higher VPF on one group than another. Yet one can understand a reluctance to admit this, for the reasons given: how can we value one person's life more than that of another? However this is largely a terminological problem, based on the confused idea that VPF puts a value on life. This, it seems to me, is a good reason for reconsidering terminology. The misleading content of the idea of the value of preventing a fatality is getting in the way of clear thinking. Perhaps it is time that this term is abandoned and replaced with another. We shall look at one such proposal shortly.

Before doing so, we might ask what the warrant would be for using different VPFs for different groups. One reason why this topic is something of a taboo is that if such differences are based on willingness to pay methods, we will find different VPFs for the rich than for the poor, as the rich are typically prepared to pay more for risk reduction, as for almost everything, than the poor. This outcome is avoided by averaging strategies, which are generally treated as justified.[4] In the cases discussed in this chapter the rationale for different VPFs is likely to be derived from judgements about higher and lower responsibility, rather than willingness to pay for different types of risk reduction, although there is room for conducting research, using willingness to pay methods. Clearly there is more work to be done here.

The value of reducing a standard risk of death

In the last section I suggested that we might wish to rid ourselves of the confusing terminology of the value of preventing a fatality. Consider a new term: the Value of Preventing a Standard Risk of Death (VPSRD). This, clearly, is parasitic on the idea of a Standard Risk of Death. There are various ways in which this, in turn, could be approached. One suggestion would be to operate by orders of magnitude. SRD1 would be certain death. SRD2 would be a one in ten chance of death, SRD3 one in a hundred, and so on. However, this is probably more complex than is needed. For regulatory purposes risks between one in ten thousand and one in a million are most relevant. It would be very convenient if we could also assume linearity in this area, which I will do for present purposes, while acknowledging that if it fails modifications to what follows would be necessary. This would then suggest that we could take a risk of one in a million per year as the base unit for a Standard Risk of Death. Translating current UK values into this terminology would suggest that, if we take a VPF of £1,000,000 then VPSRD would be £1. This would then be multiplied by the number of people involved and the probability of death as a multiple of one in a million to yield the financial value of the safety benefit under consideration. So far this would be identical in its workings and consequences to standard RCBA using a VPF figure. The only benefit so far would be transparency: that reduction of risk rather than saving of lives is more obviously at issue. However, once this step is made, it becomes possible for an industry to decide that reducing risks in one category – passengers, say – is a higher priority than another – adult trespassers. Hence it might decide to use standard figures for reducing risks to adult trespassers, but put a premium on reducing risks to passengers and to child trespassers. And once again, this could be defended not on the grounds that one category of life is more important that another, but because the industry has a greater responsibility to guard against some types of risk rather than another.

Conclusion

My purpose in this chapter has been to consider the beneficial consequences of taking seriously the distinction between saving lives and reducing risks of death. Some of the objections to RCBA seem less pressing once this distinction is made clear, for it allows us to see safely legislation as more continuous with ordinary safety decisions made by consumers. It has the further benefit of paving the way to opening up a clear debate on whether more money should be spent to reduce risks which fall into one category rather than another, even if they are of the same magnitude. Whether or not it is sensible to attempt to change standard terminology, there seems little doubt that the existing language makes the methodology of RCBA seem more vulnerable than it need be.[5]

Notes

1 Safety measures come into conflict, for example, with aesthetic values, such as in the modification of existing buildings. It is not obvious that this conflict can be translated

into economic terms without loss. For some related discussion see Wolff and Hau-brich (2006).

2 For some purposes a further 'lost output' figure of around £500,000 is also added.

3 Such difficulties were observed in Beattie *et al.* (1998), in which advocates of the contingent valuation model face up to some of the difficulties of the methodology as a preliminary to exploring a way forward. They note: 'Amongst the more worrying ... anomalies and inconsistencies are so-called "embedding", "scope" and "sequencing" effects. Essentially, embedding and scope effects refer to the tendency of many CV respondents to report much the same willingness to pay for a compre-hensive bundle of safety or environmental "goods" as for a proper subset of that bundle. In turn, sequencing effects reflect a tendency for the order in which a sequence of CV questions are put to respondents to have a significant impact on the values that are implied by the responses to such questions' (Beattie *et al.* 1998: 8).

4 It is important, however, to consider how the costs for safety measures are to be met. If safety costs come out of a public budget, funded by progressive taxation, then there is every reason for using averaging strategies as a form of distributive justice. However, if the price of safety goes on to the price of a ticket, then averaging will lead to the poor being forced to buy a level of safety they would not have chosen to. My conjecture is that at least some people will then try to return their level of risk to their preferred level by, say, every now and again evading the fare. Hence break-ing the law can function as a type of risk 'black market'. I hope to make this the topic of future work.

5 I am very grateful to Shepley Orr, Donald Franklin, Dirk Haubrich, Jesse Norman, Mike Jones Lee, Graham Loomes, Mike Robertson and Andrew Sharpe for discussions which have helped shape this paper. Written comments from Shepley Orr, Andrew Sharpe and Tim Lewens on the penultimate draft have been especially helpful.

References

Beattie, J., Covey, J., Dolan, P., Hopkins, L., Jones-Lee, M., Loomes, G., Pidgeon, N., Robinson, A. and Spencer, A. (1998) 'On the contingent valuation of safety and the safety of contingent valuation: part 1 – caveat investigator', *Journal of Risk and Uncertainty*, 17: 5–25.

Carthy, T.S., Chilton, J. Covey, J., Hopkins, L., Jones-Lee, M., Loomes, G., Pidgeon, N., and Spencer, A. (1999) 'On the contingent valuation of safety and the safety of contingent valuation: part 2 – the CV/SG "chained" approach', *Journal of Risk and Uncertainty*, 17: 187–213.

Davidson, D. (1963) 'Actions, reasons, and causes', *Journal of Philosophy*, 60: 685–700.

Department of Transport (2004) *Highways Economic Note 1*. Online. Available: http://www.dft.gov.uk/stellent/groups/dft_rdsafety/documents/page/dft_rdsafety_610642–01.hcsp (accessed 18 April 2006).

Diamond, J. (2006) *Collapse*, London: Penguin.

Hammerton, M., Jones-Lee, M.W. and Abbot, V. (1982) 'Consistency and coherence of attitudes to physical risk', *Journal of Transport Economics and Policy*, 16: 181–99.

Health and Safety Executive (2001) *Reducing Risks, Protecting People*, London: HMSO. Online. Available: http://www.hse.gov.uk/risk/theory/r2p2.htm (accessed 18 April 2006).

Jones-Lee, M. (1989) *The Economics of Safety and Physical Risk*, Oxford: Basil Blackwell.

Mishan, E.J. (1971) 'Evaluation of life and limb: a theoretical approach', *Journal of Political Economy*, 79: 687–705.

Posner, R. (2004) *Catastrophe*, New York: Oxford University Press.

Sunstein, C. (2002) *Risk and Reason*, Cambridge: Cambridge University Press.

Wolff, J. (2002) 'Railway safety and the ethics of the tolerability of risk', Rail Safety and Standards Board. Online. Available: http://www.rssb.co.uk/pdf/policy_risk.pdf (accessed April 18, 2006).

—— (2006) 'Risk, fear, blame, shame and the regulation of public safety', *Economics and Philosophy*, 22(3), November: 409–27.

Wolff, J. and Haubrich, D. (2006) 'Economism and Its Limits', in M. Moran, M. Rein and R.E. Goodwin (eds) *Oxford Handbook of Public Policy*, Oxford: Oxford University Press, 744–68.

4

ON MULTI-ATTRIBUTE RISK ANALYSIS

Martin Peterson

Introduction

The aim of this contribution is twofold. First, I wish to give a non-technical overview of multi-attribute risk analysis.[1] This will, I hope, be helpful for readers not already familiar with this widely used methodology. The second aim is more challenging: I shall explore and defend an argument to the effect that multi-attribute risk analysis is unsuitable to decision-making involving sufficiently disparate values. The argument has two parts. The first part shows that on the multi-attribute approach, it is plausible to maintain that alternatives are sometimes incomparable, i.e. that the decision-maker's ranking of alternatives is incomplete. In the second part I show that anyone who accepts the first part of the argument can be exploited, i.e. may make a sequence of choices leading to a certain loss. Exploitability is a familiar sign of irrationality, traditionally used for motivating transitivity and other structural constrains on rational choice behaviour. If correct, the present contribution shows that exploitability also poses problems for advocates of multi-attribute risk analysis.

My argument against the multi-attribute approach is of a general nature. In principle, it could be applied to nearly any kind of decision. However, in order to give some substance to the argument it is helpful to consider an example. Suppose that the following is true:

> The bird flu is here! Fortunately, a vaccine for humans has been rapidly developed. Before the vaccine can be distributed to the population, it must be approved by the medical products agency. (In Europe, the EU has prepared a 'fast-track system' for handling this kind of application quicker than usual.[2]) There are some concerns about the safety of the new vaccine. Preliminary results indicate that it may cause serious cardiovascular health risks to the elderly, even though it is likely to be safe in all other respects. No other vaccine is available. The fact that the vaccine may lead to serious adverse effects

is not sufficient reason for turning it down. As pointed out by the European Medical Agency (EMEA), 'the concept of "zero-risk" does not apply to medicinal products'.[3] This is because, '[t]he licensing of medical products needs to be assessed in the context of the benefit/risk balance concept, whereby demonstrated benefits must outweigh known risks'.[4] Given the seriousness of the threat posed by bird flu, it seems clear that even a vaccine that is far from optimal ought to be approved. But how good is good enough and which principle should be used for balancing costs against benefits?

Several academics and government officials, including the present Executive Director of the EMEA,[5] maintain that regulatory decisions on medical products ought to be guided by multi-attribute risk analysis. The official reason given by the EMEA is that 'a typical individual medicinal product will have multiple risks attached to it and individual risks will vary in terms of severity, and individual patient and public health impact'.[6] According to the EMEA this justifies the conclusion that 'the concept of risk management must ... consider the combination of information on multiple risks with the aim of ensuring that the benefits exceed the risks by the greatest possible margin both for the individual patient and at the population level'.[7]

I wish to emphasize that I use the bird flu vaccine only as an example; as explained above, my argument is more general. The structure of the chapter is as follows. In the following two sections the basic elements of the multi-attribute approach are outlined. Thereafter, in the final three sections, I develop my argument against the multi-attribute approach.

Two approaches to risk analysis

The aim of risk analysis is to advise decision-makers about how to choose among a pre-defined set of alternative acts. It is common to distinguish between single- and multi-attribute approaches. In a single-attribute risk analysis, all risks and benefits are compared on a common scale. In most cases a monetary scale is used. For example, in a decision on whether to build a new road, benefits are assigned monetary values by estimating how strongly members of society desire a new road expressed in terms of their hypothetical willingness to pay. Typically, a sample of the population is asked about their hypothetical willingness to pay, say, for getting a little bit safer and ten minutes quicker to work. The total benefit of the new road is thereafter calculated by multiplying the average amount respondents are willing to pay by the total number of people in the population. The value of increased traffic safety is also assigned a monetary value. In Britain, the monetary value of preventing a fatality (VPF) is approximately one million pounds.[8] This value has been determined by asking people about their hypothetical willingness to pay for decreasing the risk of having a fatal accident by a certain percentage, and then adding society's costs for taking care of accidents. According to the UK Health and Safety Commission, 'A VPF of £1,000,000 corresponds to a reduction in risk of one in a hundred thousand being worth about £10 to an average individual.'[9] Needless to say, it can be doubted whether people's preferences really are linear in the sense tacitly assumed in this calculation. For a detailed discussion of this, see Jonathan Wolff's contribution to this volume.

In a single-attribute risk analysis, the cost of an alternative is often easier to calculate than its benefits. In the road project example, the cost of building a new road equals the sum of money paid to the contractors and consultants hired for the project. These figures are, of course, much easer to estimate than the total benefits expressed in terms of willingness to pay.

Unsurprisingly, the single-attribute approach has been criticized.[10] A common argument is that it seems impossible to assign *non-arbitrary* monetary values to sufficiently disparate risks and benefits. The monetary value assigned to human health is often felt to be taken out of the blue. Some scholars even go as far as claiming that monetary values assigned to certain types of risk and benefit are meaningless. To take a stand on whether this is correct is beyond the scope of this article. However, I think the basic point deserves some respect – it is indeed very difficult to see how ordinary people could tell *precisely* how much money they would be prepared to pay for decreasing the risk of having a car accident or for safer medical products. (For reasons to be explained later, a rough approximation of your willingness to pay would not do – see page 80).

The multi-attribute approach avoids the criticism raised against the single-attribute approach by giving up the assumption that all risks and benefits have to be compared on a common scale. In a multi-attribute approach, each risk and benefit is measured in the unit deemed to be most suitable for that attribute. Perhaps money is the right unit to use for measuring the construction costs of a new road, whereas the number of lives saved is the right unit to use for measuring increased traffic safety. The total value of each act is thereafter determined by aggregating the attributes, e.g. money and lives, into an overall ranking of the act. Of course, the multi-attribute approach will only be a substantial improvement over the single-attribute approach if the aggregation mechanism is sufficiently simple and robust; in some cases, but not in all, it might turn out that an act scores at least as well as the others with respect to all attributes, and then it is of course reasonable to choose that act.

Before taking a closer look at the multi-attribute approach, it should be acknowledged that this methodology has a number of advantages. Some of these become particularly apparent when the multi-attribute approach is applied to decisions on social issues, rather than to decisions affecting only a single decision-maker. For example, the multi-attribute approach tends to make the decision process more transparent. Since the decision-maker adopting the multi-attribute approach is forced to divide all advantages and disadvantages of an alternative into different attributes, external observers can easily find out which factors are considered as relevant by the decision-maker. Given that the aggregation process is equally transparent, external observers can furthermore find out how important each attribute is relative to the others.

Another virtue of the multi-attribute approach is that it makes the outcome of the decision-making process more predictable. This is mainly because the multi-attribute process is more transparent than other methodologies – transparency entails predictability. Of course, predictability is important for those affected by the decision. For example, for drug companies developing new vaccines, predictability can be a very important factor to consider. Since the costs of developing new drugs are enormous, it is important to know in advance what kinds of adverse effects are, and are not, accepted by regulators.

What is multi-attribute risk analysis?

The theoretical foundations of the multi-attribute approach were developed a few decades ago by, among others, Debreu (1960), Krantz (1964) and Fishburn (1970). In the 1970s Keeney and Raiffa wrote a very influential textbook, which appeared in a second edition in 1993; see Keeney and Raiffa (1976/1993).

Sometimes a distinction is drawn between multi-criteria decision-making (MCDM) and multi-attribute utility theory (MAUT).[11] The aim of MCDM is to establish criteria for making multi-attribute decisions, whereas MAUT seeks to find mathematical structures that measure how attractive one multi-attribute alternative is in relation to another. However, the distinction between MAUT and MCDM is of little relevance in the present context. If one can measure which alternative is best, one can of course take this to be a criterion of what to choose. Conversely, if there is a criterion that ranks all alternatives from the best to the worst, this means that the alternatives can be measured at least ordinally. Therefore, the distinction between MAUT and MCDM will be ignored here.

Let us suppose that the decision-maker has been able to divide the relevant objectives of her decision problem into a list of attributes. Keeney and Raiffa (1993) devote an entire chapter to this issue, but like most advocates of MCDM and MAUT they have surprisingly little to say about the theoretical aspects of this problem. Ultimately, decision-makers would wish to use an algorithm for generating a list of attributes. However, for the time being we ignore this problem, as well as the obvious problem that there might be more than one way to construct an optimal list of attributes. (We shall return to the latter problem on page 74.)

For illustrative purposes, we assume that the list of relevant attributes in the vaccine example includes: (i) the number of people protected by the vaccine; (ii) adverse effects for children; (iii) adverse effects for adults; and (iv) economic aspects of the decision. In order to make a decision, the decision-maker has to gather information about the degree to which each attribute can be realized by each alternative. At this point, issues about risk and uncertainty become important – a rational decision typically requires that one is able to say at least something about the likelihood that each attribute will be realized by a given alternative. Table 4.1 illustrates an example with four attributes and three alternatives.

The vaccine example helps us to understand Table 4.1. In this illustration, the four attributes are the ones previously described, whereas the three alternative acts might be taken to be: (A) limited approval of the vaccine (give to adults, but not to kids); (B) full approval of the vaccine; and (C) reject the application.

The numbers represent the degree to which each attribute is fulfilled by a corresponding alternative; in the leftmost column, the numbers show that the second alternative fulfils the first attribute to a higher degree than the first alternative, etc. So far the ranking is ordinal, so nothing follows about the 'distance' in value between the numbers. However, in many real-life applications it is of course natural to assume that the numbers represent more than an ordinal ranking. For example, the number of people protected by a vaccine can be measured on a ratio scale. This also holds true for the number of adverse drug reactions of a certain type, as well as the amount of money saved by distributing vaccine to the population. Nothing prevents the advocate of the multi-attribute approach to use a ratio or interval scale if he so wishes.

In the literature, several criteria have been proposed for choosing among alternatives with multiple attributes (see, e.g., Keeney and Raiffa 1993: Chs 3–6). It is helpful to draw a distinction between two types of criterion, viz. additive and non-additive criteria. Additive criteria assign weights to each attribute, and rank alternatives according to the weighted sum calculated by multiplying the weight of each attribute with its value. The weights are real numbers between zero and one, which together sum up to one. Obviously, this type of criterion makes sense only if the degree to which each alternative satisfies any given attribute can be represented on an interval scale, i.e. if it makes sense to measure value in quantitative terms. Let us, for the sake of the argument, suppose that this is the case for the numbers in Table 4.1, and suppose that all attributes are assigned equal weights. This implies that the value of alternative A is $1/4 \cdot 2 + 1/4 \cdot 2 + 1/4 \cdot 3 + 1/4 \cdot 1 = 2$. Analogous calculations show that B = 9/4 and C = 7/4. Since we defined the ranking by saying that a lower

Table 4.1

	Attribute 1	Attribute 2	Attribute 3	Attribute 4
Alt. A	2	2	3	1
Alt. B	1	3	2	3
Alt. C	3	1	1	2

number is better than a higher, it follows that C is better than B, which is better than A.

Of course, one might question the 'method' used for determining the weights in the example above. How can the decision-maker determine the relative importance of each attribute? The obvious approach is, of course, to ask the decision-maker to directly assign weights to each attribute. A slightly more sophisticated approach is to let the agent make pair-wise comparisons between all attributes, and thereafter normalize their relative importance. However, from a theoretical point of view the second approach is no better than the first. None of them can overcome the objection that a direct approach makes the assignment of weights more or less arbitrary. It is indeed very optimistic to believe that decision-makers can come up with adequate numerical weights in this way. So perhaps the multi-attribute approach is no better than the single-attribute approach. It seems extremely contentious to measure the value of very different risks on a common (monetary) scale, but it is probably equally contentious to assign numerical weights to attributes in the way suggested above.

Most advocates of multi-attribute risk analysis favour a different, implicit approach for making trade-offs between attributes. The basic idea has been imported from economic theory. Instead of directly asking the decision-maker how important one attribute is in relation to another, we may instead ask the decision-maker to state preferences among a set of hypothetical alternatives, some of which include more of one attribute but less of another. One can then establish 'indifference curves' for the attributes, showing how much of one attribute the decision-maker is willing to give up in order to get one extra unit of another attribute. Given that the decision-maker's preferences among alternatives are rational in the sense assumed by economists – that is, complete, asymmetric, and transitive – it can be proved that the decision-maker behaves *as if* he is choosing among alternatives by assigning numerical utilities to alternatives, e.g. by assigning weights to the attributes and then adding all the weighted values (see Debreu 1960; Keeney and Raiffa 1993: Ch. 3).

Unfortunately, the implicit approach seems to put the cart before the horse in normative contexts. If one *merely* wishes to describe and predict the decision-maker's future choices, it certainly makes sense to observe preferences among a set of alternatives and then assume that the trade-off rate between attributes implicit in those choices will be the same in future choices. However, if one wants to say something more than this, the implicit approach becomes more questionable. A decision-maker who knows his preferences among alternatives with multiple attributes does not need any action guidance – so why divide the decision into a list of attributes in the first place? Furthermore, according to the implicit approach, it is false to say that one alternative act is better than another *because* its utility is higher. All one is entitled to say is that the decision-maker, as a matter of fact, behaves *as if* he was assigning numerical utilities to alternatives. From a normative point of view, this is of little help.

Non-additive aggregation criteria do not assume that the total value of an alternative can be calculated as a weighted sum. A large number of different criteria have been proposed in the literature.[12] For an example of a non-additive criterion, consider the suggestion that the value of an alternative is obtained by multiplying the value of each attribute. Obviously, multiplicative criteria tend to put emphasis on the minimal degree to which each attribute is satisfied – a large number times zero is zero, no matter how large the large number is. Suppose, for example, that only two attributes are considered, and that the value of the first is zero and the value of the second is 999; then the product is of course also zero. An additive criterion would give at least some weight to the second value (999) so the overall value would in that case be strictly greater than zero, depending on the weight assigned to the second attribute.

Another example of a non-additive criterion is to impose 'aspiration levels' for each attribute. The basic idea is that in case an attribute falls below a certain minimal level, the aspiration level, that alternative should be disregarded, no matter how good the alternative is when evaluated according to the other levels (see Keeney and Raiffa 1993: Sect. 3.2.3). An obvious problem is, of course, that it might be difficult to specify the aspiration level. Furthermore, contrary to what is assumed by Keeney and Raiffa, it may be questioned whether it is reasonable to assume that aspiration levels are sharp. Perhaps there is an area of vagueness, in which some outcomes are neither below nor above the aspiration level.

Some attributes are incomparable

Before stating the first part of my argument against the multi-attribute approach, I wish to elaborate on a point mentioned earlier, namely that there might be more than one way to construct a list of attributes for a given decision problem. As far as I am aware, advocates of the multi-attribute approach are not familiar with this problem.

The point of departure is the observation that in many cases there are several equally plausible but different ways of constructing the list of attributes. Furthermore, the outcome of the decision process sometimes depends on which set of attributes is chosen – an alternative that is ranked as optimal according to a given decision criterion relative to one set of attributes might be ranked as sub-optimal according to the same decision criterion relative to another equally reasonable set of attributes. This gives rise to deep problems. For an example, consider the highly controversial drug Herceptin. As I write this, it has not yet been approved by the EMEA for treatment against early stages of breast cancer. The long-term effects are still partly unknown, and there is a concern that Herceptin may lead to increased cardiotoxicity. Cardiotoxicity might thus be taken to be a relevant attribute. However, let us make a thought experiment, which is purely hypothetical and not based on any existing scientific evidence. Suppose that for half of the population, the intake of Herceptin

leads to an increased risk of cardiotoxicity, whereas for the other half Herceptin actually leads to a decreased risk. It is plausible to assume that the explanation of this difference is to be found in our genes. Now, if cardiotoxicity is
conceived as one attribute, Herceptin might very well be approved by the
regulatory agency, since no increased risk could be detected in a clinical trial –
the two effects will cancel out each other. However, had we instead distinguished between two different attributes, 'cardiotoxicity for people with
gene A' and 'cardiotoxicity for people with gene B', the result might have been
quite different. If the increased risk for people with gene B is sufficiently large,
the regulatory decision might be radically affected, depending on which criterion is used for aggregating risks.

Perhaps it could be argued that the second individuation of attributes is better
than the first, because it is more fine-grained. However, this does not solve the
general problem. One can easily imagine another, equally fine-grained individuation of attributes that would rank alternatives differently. So it seems difficult to avoid the conclusion that there sometimes exist no unique way to
divide all relevant aspects of a decision problem into a single list of attributes.[13]

However, my main argument against the multi-attribute approach is not
about the individuation of attributes. As explained earlier, the first part of my
argument holds that some intra-attribute comparisons might be impossible to
make, even in principle. For people wishing to assign weights to attributes, this
is equivalent to saying that there are no weights one could assign to some
possible lists of attributes. A paradigmatic example is a decision problem in
which both human health and economic aspects are included in the list of
attributes – many scholars have defended the view that it is makes no sense to
compare money with human well-being.[14] For another example, consider the
claim that some adverse drug reactions are incomparable with others. Perhaps a
drug causing ten heart attacks in a sample of a thousand patients is neither
better, nor worse, nor equally good as a drug causing one hundred gastric ulcers
in an equally large sample. Formally, the claim that two attributes A and B are
incomparable means that there is some x,y such that (i) it is false that x units
of attribute A are better than y units of attribute B, (ii) it is false that y units of
B are better than x units of A, and (iii) it is false that x units of A are equally
good as y units of B.

Arguably, the strongest evidence we have for believing that some attributes
are incomparable is the small-improvement argument.[15] It runs as follows.
Consider a choice between one million pounds and a human life. Suppose that
the decision-maker prefers neither one million pounds to a human life nor a
human life to one million pounds. Then it might be tempting to conclude that
the decision-maker is indifferent between the two alternatives, i.e. considers
them to be equally good. However, as pointed out by Savage, 'If the person
really does regard [one million pounds] and [a life saved] equivalent, that is, if
he is indifferent between them, then, if [one million pounds] and [a life saved]
were modified by attaching an arbitrary small bonus to its consequences the

person's decision would presumably be for whichever act was thus modified.'[16] According to the small-improvement argument, the addition of a small bonus to one the alternatives would *not* have such a dramatic effect on the decision maker's preference. In a choice between one million *and one* pounds and a human life, the decision-maker would *also* be unable to muster a preference between the two alternatives. Hence, the decision-maker was not indifferent between one million pounds and a human life. So one million pounds is neither better, nor worse, nor equally good as a human life. Hence, the two alternatives are incomparable, in the sense defined above.

Advocates of the multi-attribute approach try to escape the problem of incomparability by emphasizing that no *precise* preferences between conflicting attributes have to be stated by the decision-maker. Keeney and Raiffa (1993: 96ff) point out that it is enough that the risk analysist, in an initial phase, can establish an approximate 'trade-off rate' between two or more attributes. By applying some clever technical tricks, that approximation can thereafter be rendered more precise. Note, however, that this reasoning does not constitute a good answer to the small-improvement argument. The problem is that Keeney and Raiffa tacitly assume that decision-makers always have a 'true' preference between each possible combination attributes, that is, a complete preference ordering that correctly mirrors subjective tastes and values. In light of the small-improvement argument, that assumption seems to be unjustified and implausible. For some pairs of attributes, such as money and human well-being, it reasonable to believe that a certain amount of one attribute is neither better, nor worse, nor equally good as a certain amount of another attribute.

Perhaps a government official is asked whether he is prepared to sacrifice one million pounds of tax payers' money for saving one extra individual from dying in a clinical trial of a new drug. If forced to make a choice between the two attributes, he would of course do so. But there is no reason to assume that such a forced choice would reflect any deeper values and feelings. The choice might very well be arbitrary. Hence, an actual choice is not a valid proof of a determinate preference, as illustrated by the story of Buridan's ass.

The fact that the decision-maker considers one million pounds to be incomparable with a human life does not imply that the same holds for all amounts of money. Of course, ten pounds is worth less than a human life, and a hundred billion pounds is arguably worth more than a human life.

The claim about incomparability I defend is best conceived of as a metaphysical claim about the nature of value. The fact that certain amounts of one attribute are not better, or worse, or equally good as a certain amount of another attribute is not a matter of limited epistemic capabilities. No matter how hard we try, we will never find a monetary amount that is exactly as valuable as a human life – because there is no such amount.

Advocates of the multi-attribute approach would perhaps say that my objection can be rebutted by first observing actual choice behaviour and then determining the actual importance of each attribute, as revealed in choice behaviour, by reasoning 'backwards', as briefly described on page 73. However, this is not an acceptable solution. Once again, it should be emphasized that the fact that a decision-maker actually chooses one alternative rather than another, and thereby 'reveals' his trade-off rate between different attributes, does not mean that he considers the chosen alternative to be at least as valuable as the non-chosen one. Even a decision-maker who considers some attributes to be incomparable will, of course, choose among alternatives if forced to do so.

In the literature on the multi-attribute approach, incomparability has been rarely touched upon. This is surprising, especially since the main reason for invoking the multi-attribute approach in the first place is to avoid the type of 'hard' comparisons required in the single-attribute approach. The motivation for dividing a decision into a list of different attributes in the first place was to reduce the complexity of the decision problem and facilitate comparisons between disparate values – I am now making the point that this is impossible, even in principle. The multi-attribute approach has not solved the problem it was designed to take care of.

Incomparability and the money-pump

The first part of the argument against the multi-attribute approach, outlined above, is not new. Others have made similar points about incomparability.[17] However, I think the importance of this observation has been severely underestimated. In this section I try to spell out this concern by proving that it is impossible, in a strong sense, to choose rationally among incomparable alternatives. The basic idea is that anyone facing incomparable alternatives can be exploited in a money-pump, i.e. end up in a situation in which he is certain to lose everything he thinks is important, without gaining anything that compensates for this.

The money-pump argument goes as follows. Suppose that one million pounds is incomparable with a human life. Also suppose that a slightly improved version of the first alternative, say one million and one pounds, is incomparable with a human life. Incomparability is a non-transitive relation, so even though one million pounds is incomparable with a human life and a human life is incomparable with one million and one pounds, it is of course not inconsistent to assume that one million pounds and one million and one pounds are fully comparable. Now suppose that you are in possession of one million and one pounds, and that I offer you to swap one million and one pounds for saving a human life. Since the two alternatives are incomparable, rationality permits you to swap. So you swap, and temporarily save a human life. You are then offered to swap a saved human life for one million pounds, which you do, since the two alternatives are incomparable. Finally, you are offered to pay a small amount of money, say one penny, for swapping one million pounds for one million and one pounds. Since one million and one pounds is strictly better than one million pounds, even after you have paid the fee for swapping, you accept the offer and end up where you started, the only difference being that you now have one penny less. This procedure is repeated again and again. After a billion cycles you owe me ten million pounds, for which I have given you nothing in return.

On first acquaintance, this argument may leave a strange impression. After all, it is very unlikely than anyone will *actually* face a money-pump of this kind. So why bother? In my view, this response reveals a lack of understanding of theoretical arguments. A plausible theory of rationality, which the multi-attribute approach attempts to be, should give reasonable recommendations also in hypothetical and very 'strange' examples. If we are looking for something that is more than just a rule of thumb, extreme examples are no less important than more 'natural' examples. Furthermore, I do not think that real-life money-pumps are as unlikely as some people might think. For example, imagine a group of politicians who face a sequence of decisions and hire a new decision consultant for each decision. If the politicians are unlucky, they might end up in an extended money-pump, in which they choose between the same incomparable alternatives over and over again (say, more or fewer private hospitals). Each time they change their mind, they pay a fee to a consultant for justifying their latest decision, so after a couple of iterations tax payers will be significantly poorer but the outcome will not be any better than the initial one.

Let us now examine the anatomy of the money-pump argument in more detail. It will be helpful to state the premises of the argument in a way that entails a contradiction. If all premises are judged to be plausible, it then follows that the incomparable alternatives generated by the multi-attribute approach *cannot* exist. Arguably, this shows that there is something wrong with the multi-attribute approach.

The first premise of the money-pump argument holds that value is choice-guiding. Therefore, if one object is more valuable than another, then it is not permitted to choose the less valuable object; and if two objects are equally valuable it is permitted to choose either of them; and if two objects are incomparable it is also permitted to choose either of them. This premise is not entirely innocent. Wlodek Rabinowicz has suggested that in case two objects are incomparable, it is neither permissible nor forbidden to choose any of them.[18] Instead, if two objects are incomparable we may say that there is a corresponding 'lack of precision' on the normative level. However, in my view Rabinowicz's objection is problematic. First of all, it forces us to give up one of the most fundamental assumptions of deontic logic, namely that every alternative action is either permissible or forbidden (but not both). Rabinowicz's revision of deontic logic is simply too drastic. Second, Rabinowicz's proposal is of little help for an agent wishing to find out what to do. The point is that value is supposed to be choice-guiding – that is why we care so much about value – but on Rabinowicz's account it is not.

The second premise of the money-pump argument is the principle of no payment. It holds that it is never permissible to pay for something, if that something could have been obtained for free. This premise is not universally valid, since the value of things may change over time. For example, though you now could get a copy of my PhD thesis for free, it might be rational to pay a huge amount for it in the future, if I become as famous as Jean-Paul Sartre. However, given that the principle of no payment is restricted to short periods of time, it can hardly be rejected. For the sake of the argument, I assume that the principle of no payment holds at least in the following situation: The decision-maker will shortly receive exactly one of three valuable objects. He knows that these three objects are the only objects he can ever obtain; there are no better outcomes. He is then offered a sequence of pairwise choices between the three objects. Now, if it is permissible to choose the first object at one point during the course of the experiment, then it can hardly be permissible to choose a strictly worse outcome, the same object minus some small amount of money, at a later point.

The third and last premise of the money-pump argument is the technical assumption that whenever one object is strictly better than another, then there exists some small amount of value such that the first object is better than the second, even if one has to pay that small amount for getting it.

It can easily be proved that the three premises of the money-pump argument are logically inconsistent: Suppose for *reductio* that x, y, z are three objects such that x and y are incomparable, and y and z are incomparable, and x is strictly better than z. Let t_1, t_2, t_3 be three points in time such that the agent is offered a choice between x and y at t_1, and between y and z at t_2, and between z and x at t_3. It follows from the first premise that it is permissible to choose x at t_1 in the choice between x and y, since x and y are incomparable. For the same reason, it is permissible to choose z at t_2 in the choice between y and z. Now consider the choice made at t_3. The third premise guarantees that there is some small amount of value such that x is better than z even if one has to pay that small amount for getting x. Therefore, in the choice made at t_3, the first premise implies that it is permissible to choose x minus the small amount. However, since it was permissible to choose x without paying anything at t_1, the second premise implies that it is not permissible to choose x minus the small amount at t_3. This contradicts the previous conclusion about the choice made at t_3.

The money-pump argument proposed here is parallel to the traditional money-pump argument for transitivity, showing that an agent whose preferences are not transitive can be exploited by repeatedly offering him to pay a small amount for swapping one object for a better one. Some of the criticism raised against the traditional money-pump argument affects the new version of the argument discussed here. For example, Schick has famously pointed out that a clever decision-maker facing a money-pump would see 'what is in store for him [and] reject the offer and thus stop the pump'.[19] Thus, it cannot be taken for granted that someone who knows that he will be offered to swap several times should be prepared to do so, since he can simply see what is going to happen.

Schick's idea can be rendered more precise by using backwards induction, as shown by McClennen.[20] However, Rabinowicz has pointed out that even a decision-maker who reasons backwards, from the end node of the decision tree up to the top, and then decides what to, can be exploited in a modified (more complex) money-pump.[21] It is beyond the scope of the present contribution to comment on Rabinowicz's modified money-pump. Let me just point out that there seems to be another way of avoiding the criticism raised by Schick. Suppose that the agent has no reason to believe that he will be offered to make any more choices. Each new offer to swap comes as a surprise to him. All he knows is that x, y, and z are the possible outcomes (plus a finite number of small payments). It still seems plausible to maintain that a reasonable theory of rational choice should guarantee that it is not permissible to pay for x at t_3 if x could have been chosen at t_1. If one knew from the beginning that one could choose x and stay with it, and that there was no other strictly better object, why should one then accept to end up with x minus some small amount?

Is the argument too broad?

The money-pump argument may be too broad. The problem is that it also seems possible to raise the money-pump argument against the single-attribute approach because, as pointed out on page 70, advocates of the single-attribute approach could argue that some alternatives are incomparable. For example, how could one possibly assign a precise amount of money to the value of a human life? If there is no such precise amount of money, a money-pump could easily be constructed along the lines indicated above. Therefore, it would be tempting to conclude that the money-pump argument is just an interesting general problem, but not an argument that poses a problem that is unique for the multi-attribute approach.

However, in my view the problem of incomparability is, contrary to what is suggested above, significantly more relevant in the multi-attribute approach than in the single-attribute approach. This is because advocates of the single-attribute approach put so much emphasis on 'revealed preferences' – they believe that the monetary value of a human life can be calculated by observing how much we do actually spend on preventing fatalities today. Then, since people's actual choices are taken as evidence for underlying preferences, and since we do actually spend a certain amount of money on preventing fatalities, advocates of the single-attribute approach become less susceptible to problems raised by incomparability. They tend to simply deny that some values are incomparable, despite the overwhelming philosophical evidence for believing the opposite. Hence, the money-pump objection is a significantly more relevant when raised against the multi-attribute approach, compared to the single-attribute approach. Of course, this does not mean that the single-attribute approach should be preferred over the multi-attribute approach – the single-attribute is even further removed from reality, since it implies that all outcomes can be compared on a single scale.

So what conclusion should one draw from the money-pump argument, then? I shall briefly mention three alternatives. The first alternative is to simply deny that attributes are sometimes incomparable, contrary to what I have argued. However, to maintain that *all* attributes, even very disparate ones, are *always* comparable is a very strong claim. I think anyone who pays attention to his normative intuitions will find this solution unacceptable. The second alternative is to replace the notion of incomparability with the notion of 'parity' introduced by Chang (2002). Two alternatives are 'on a par' if and only if they are comparable and it is false that one is better than the other and false that they are equally good. Hence, parity is a unique, fourth, positive value relation, which cannot be defined in terms of the traditional value relations 'better', 'worse' and 'equally good'. Derek Parfit's and James Griffin's concept of 'rough equality' is designed to capture essentially the same intuition about evaluative comparisons between very disparate items.[22] However, it should be noted that the concept of parity cannot solve the problem outlined above, because from a deliberative point of view the notions of parity and incomparability appear to be equivalent. Let x be on a par with y, and let the same be true of y and x^+, where x^+ is a slightly improved, strictly better version of x. Suppose you are in possession of x^+, and that you are offered to swap x^+ for y. Since the two objects are on a par, it is permissible to swap. So you swap, and get y; you are then offered to swap y for x, which you do, since they are on a par. And so on.

The third conclusion, which I am inclined to accept myself, is that our present theories of rationally are not sufficiently well developed. None of the theories discussed here provides acceptable answers. Therefore, we ought to drastically reconsider our theories of rational choice, and in particular theories of rational choice between incomparable alternatives.

Notes

1 The terminology in the literature is very liberal. Some authors prefer to use slightly different terms: 'multi-attribute risk–benefit analysis', 'multi-attribute decision analysis', 'multi-criteria risk analysis', or 'multiple objective decision analysis'.
2 UK Health Departments (2005: 41).
3 EMEA (2005: 3).
4 Ibid.
5 In an interview in February 2006, Mr Tomas Lonngren of the EMEA confirmed to me that he supports the multi-attribute approach.
6 EMEA (2005: 4).
7 Ibid.
8 HSE (2001: 65).
9 Ibid.
10 See, e.g., Jones-Lee (1992), Hansson (2004) and Wolff (2006).
11 See, for example, Dyer *et al.* (1992).
12 See Zanakis *et al.* (1998) for an overview. They also make an interesting comparison with additive criteria.
13 A related problem is that one can never be sure that the list of attributes is complete, i.e. that one has actually identified all relevant aspects of a decision problem.

One can, of course, always add an attribute like 'all remaining relevant aspects', but as long as one does not know what to put in there, that is of little help.

14 For an excellent overview, see Dorman (1996). See also Card and Mooney (1977).

15 See Chang (2002) and Espinoza (2006).

16 Savage (1954/1972: 17).

17 See Dorman (1996).

18 In conversation.

19 Schick (1986: 117).

20 McClennen (1990).

21 Rabinowicz (2000).

22 Parfit (1984: 431) and Griffin (1986: 96–98).

References

Card, W.I. and Mooney, G.H. (1977) 'What is the monetary value of a human life?', *British Medical Journal*, 2(6103): 1627–9.

Chang, R. (2002) 'The possibility of parity', *Ethics*, 112: 659–88.

Debreu, G. (1960) 'Topological methods in cardinal utility theory'. In Arrow, K. J., Karlin, S. and Suppes, P. (eds) *Mathematical Methods in the Social Sciences, 1959: Proceedings*, Stanford, CA: Stanford University Press.

Dorman, P. (1996) *Markets and Mortality: economics, dangerous work, and the value of human life*, Cambridge: Cambridge University Press.

Dyer, J. S., Fishburn, P.C., Steuer, R.E, Wallenius, J. and Zionts, S. (1992) 'Multiple criteria decision making, multiattributive utility theory: the next ten years', *Management Science*, 38: 645–54.

EMEA (2005) 'Action plan to further progress the European risk management strategy', Doc. Ref. EMEA/115906/2005/Final.

Espinoza, N. (2006) 'The small improvement argument', mimeo, Lulea University of Technology.

Fishburn, P.C. (1970) *Utility Theory for Decision Making*, New York: John Wiley & Sons.

—— (1991) 'Nontransitive preferences in decision theory', *Journal of Risk and Uncertainty*, 4: 113–34.

Griffin, J. (1986) *Well-Being*, Oxford: Oxford University Press.

Hansson, S.O. (2004) 'Weighing risks and benefits', *Topoi*, 23: 145–52.

Health and Safety Excecutive (2001) *Reducing Risks, Protecting People*, London: HSE Books.

Jones-Lee M.W. (1992) 'Paternalistic altruism and the value of statistical life', *The Economic Journal*, 102: 80–90.

Keeney, R.L. and Raiffa, H. (1976) *Decisions with Multiple Objectives*, New York: John Wiley & Sons; 2nd edn (1993) Cambridge: Cambridge University Press.

Krantz, D.H. (1964) 'Conjoint measurement: the Luce–Tukey axiomatization and some extensions', *Journal of Mathematical Psychology*, 1: 248–77.

McClennen, E. (1990) *Rationality and Dynamic Choice*, Cambridge: Cambridge University Press.

Parfit, D. (1984) *Reasons and Persons*, Oxford: Oxford University Press.

Rabinowicz, W. (2000) 'Money pump with foresight', in Almeida, M.J. (ed.) *Imperceptible Harms and Benefits*, Dordrecht: Kluwer.

Savage, L.J. (1954) *The Foundations of Statistics*, New York: Wiley & Sons; 2nd edn 1972, New York: Dover.

Schick, F. (1986) 'Dutch bookies and money pumps', *The Journal of Philosophy*, 83, 112–17.

UK Health Departments (2005) 'Influenza pandemic contingency plan', October edition.

Wolff, J. (2006) 'Risk, fear, blame, shame and the regulation of public safety', *Economics and Philosophy*, 22(3): 409–27.

Zanakis, S. H., Solomon A., Wishart N. and Dublish S. (1998) 'Multi-attribute decision making: a simulation comparison of select methods', *European Journal of Operational Research*, 107: 507–29.

5

GREAT EXPECTATIONS

Adam Morton

As you leave a bar in the early hours you are approached by a shifty character who offers you the following deal. If you first pay him $100 you can choose a number and he will roll a die, this die here. If it lands with your chosen number up he will pay you $1,000. If it lands with any other number up, well, it's goodbye to him and to your $100. Of course you worry a bit about whether the deal really is as described, even though he throws the die a few times and it doesn't seem loaded, and you have a quick glimpse of ten $100 bills in his hand. On the other hand, it's a good deal. You are being offered a one in six chance of $1,000, which you take to be worth one hundred and sixty seven, for only one hundred. And yet, a vague worry flashes through your mind, elusive enough that you cannot quite state it, but strong enough to make you decline the deal.

The next morning, sober and well-slept, though slightly hung-over, you try to pin down the worry. Finally you see it. The disturbing thing about the gamble is that even if it is played honestly *most people who play it will lose* – five-sixths of them, in fact. And this is in spite of the fact that the odds suggested are strongly, almost worryingly, in the player's favour.

This chapter is concerned with the reasons we can give for our choices between risky options. It focuses especially on the phenomenon described in the previous paragraphs. I shall argue for a close connection between this phenomenon and some pervasive facts about human attitudes to risk. My aim is to say something helpful about the ways in which we ought to approach risky choices, the strategies and attitudes that can benefit us. There is an enormous literature in philosophy, economics and psychology on decision-making in risky circumstances. I am not aiming to improve or correct any of this tradition, but rather to bring out some points that it misses or hides. One usually neglected theme that becomes increasingly important as this chapter progresses is that of decision-making *virtues*, traits and abilities that a person has to have in order to make the most of whatever attitude to risk she has adopted. As I develop this theme it is closely related to another, that of the tensions between the interests of an actual person and of the possible people who would have gained or suffered had the person's choice turned out differently. To see the relevance of this second theme to risk-taking suppose that you had taken the gamble offered by the shifty character and, as was most likely, lost. The next morning you are berating your self of the night before. 'Why did you lose me the hundred dollars I need to take my friend to an impressive brunch?' you ask. And in your imagination your past self replies, 'Because although you in fact lost, in one sixth of all the possible futures you won big – wasn't that worth it?' To which your present impoverished self groans, 'I wish you were less considerate of our possible selves, when the probable cost to my actual self is so high.'

Variability and expectation: three facts

An agent, A, is facing a choice between two options. The options could be taking the right or left fork in the road. How things will turn out after her choice depends on some facts that she does not know. (Perhaps whether there are still bandits in this territory, who will attack travellers who take the short-cut path.) Suppose that one of the options is riskier than the other, in that it might turn out much better than the other, and also might turn out much worse, depending on the unknown facts. But suppose that she does have ideas about how likely these facts are to be true. (She knows that there have been no attacks for years, though not all of the known bandits have been caught.) Then she can ask, 'Do the potential benefits of taking the first option outweigh its potential costs?' She has to ask herself this, because this is the essence of the situation she faces. But the concept of outweighing demands a lot. It asks her to count for an action its benefits and the probability that these will follow, to count against it its costs and the probability that these will follow, and to combine these probabilities and values in a way that allows them to be compared. The result of the combination is the *expectation* of the action: its benefits weighted by the likelihood they will occur reduced by its costs weighted by the likelihood they will occur.

How can we calculate expectations? The standard model of a situation in which the calculations are unproblematic is given by games of chance. Suppose that instead of a fork in the road our agent faces a choice between two gambles, o_1 and o_2. In o_1 a fair coin will be tossed: if it lands Heads she wins $200, and if it lands Tails she loses $100. In o_2 she gets $30 whatever. (She might have paid to be in the situation where this choice is open to her. The person offering the gambles does not have to be benevolent.) If the gamble were repeated many times and she took o_1 every time her gains would approach $50 times the number of repetitions, since she would win roughly half the time and lose roughly half the time. And if she took o_2 every time her gains would approach $30 times the number of repetitions. (Or, equivalently, if a zillion duplicates of her were to take o_1 they would end up with 50 zillion dollars, and if they took o_2 they would end up with 30 zillion.) So this aspect of the gamble, the average amount that it would yield if repeated indefinitely, is clear. For each option it is the probability of Heads times the benefit from Heads for that gamble plus the probability of Tails times the benefit from Tails. Then it is just a small step to taking this expected or average value to be 'what the gamble is worth', to specify how the agent should rank it in comparison with other options. (Standard expositions of this idea are in Jeffrey 1983: Ch. 1; Raiffa 1968: Ch. 2; Resnik 1987: Ch. 3. For some history see Hacking 1975, especially Ch. 11.)

Suppose that the agent takes this small step, and evaluates the options by their expected value. Then the 'average' amount she will gain from the risky option will be $50, which is better than the $30 she will get if she takes the less risky one. 'Average' here means average over some indefinitely large set of possible occasions. It could be all the ways things might turn out if she takes the option, or it could be the way things would turn out if she (impossibly) were to repeat the choice over and over again. Thought of either way, the benefits to the assembly of her possible selves will be greater if she takes the risk. But there is also a price for this: some of these selves will end up richer than others. After the risky choice her possible selves will fall into two classes. Half of them will be $200 better off and half $100 poorer, and after the riskless choice all her possible selves will have the same profit of $30. So the downside for the greater expected outcome is the greater variability of actual outcomes.

This fact is completely general. Take one gamble to be riskier than another when its possible outcomes are more varied. (There are several ways of making this precise, and their differences do not matter here. For simplicity take a riskier gamble to have a greater variance of distribution of outcomes.) It will follow that people who make riskier choices will experience more varied outcomes than those who make safer ones. Consider the effects of this on a population of people in a gamble very similar to the one just described. A coin is tossed: if it lands Heads players gain $1, if Tails they lose $1. The game can continue, and then after the second toss each player may have $2 (after two successive Heads), $0 (after Heads–Tails, or Tails–Heads) or –$2 (after two successive Tails). And so on. Call this game 'g-risky' and compare it to an alternative game, 'g-safe', in which the players win or lose nothing. The two games have the same expected value, 0. Consider two sub-populations of players, one playing each game. After one round of g-risky roughly half of the first sub-population will be richer by $1 and roughly half will be poorer by $1. No one's wealth will have been unchanged. After two rounds about one quarter will be richer by $2, one half will have returned to zero, and one half will be poorer by $2. And of course the whole of the second sub-population, playing (or perhaps not-playing) g-safe will have remained at zero. And if we continue to play the game with more and more rounds then though the average wealth of the two populations is the same, it is distributed very differently. In the first population there are eventually some extremely wealthy people and some grotesquely indebted ones, while in the second population no one has changed their wealth more than anyone else.

Some very general facts are beginning to emerge. Fact number one: *when two gambles have the same expected value the riskier one will also produce a wider distribution of results* – more or greater winners and also more or greater losers.

There are social consequences of this fact, though they are not the focus of this chapter. A society in which people are free to take risks for their own benefit will often end up with a higher average wealth, but it will also end up with a greater variation in wealth, so that it is quite easy for many people to be worse off as a result of the choices that lead to an increase in the average well-being. (And the people who emerge well off will compliment themselves on their wise choices and their sense of opportunity, when often the fact will be that they are the few for whom the coin came down Heads many times.) More to the present point is the consequence that a riskier gamble can make it more likely that one does badly. Or, to put it more carefully, given two gambles with the same expected value, the riskier one will sometimes present a larger probability of emerging with less than the expected value of the gamble. And, more generally, sometimes though one gamble has a higher expected value than another it also makes it more likely that you will do worse than you will if you had taken the other. (Two ways: it can be more likely that you will do worse than the expected value of the other, and it can also be more likely that you will do worse than the most likely outcome of the other gamble.) This can be illustrated by variants of the g-risky game just considered or by cases like the shifty character story at the beginning of this chapter. Fact number two: *by choosing a gamble which has a higher expected value but also a greater risk, one can often increase the probability of doing badly.*

My examples have been gambles with money, and I have been measuring expected value in money. Most choices are not like this, and the person approaching the fork in the road in bandit country, for example, will not frame her problem in money terms. But the same facts apply. The real dilemmas of risk will occur when two options are roughly equal in their overall attractiveness, balancing possible benefits against possible losses, but where one, the riskier one, offers greater possible benefits at the price of greater possible losses. (Or, to put it more subtly, the element of risk only arises as a factor in comparing options when one can make some sense of the balancing of benefits and losses, but the possible losses of one option are greater than those of another otherwise equally attractive one.) And then analogs of the two facts just mentioned above will be true. People who take more risks, in order to get more benefits, will get more variable results than those who take fewer, so that over time risk-takers will be both better and worse off. And if they make clever choices among a wide range of options people who take more risks will be more likely to do badly, though on average they will do better.

What you really prefer

In the next section I will consider the pros and cons of some ways of steering between the competing pulls of safety and benefit. But first I shall formulate things in slightly greater generality, in a way that allows me to bring out a third important fact. It also allows me to engage with a standard economists' line about risk.

An option is risky, I said, in comparison with another, when it might turn out better but also might turn out worse. I have been illustrating risk in a traditional way with gambles between sums of money. But it has also been clear that one cannot react to such gambles without considering *how much* one wants the possible gains and losses. And it is pretty clear that we cannot measure how much one wants things, not even amounts of money, in direct proportion to their monetary values. The standard example is that a gift of $1,000 is wonderful for a street person, but almost irrelevant to a billionaire. So for the street person a gain of $1,000 will be something like ten times as desirable as a gain of $100, while to the billionaire it is hardly better at all. So consider someone for whom, say, $10,000 is about ten times as good as $1,000, but $20,000 less than twice as good as $10,000. (This might be because for each extra $1,000 up to about $10,000 the person can improve their life in basic ways, but after that the money would go for luxuries.) For that person a Heads/Tails gamble between $20,000 and $0 will not be the same value as a certainty of $10,000, since the $10,000 that would be lost if the coin comes down the wrong way would be missed more than the $10,000 that would be gained if it came down the right way. It is standard in economics to express this by describing agents in terms of 'utility functions', measures of the benefit to them of different amounts of goods, in particular money. (I shall use the terms 'benefit' and 'utility' interchangeably: 'benefit' when it makes more natural English, 'utility' when it makes a clearer connection with the literature.) It is usually assumed that money has a diminishing marginal utility, that is, that all people's utility functions give higher values for more money than for less, but increase less and less as the amounts get larger. (For expositions of the utility of money see Raiffa 1968: Ch. 4; Morton 1991: Ch. 6; Hargreaves-Heap *et al.* 1992: Ch. 1; and, going back to a source of much later work, Friedman and Savage 1948.)

A person whose utility function is of the diminishing marginal utility kind, and who evaluates gambles in terms of their expected utility or benefit rather than their expectation in money or other goods, will automatically show a certain kind of risk-aversion; that is, given two money gambles with the same *monetary* expectation, one of which has a wider spread of possible outcomes than the other, the person will prefer the one with the less wide spread. Such a person will for example usually take a Heads/Tails gamble between two amounts of money to be less valuable than a certainty of an amount half way between the two, since the value to the person of increasing by that half-way amount is less significant to them than the disvalue of decreasing by it.

There is clearly something right about this. The value of money, and most goods, does increase at a decreasing rate. In the hands of some economists, though, the point has become expanded into the following thought: 'Whatever choices someone makes, unless they are blatantly irrational, we can find a utility function so that the person is choosing the options with the greatest expected value in terms of that utility function. So in a way, no one is risk averse in terms of their own preferences.' This view is sometimes called the 'revealed preference' theory. (A person's 'real' preferences are revealed by their choices, not by what they say or think they want.) I think it is a misguided position. Though this is not the place to argue the issue, I do not think the resulting theory can give real explanations of why individual people make particular choices. And, quite evidently, it is no use to people trying to think their way through risky situations, since it says, 'Whatever you eventually do will have been the rational choice, in terms of the preferences you revealed in choosing it.' In focusing on which are the rational actions given a person's preferences, it loses sight of the more interesting question of what are the rational ways for people to think out what their preferences and hence their actions should be. (For a brief discussion of revealed preference see Hargreaves Heap *et al.* 1992: Ch. 2. A source of the view is Samuelson 1947.)

One complication that makes it harder to get a revealed preference theory off the ground, and which is directly relevant to the main themes of this chapter, is the fact that a person will sometimes be best off *not* evaluating gambles in terms of her utility functions, but in terms of money. This is true even if 'best off' is understood in terms of her personal utility rather than money or other goods. This paradoxical-sounding situation can be best understood through an example. Suppose that a person is facing a series of choices between gambles in a fixed period of time, all with monetary outcomes. Suppose to make it simple that the person has paid a fixed amount for the opportunity of making the choices, and that none of them involve losses. Suppose that the person wants to come out of the process doing as well as possible. Then she has two strategies, consistent with the general aim of trying to maximize expected utility: (a) take each gamble as it comes, evaluating them in terms of her utility function; (b) decide in advance how she will choose at each possible stage of the process, in such a way that her expectation of gain at the end is maximized. One might think that these amount to the same, but they do not have to. Our person is not extremely rich, so she regards sums up to $10,000 as serious amounts and values them linearly, so that gaining twice as much money within this range is twice as good. Above $10,000, though, the importance of increases in money begins to tail off, so $20,000 is just more than half again as valuable as $10,000. I'll express this by assuming that she has a utility function, u, such that u($0) = 0, u($10,000) = 1, u($20,000) = 1.6, and that u follows a straight line between the values of $0 and $10,000 and then curves smoothly to the value of $20,000 and onward, increasing at a decreasing rate. (The exact numbers could be changed quite a lot while still supporting the point I shall make. By the utility of x dollars I mean the value of an increase of her pre-game wealth by $x, not the value of having a wealth of $x.) She is faced with a series of twenty choices between gambles, in rapid succession. Each will consist of a choice between the risky option of 'Heads $20,000;

Tails nothing' and the safe option of $9,000 for sure. What should she do? Suppose that in accordance with the suggestion (a) just above she first considers the first choice. The expected value in utility terms of the risky gamble is ½u($20,000) + ½u($0) = 0.8, and the expected value of the safe gamble is u($9,000) = 0.9. So she will choose the safe gamble, and then for the same reasons choose the safe gamble on the following choices. And at the end of the series she will have $9,000 x 20 = $180,000. Now contrast this with what happens if in accordance with suggestion (b) she thinks of the whole series as a single unit. A little calculation shows that the expected monetary value of the gamble is $200,000, which is definitely more than $180,000, measured either in utility or in money. (In this case, then, it makes no difference whether she goes for money or for utility.) So if she thinks in this second way and values gambles in terms of their expected values she will commit herself to taking the risky gamble each time. So (a) and (b) are not the same; evaluating a series of gambles as they come along leads to different choices from evaluating them as a single process. Moreover, it is clear which is the better way to think. If she makes the (a)-style series of choices she ends up with $180,000. Suppose on the other hand she makes the (b)-style single choice. Then she will on average end up with $200,000. Moreover – as slightly longer calculations will show – there is an approximately 0.6 chance that she will gain $200,000 or more and an approximately 0.4 chance that she will gain $180,000 or less. (At 20 trials the next worst possible outcome after $200,000 is exactly $180,000.) So she is more likely than not to do better by following (b) than (a). So – however she balances utility against money and whichever way she evaluates the advantages of a decision-making method – she is better off thinking of the series of gambles as a single choice.[1]

The point here can be summed up as another fact. Fact number three: *avoiding risk by valuing money or other goods in a risk-averse way – one that makes the value of greater amounts less than proportionately greater than that of smaller amounts – can, if one does not carefully pick the way one frames one's choices, lead to choices that are less valuable, even in terms of the chosen valuation.* Canny expectation-oriented agents will choose their utility functions carefully, with an eye to the choices that are imminent.[2]

Choosing how to choose

The main character in the story so far has been the rule 'evaluate gambles – or risky options in general – in terms of their expected values'. (Henceforth often 'the expectational rule' or 'expectational thinking'.) This rule can be stated in considerable generality as a basic principle of decision-making. In fact formal decision theory is essentially an elaboration of the expected value principle into a description or prescription applying to all aspects of decision. The rule is not easy to use, though. It requires us to put our preferences into numbers: and besides the difficulties of knowing and quantifying how much one wants something fact number three shows a deep complication in doing this. It also requires us to express our estimates of likelihood or degrees of belief as numerical probabilities, also very demanding in terms of self-knowledge and the assessment of evidence. And it requires us to make probability and utility calculations of a kind that can easily become very complicated and easy to bungle. I think – I just don't know whether the suggestion would meet with general agreement – that to recommend thinking of risk in terms of expectation is to suggest an intellectual virtue, that of being able to produce numerical estimates, of how likely events are and how much one would gain from outcomes, which give one an accurate grasp of the relative frequencies and acceptabilities of potential outcomes. (Or at any rate a virtue that will give a grasp of these things that leads to decisions that one tends not to regret.) There's not much point deciding by expected values unless you have acquired this virtue, and acquiring it may require a major reorganization of your thinking. One of the signs of being a member of a society with a market economy, perhaps.

We may well ask: why follow this rule? We might ask this with respect to the choices we will have to make in a particular situation – 'how am I to think this one through?' – or with respect to the choices people should make generally. Here are three reasons that might be given for valuing gambles by expectations, together with problems with the reasons.

Reason 1: if an agent values gambles by their expectations then she will probably do better than if she chooses in accordance with some other rule.

Explanation: if a person makes a long series of choices between gambles, and always chooses the gambles that have the greatest expected value, then her total gains will approximate, the more so the longer the series, to the sum of expected values of her choices, and this will be greater than any other policy is likely to result in. Therefore evaluating risks by expectations is the best possible policy.

Problem (1): *it may not be true*. Agents operating on perfect information, with perfect calculating ability and perfect self-knowledge may make the best decisions this way, but it just is not evident that an imperfect agent facing a long series of choices will come out best by thinking expectationally. This is so for two reasons. First, the effect of mistakes in evaluation and calculation. Second, fact number three above: if by expectational thinking we mean valuing each gamble one meets in terms of its expected value according to one's preferences then it is not true that this will give one the best results one can get. (And if we mean to include just the right combinations of acts and choices of utility functions, then we are adding a completely new level of considerations, an additional set of rules, which have never yet been carefully formulated.)

Problem (2): *death*. No real agent goes through more than a limited number of choices before dying. And some of the gambles we consider have death (or the commercial equivalent, bankruptcy) as a possible consequence. So the problem of getting from what would be best on an indefinitely long series of choices to what would be best in a finite life span is as difficult as that of getting from a range of possible choices and outcomes to an actual one.

Problem (3): *equivocation.* As fact number two shows, in some situations most people who choose in terms of expected value will do badly (though a minority will do well enough to raise the average). So it is simply not true that to choose by expected value is always to make it more probable that you will do well. Will people who choose by expected value in general do well? That depends on what gambles the human race happens to be faced with, and in what proportions. Will possible people meeting all possible gambles do best if they think in expectational terms? In the absence of some probability distribution over all possible occasions of person-meets-gamble the question is not well defined.

Reason 2: if you evaluate risks in accordance with their expected values the probability that you will regret your decision is minimized.

Explanation: the benefits of expectational decisions tend to be greater than those of decisions made in other ways, and so the difference between the outcome of such a decision and the outcome had an alternative been chosen tend to be in the favour of the expectational decision.

Problem: the argument just given does not support expectational thinking. Instead it supports the quite different idea that the best decision is the one that will probably give the best results. That is a different idea because, as in the example in the midnight gamble at the beginning of this chapter, the option with the greater expectation can probably give the worse results. Some people might take it as a better idea, but there are cases where it is clearly wrong. Consider a choice between on the one hand a gamble which leads to $1,000 nine hundred and ninety nine times out of a thousand and death one time in a thousand, and on the other hand a 'gamble' that gives no money and no danger. Then the first gamble will probably give better results, but the risk of being in the minority of dead people is clearly not worth it.

Reason 3: people who evaluate risks in accordance with their expected values will generally do better than those who do not, so you should encourage this mode of evaluation.

Explanation: one way of thinking of what you should do is as an instance of a general pattern which it makes sense for people to adhere to. And you can hardly recommend it for others without following it yourself.

Problem (1) as with the first problem with reason 1 above: it is not obviously true that people who go by expected value do generally do better.

Problem (2) assuming that the assumption is true, it must mean that people on average do better if they evaluate by expectations. Grant the further assumption that you should encourage the general adoption of practices that on average are good for people. It does not follow that these are the practices that will do best for you on this occasion. (Compare: you should encourage people to be truthful and cooperative, and your own truthfulness and cooperation may be a necessary means to this. But on any given occasion a lie or a cheat may be your best choice.)

Since I have been finding holes in justifications for the expectational rule, I should mention an objection to it, which also has problems.

The reliability objection: Grant that in many circumstances if we evaluate gambles by their expectations we will get results that on average are in our best interests, *if* our estimates of probability are accurate. It does not follow that, given our human propensity to mis-estimate and mis-calculate, gambles evaluated in terms of the consequently inaccurate probabilities will be similarly well chosen. Expectational thinking may be fine for ideal agents, but we need something that works for us human bunglers.

Problem (1) Expectational thinking is surprisingly tolerant of approximate probabilities. Consider for example a case in which one is pondering a Heads/Tails gamble with a coin that one takes to be fair, with payoffs of $1 for Heads and $0 for Tails, so that one evaluates the gamble as worth ½$1 = $0.5. Suppose that in fact the coin is not fair, but biased so that the probability of Heads is 0.7. Had one known this one would have given the gamble a value of $0.7. The difference in the expected value of the gamble is linear in the error: if one's probabilities are out by 30 per cent one's valuations are out by just 30 per cent. The expectational rule is even more tolerant when we consider embedded or repeated gambles, in which the expectation depends on the probability of an outcome which is itself probabilistic. In a simple embedding the expectation will be a function of the square of the probability, so if that is out by, say, 30 per cent, then the expectation will be out by only 11 per cent. (Remember that probabilities are less than one, so that when raised to a power they become smaller rather than larger.)

Problem (2) Moreover estimates of risk are also quite tolerant of errors in probability. One's estimate of the probability of the worst case outcome of a gamble will be inaccurate only to the degree that one's estimate of the basic probabilities is inaccurate. It will not amplify the error. (And, more generally, the fact that one's estimates of probability may be in error increases the variance of gambles. But, considering them now as weighted sums of gambles where the weights are proportional to a distribution of errors assumed to have one's original estimate as its mean, the variance of this new distribution is not so different from that of the original one. I find this fact surprising.)

And, to end this section, here is a direct objection to using the expectational rule, that does have some force, though it could be exaggerated.

The unpredictability objection: We need to be able to predict the future, and riskier choices, even when accompanied by higher average payoffs, are less predictable in their outcomes.

Explanation: Consider someone facing a series of choices like the ones that illustrated fact number three. (Heads/Tails between $20,000 and $0, versus certainty of $9,000; repeated several times.) If he takes the risky option each time his wealth will probably increase, but will do so in an unpredictable way. If he takes the safe options he can know in advance that he will be $9,000 richer at the end of each play. This might for example allow him to make plans to invest the money, or to keep it safe from thieves, or to purchase things expecting that the money will be available when the bills arrive.

Qualification: The main disadvantage of expectational thinking that this reveals is the bad combination of risk-taking and unpreparedness. Someone who chooses with an eye to average rather than probable benefits should also have contingency plans, both for winning and for losing, and ways of using winning occasions to palliate the effects of losing occasions. The disposition to do these things is a practical virtue that has to accompany the expectational mentality, rather like the virtue of ordering one's beliefs and desires to fit that mentality, mentioned earlier.

Against rules

What we have seen is a tension between three intuitively appealing ideas about good decision-making. We can't hold all three of these as general rules:

1 Choose so that you are likely to get what you want. (Maximize the chance of good consequences).
2 Choose so as to minimize the probability of bad consequences.
3 Choose so that you will on average get as much as you can of what you want.

(3) is the expectational rule. (2) is a general principle of risk-aversion, in the same general spirit as what is sometimes called the precautionary principle (see Chapter 6 in this book by Per Sandin). (1) is a general principle of practical reasoning, which we often appeal to as if it were obviously true. But it is clear that no sensible person would always obey (1) or (2). (1) ought to be violated – for people with normal preferences about the kinds of choices they want to make – when there is a small but unlikely chance of something extremely desirable. (You are trapped in a canyon as the river rises. Your only hope is to climb a fragile vine. Probably this will fail, but it might just succeed. The alternatives are staying where you are and drowning in five minutes or moving to a ledge and drowning in ten minutes.) (2) ought to be violated when the same course of action leads to an extremely good outcome and an extremely bad one. (If the vine breaks the crocodiles will get you – but then if you don't take the chance you'll drown.)

When should (3) be violated? We have seen a number of situations where sensible people would be very reluctant to choose the act with the greatest expected value. They are all risky situations, of course, but I think it helps to distinguish two kinds of risk.

The first – call it *wide consequences risk* – comes when an act has both good and bad consequences. Since the interesting cases, the ones that make for hard decisions, are those where the risky option is a serious rival to a safer one, the hard problems involving wide-consequence risk arise when one option gives a higher expected value than another, but also gives a possibility of a worse outcome. Is the chance of the better payoff worth the risk of the worse one?

The other kind of risk – call it *probable trouble risk* – comes when an act will most likely lead to bad results. The hard problems with probable trouble risk arise when one option will on average give a better result than another, but more often than not will do worse. We can have wide-consequence risk without probable trouble risk when it is most likely that one will come out with the average or even the best result, but there is a small yet non-negligible chance of a much worse one (see Figure 5.1). We can also have hard choices between risks of the two kinds, in which one option will probably turn out well but might well turn out disastrously, and the other option will probably turn out badly, though not disastrously, but might turn out well. These two options might be identical in expected value, but one person might be more averse to one and another person to the other. This is something more complex than

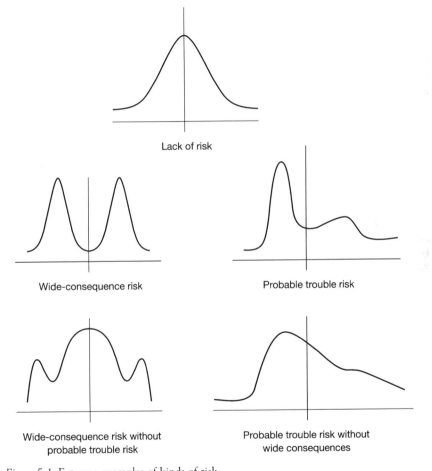

Lack of risk

Wide-consequence risk

Probable trouble risk

Wide-consequence risk without probable trouble risk

Probable trouble risk without wide consequences

Figure 5.1 Extreme examples of kinds of risk.
Note: The vertical axis is probability, the horizontal is value, with worse to the left and better to the right.

risk-aversion; it is an aversion to a particular kind of risk, to a particular profile of desirable and undesirable consequences.

I do not think there is anything rationally wrong with someone who chooses in a way that avoids particular kinds of risk. There is nothing wrong, that is, as long as the person also exhibits other traits, virtues as I have been calling them, that are necessary in order to make a success of that style of choice, and as long as the person finds the general consequences of choosing in that way acceptable. This applies to choosing in terms of expected value too. In the course of this chapter I have mentioned a number of virtues that expected-value-choosers should have: the ability to think of one's preferences and one's degrees of confidence in numerical terms, the ability to make contingency plans for the inevitable times when a gamble with a high expected value has a low actual one, and the ability to schedule and gather together one's choices for the best overall outcome. If you don't have these virtues, then you should stay away from expectational thinking. You should also stay away from expectational thinking if you are not prepared for frequent losses which will accompany your gains.

In fact, I put this last point too gently. Suppose that the gambles available to you include many probable trouble risks. Then if you choose in purely expectational terms you will have more losses than gains, although if you are lucky you will have the occasional big gain. If you are not lucky you will have just the losses, while just a few of your like minded friends get the big gains. I doubt that very many people are really prepared for this. Most people's general preferences about the outcome of their choices, I am sure, countenance a mixture of losses and gains, but resist the possibility of unmitigated losses. That suggests that to the extent that people reason expectationally, they do so in contexts in which they are reasonably sure that the risks tend to the wide consequence rather than the probable trouble profiles. And this suggests yet another virtue, or rather yet another combination of a decision-making style, a preference for kinds of outcomes and a virtue. If you want to do well on average, are prepared to take losses along with your gains, but are not prepared for the prospect of far more and more likely losses than gains, then you must learn to find wide consequence risks, and avoid situations in which they are not to be found.

There are virtues associated with other attitudes to risk, too, though the focus of this chapter is on expectational thinking. If you are averse to losses even as the price to pay for the possibility of gains then you will need the virtue of equanimity as gambles you turned down pay off grandly. (And it would help to have the virtue of tact when gambles you turned down prove disastrous for others.) And above all you will need the virtue of finding non-risky options with reasonable payoffs: you will have to spend a lot of time looking. If you want to gain most of the time, accepting the possibility of frequent losses as a price for this, in effect submitting your choices to principle (1) at the beginning of this section, then too you will have to acquire the virtue of finding wide-consequence risks where at first you see only probable trouble ones.

The central point is this: don't think in terms of rules alone. They are not that important. What matters is the fit between a person's general aims in decision-making, the procedures they have for comparing and deciding between options, and the skills of judgement, perception and long-term self-control that they have or can acquire. These last, what I have been calling virtues, play a much larger role than is generally appreciated. One reason they are easily ignored is that we often frame questions about decision-making as if people were faced with a set of options, over whose composition they have no control, from which they must choose. But in fact we *search* for options, digging out facts and using our imaginations, and one of the central virtues of a good decision-maker is the capacity to find the right set of options to choose between. A situation studded with probable trouble risk, for example, is not one in which comparison by expected value is very appealing. So what should you do if you seem to be in such a situation? The first thing you should do is look for more options.[3] The main focus of advice concerning risk should be not how to compare the options that you have but what sorts of options to search out before comparing them.[4]

Notes

1 The point could be made with a shorter series of choices by using gambles in which the expected monetary value is just greater than that of the certain alternative, but in which the agent is more likely than not to get more than the expected value. Though discrepancies between expectation and most likely outcome are important in this essay, I thought it would be simpler to make the point with more familiar-shaped gambles.

2 Really canny agents can have very complex utility functions. One aspect I have not discussed is that they may make their evaluation of an outcome depend on whether the process that led to it was a risky one (see Broome (1991), especially Ch. 5). I do not think this affects the point I am making here. My point is related to what Savage (1954) called the 'small world problem'. See also Pollock (2002).

3 Risk-management in terms of procedures for searching for options is discussed in Ch. 7 of Morton (1991).

4 James Hawthorne and John Simpson gave me good advice about this essay.

References

Broome, J. (1991) *Weighing Goods*, Oxford: Blackwell.

Friedman, M. and Savage, L. (1948) 'The utility analysis of choices involving risk', *Journal of Political Economy*, 56: 279–304.

Hacking, I. (1975) *The Emergence of Probability*, Cambridge: Cambridge University Press.

Hargreaves Heap, S., Hollis, M., Lyons, B., Sugden, R. and Weale, A. (1992) *The Theory of Choice*, Oxford: Blackwell.

Jeffrey, R. (1983) *The Logic of Decision*, 2nd edn, Chicago: Chicago University Press.

Morton, A. (1991) *Disasters and Dilemmas*, Oxford: Blackwell.

Pollock, J.L. (2002) 'Rational choice and action omnipotence', *Philosophical Review*, 111: 1–24.

Raiffa, H. (1968) *Decision Analysis*, Reading, MA: Addison-Wesley.

Resnik, M.D. (1987) *Choices*, Madison: Wisconsin University Press.

Samuelson, P.A. (1947) *The Foundations of Economic Analysis*, Cambridge, MA: Harvard University Press.

Savage, L.J. (1954) *The Foundations of Statistics*, New York: Wiley.

6

COMMON-SENSE PRECAUTION AND VARIETIES OF THE PRECAUTIONARY PRINCIPLE

Per Sandin

Introduction

I am hiking in the mountains, and I am thinking of having a drink of water from a small stream. I do not know that the water is safe to drink. There just might be a reindeer carcass a short distance upstream, poisoning the water. Thus, as the saying goes, 'When in doubt, don't.' I abstain from drinking the water, or at least boil it before drinking it.

Back home, I am asked for an opinion about whether crops that have been genetically modified to resist pesticides should be allowed to be cultivated on a large scale in the southernmost part of Sweden. I do not know that the practice is safe. The crops might somehow spread this resistance to the pests themselves. Furthermore, we know little about what other unpleasant surprises GM crops might have in store for us. Thus, I recommend that the cultivation of GM crops should not be allowed to proceed, or at least that it should proceed only in a completely sealed-off environment. My reasoning is similar to that in the mountains.

Those stories capture the seemingly simple idea behind the precautionary principle, which in the last twenty years or so has found its way into national and international legal documents and policy statements concerning diverse areas of health and environmental protection in risk situations. It has been invoked in highly diverse contexts: from regulation of chemicals and genetically modified organisms to research into life-extending medical therapies.[1] There are numerous versions of the precautionary principle around. The most prominent and oft-cited one is probably the version found in Principle 15 of the 1992 Rio Declaration:

> In order to protect the environment, the precautionary approach shall be widely applied by States according to their capabilities. Where

there are threats of serious or irreversible damage, lack of full scientific certainty shall not be used as a reason for postponing cost-effective measures to prevent environmental degradation.

(UNCED 1993)

Interestingly, the English text of the Rio Declaration does not mention the term 'principle' at all. It has, as one author expresses it, been 'demoted to a "precautionary approach"' (Dommen 1993: 2). However, translations into several other languages use the expression directly corresponding to 'precautionary principle', and the passage cited here is commonly referred to as expressing the precautionary principle. I follow that practice.

Another example is from the Third Conference on the North Sea, The Hague, March 1990. The version here is specifically about toxic substances:

[...] the precautionary principle, that is to take action to avoid potentially damaging impacts of substances that are persistent, toxic and liable to bioaccumulate even when there is no scientific evidence to prove a causal link between emissions and effects.

(Quoted in Haigh 1994: 244)

When thus transformed into a principle, the intuitively simple idea of 'when in doubt, don't' or perhaps 'better safe than sorry' is not so simple anymore. Despite extensive discussions, there is still considerable disagreement about what the precautionary principle means, should mean, or might reasonably mean.

The different versions of the precautionary principle can be classified in at least three groups. These contain precautionary principles as (1) rules of choice, (2) epistemic rules or principles, and (3) procedural requirements. In this chapter, I will treat these in turn and discuss some problems with each. I will present an analysis of the everyday or common-sense concept of precaution, and attempt to show how an understanding of it can be useful in the debate around the precautionary principle.

Rules of choice

Several authors have interpreted the precautionary principle as a rule of choice, stating that in particular types of situation, certain courses of action should be chosen. An example of a version of the precautionary principle that is reasonably interpreted as a rule of choice is found in the Wingspread Statement:

When an activity raises threats of harm to human health or the environment, precautionary measures should be taken even if some cause-and-effect relationships are not fully established scientifically.

(Raffensperger and Tickner 1999: 354–55)

Taken literally, this type of rule of choice is obviously problematic. The reason is that there are always some cause-and-effect relationships that are not fully established scientifically. And every action might – just might – raise threats to human health and the environment, if possibilities that are remote enough are taken into consideration. If the precautionary principle is understood as prohibiting those courses of action that *might* lead to harm, then the precautionary principle will prohibit *every* action, including the action of taking precautionary measures, since any action, in a sense, might have unforeseen harmful consequences. Perhaps, through a long, winding and unlikely but possible causal chain, you will cause a new world war by eating asparagus, and so on. Decision-makers will thus be paralysed.

According to this argument, the precautionary principle is self-refuting or incoherent.[2] This is something that has been pointed out, repeatedly, by a number of commentators.[3] Most recent, to my knowledge, and nicely summing up the argument, is Sunstein (2005). One of his many examples will serve as an illustration: There is not full agreement among scientists about the dangers of global warming. Many people believe that reductions of emissions as required by the Kyoto Protocol may mitigate the consequences of global warming. But others argue that such measures are extremely costly, and that the costs would hit the poorest and worst-off in society hardest. If we are to apply the precautionary principle and avoid the course of action that might lead to great harm, both alternatives will be prohibited. Sunstein contends: 'The real problem is that the principle offers no guidance – not that it is wrong, but that it forbids all courses of action, including regulation' (Sunstein 2005: 26).

In fact, the argument is older than the spreading of the phrase 'precautionary principle'. An early example, from the early days of DNA technology, is Stich's critique (1978) of what he calls 'the "doomsday scenario" argument'. And Stich himself – as other authors – mentions Pascal's Wager and the Many-Gods Objection.[4] Just like the incoherence charge against the precautionary principle, the Many-Gods Objection points out that a prescription to act on the basis of mere possibilities will lead to paralysis.

The claim that the precautionary principle is self-refuting or incoherent is a strong one. There also is a related but weaker claim, according to which the precautionary principle is not necessarily incoherent, but is *counterproductive*. That is, even if the precautionary principle could be action guiding, the precautionary measures it prescribes would lead to more risk-taking, rather than less.[5] This could for instance come about through increased cost induced by regulation. To take an example: Some proponents of the precautionary principle have been sceptical of GM foods and have argued that, as precautionary measures, restrictions should be put on such foods, because of the uncertain but potentially catastrophic consequences they might have. However, as several commentators have noted, those precautionary measures might themselves have catastrophic consequences, directly or indirectly. For instance, rejection of GM foods in developing countries may have the consequence of famine (Turvey and Mojduszka 2005: 150–52). It should be said that the example is meant as an illustration only. I am well aware that there are probably better ways of combating famine than distributing GM crops.

The argument to the effect that the precautionary principle, on one interpretation, is incoherent is a sound argument. But how is one to react to it? One possible reaction is to regard the precautionary principle as simply refuted. This, I believe, is too rash. A better way is to see the argument as indicating necessary refinement and further specification of the precautionary principle. There is a reason for this: the incoherence argument is, in fact, so obvious a problem that it is unlikely that anyone would propose a principle that is vulnerable to it. Thus, applying the principle of charity, one may suspect that proponents of the precautionary principle have something more sophisticated in mind than a principle demanding that one should act upon mere possibilities. This 'something', however, needs spelling out.

Some philosophers who have commented upon the precautionary principle as a rule of choice translate it into something more manageable in the form of one or other decision rules recognised from decision theory. One example of that approach is Hansson (1997).[6] He interprets the precautionary principle as the maximin rule. (It should be noted that Hansson's views have evolved since then.) According to the maximin rule, an agent should choose the action where the *worst* possible outcome is least bad. Suppose that you are choosing between betting £5 on Long Shot or abstaining. If you bet your fiver and Long Shot wins the race, you will be rich, but if he doesn't, you will lose £5. If you choose not to bet, you will lose nothing. The worst case if you do not bet £5 is thus better than the worst case if you do. Maximin tells you not to bet.

The problem with this approach is that the precautionary principle is not readily translatable into, say, maximin (see Sunstein 2005: 61). An example might illustrate. In Sandin (1999) I surveyed several (then) existing versions of the precautionary principle and attempted to find common elements and a common structure. I argued that four core elements or 'dimensions' of the precautionary principle could be identified: (1) the threat dimension, (2) the uncertainty dimension, (3) the action dimension and (4) the prescription dimension. The actual phrasing in (1)–(4) varies between different versions of the principle, of course. I further argued that the precautionary principle could be recast into the following if-clause, containing these four dimensions:

If there is (1) a threat, which is (2) uncertain, *then* (3) some kind of action (4) is mandatory.

While maximin simply dictates that choosing the option where the worst possible outcome is least bad is mandatory, the four-part version is richer. For instance, the four-part version contains *triggering conditions*, which maximin does not. Thus, the precautionary principle is not identical with maximin. Neither does it imply maximin. Furthermore, one could ask, if the precautionary principle is maximin, what's all the fuss about?

On one view, the precautionary principle as a rule of choice can be saved, if properly restricted. For example, it can be requested that a precautionary principle of the Wingspread type be supplemented with some requirement of the likelihood of the harm before precaution is triggered, and that it is only applicable to certain types of threat. Whether this approach is fruitful is disputed.[7]

A different approach is to give up the idea of a precautionary principle as an *action-guiding* principle. The argument that it fails to be action guiding then obviously loses its force, since it does not purport to be so. Let us then turn to the alternative ways of understanding the precautionary principle I mentioned at the outset: if it is not a rule of choice, it may be an epistemic rule or principle or a procedural requirement.

Epistemic rules and principles

I will not say very much about the precautionary principle as an epistemic rule. It is discussed by Harris and Holm (2002).[8] By an epistemic precautionary principle they mean a principle that requires that evidence suggesting a causal link between an activity and possible harm should be given greater weight than it would in other circumstances. They reject such principles, for the reason that 'systematic discounting of evidence would systematically distort our beliefs about the world, and would necessarily, over time, lead us to include a large number of false beliefs in our belief system' (Harris and Holm 2002: 362). This is perhaps not a sufficient condition for rejecting such an epistemic principle, at least not in applied contexts. In intra-scientific decision-making, there is arguably a premium on not including false beliefs in a belief system, for the reason that it is likely to make us err in future. In applied or policy contexts, other considerations come into play as well, such as the importance of beliefs and the consequences of being wrong. However, as Holm (2006) points out, in the context where the precautionary principle is invoked, the false beliefs would be false beliefs about very important matters.

I do not think that the precautionary principle is reasonably interpreted as an epistemic principle, that is, not as a pure epistemic principle. It would be strange to prescribe what to actually believe, on the basis of non-epistemic consequences. However, it would be less strange to prescribe that we should act *as if* certain things were true, pending further information. One possible version of the precautionary principle along these lines is the precautionary default approach discussed in Sandin *et al.* (2004). A precautionary default is a cautious or pessimistic assumption that is used in the absence of adequate information and to be replaced when such information is obtained. But that is not a (pure) epistemic principle. Rather, we are led to the third way of understanding the precautionary principle, namely the precautionary principle interpreted as a procedural requirement.

Procedural requirements

This category recognises the starting point of several proponents of precaution – whether called 'precautionary principle', 'precautionary approach' or something else: a deep dissatisfaction with earlier decisions. Things went woefully wrong in the past, and by using the precautionary principle we could, it is hoped, avoid or at least mitigate that with which we are dissatisfied. Perhaps the clearest example of this approach is found in a book aptly titled *Late Lessons from Early Warnings* (Harremoës *et al.* 2002). This dissatisfaction is not *only* concerned with the chosen course of action and the outcome, but also with *how* the decision was made.[9]

What is sought after is perhaps not an algorithm for choosing a particular course of action, but rather a set of requirements for how such decisions are to be made. This might be termed procedural precaution, reflected in procedural versions of the precautionary principle.[10]

On one such interpretation, the precautionary principle is a principle for what arguments are admissible in decision-making. The most prominent example is to be found in Principle 15 of the Rio Declaration (UNCED 1993), probably the most frequently referred to instance of the principle. This version, which is included almost verbatim in several other documents, requires that 'lack of full scientific certainty shall not be used as a *reason* for postponing cost-effective measures to prevent environmental degradation' (emphasis added). The requirement that the measures be cost-effective adds a complication, which I will disregard here. The problem with such 'argumentative' versions of the precautionary principle is that they are rather undemanding. They say little more than that arguments from ignorance should not be used, which is not a particularly controversial condition. Sunstein calls them 'the most cautious and weak versions' of the precautionary principle (Sunstein 2005: 18). Another example of a procedural version of the precautionary principle is the oft-quoted requirement of reversal of burden of proof – that the proponent of an activity should be required to show that it is safe in order for the activity to be permissible.[11]

The problem with procedural versions of the precautionary principle is that they comprise a category that is significantly more heterogeneous than, for example, the precautionary principle as a rule of choice. Furthermore, procedural versions of the precautionary principle are intermingled with other legal principles, rules, questions of legitimate authority and other procedural requirements. Elizabeth Fisher (2002) emphasises that the precautionary principle is a legal principle, in the Dworkinian sense of a principle that 'states a reason, that argues in one direction, but does not necessitate a particular decision' (Dworkin 1978: 26). Thus it is not a 'rule that dictates a particular outcome in a certain set of circumstances' (Fisher 2002: 15). She argues convincingly, while ridiculing 'precaution spotting' and 'mining' of examples of precaution, 'the discussion so far has tended to characterize the precautionary principle in a way that is at odds with the actual legal nature of the precautionary principle and how it operates in particular contexts' (ibid.).

There seems to be precious little that unites different versions of precaution, and any principle, let alone a tenable one, is hard to isolate. Compare the possible plethora of precautionary principles presented in Sunstein (2005: 120). He suggests that '[f]or every regulatory tool, there is a corresponding precautionary principle'. Examples he mentions are a 'Funding More Research Precautionary Principle', an 'Economic Incentives Precautionary Principle' and an 'Information Disclosure Precautionary Principle'. There are in fact even more possibilities. Fisher (2002: 18) emphasises context and legal culture: 'how the principle will be formulated, interpreted, and implemented will be largely a product of legal culture'. Thus differences might be deeper than 'precaution spotting' suggests. How many precautionary principles might there be? Multiply the number of legal cultures with the number of regulatory tools, and things soon start to get out of hand.

So is there anything left of the precautionary principle? Interpreted as a rule of choice, the precautionary principle seems to be untenable. Neither is it reasonably interpreted as a purely epistemic principle. Interpreted as one or other procedural rule or principle, 'the' precautionary principle soon dissolves beyond recognition. In any case, it is hard to say anything about 'the' principle as such, given the intricacies presented by the context in which it occurs. Such rules and principles can and should, of course, be discussed and evaluated, but that will have to be done on a case-by-case basis.

The everyday concept of precaution

The precautionary principle is commonly thought, rightly, I believe, to be intimately linked to the everyday concept of precaution.[12] This is illustrated by the fact that proverbs like 'better safe than sorry' (Greenpeace 2000) or 'an ounce of prevention is worth a pound of cure' (Bodansky 1991) often are used to explain what the precautionary principle contains. Even the Hippocratic Oath has been mentioned as a parallel to the precautionary principle (Ozonoff 1999: 100). Furthermore, several authors who have commented on the precautionary principle make explicit reference to the everyday concept of precaution.[13]

Others claim that someone has applied the precautionary principle, when it is far from clear that any principle was operative at all. To take one example: Dr John Snow's recommendation in 1854 to remove the handle of the water pump in Broad Street, London, in order to stop a cholera epidemic has been cited as an early use of the precautionary principle (Harremoës et al. 2002: 5ff.). At the time, it was not proved beyond reasonable doubt that cholera was transmitted by polluted water, and the majority view among scientists was that cholera contamination was airborne. In this case, Dr Snow arguably initiated precautionary action, but it is not obvious that any precautionary *principle* was present when the action was carried out. (This is somewhat similar to the problem in Kantian ethics of inferring a maxim on which an action supposedly is based.) Snow himself may have been rather convinced that cholera is transmitted via contaminated water. He had published on the subject previous to the Golden Square outbreak of 1854, and it is quite possible that he himself did not regard the removal of the pump handle as merely precautionary (Brody *et al.* 2000).

Nevertheless, this type of example suggests that there is indeed an intimate link between precaution in the everyday sense and the precautionary principle in its various guises. However, apart from the mentioning of 'common-sense' instances of precaution, this link has rarely been explored. I will therefore now turn to precaution in its everyday sense. In everyday language, several things can be characterised as precautionary. Actions are the most obvious candidates. But what makes an action precautionary?

Intention

First, in order for an action to be precautionary, there has to be present an *intention* to take precautions. An action cannot be precautionary by accident, so to speak. Consider a person bringing a fire extinguisher to a fancy-dress party as a part of his dress. A fire breaks out, which fortunately is put out with the aid of the fire extinguisher. We would not call the action of bringing the fire extinguisher a precautionary action.

However, there are several undesirable things, and an action performed with the intention of preventing one undesirable thing might well fail to prevent other undesirable things. The action might even promote these other undesirable things. This is precisely what opponents of the precautionary principle have been pointing out when claiming that precautionary measures may lead to worse problems than they were intended to solve.

The key here lies in the phrase 'with respect to'. When we speak of precautionary actions, we *assume* that there is something undesirable *with respect to which* we take precautions. This does not rule out that there are other things with respect to which we are not taking precautions.

Thus, the first criterion for precaution can be stated:

> An action *a* is precautionary with respect to something undesirable U only if *a* is performed with the intention of preventing U.

This is the *Criterion of Intentionality*. It shall be assumed that it follows from this criterion that the agent believes, first, that U might occur and, second, that *a* will in fact at least contribute to the prevention of U.

Uncertainty

Secondly, we typically consider precautions in situations when we are not certain that the undesirable thing will in fact befall us. We might in fact believe that the bad thing happening is highly unlikely, but nevertheless take precautions. (One example might be irradiating vast quantities of mail as a precautionary measure against anthrax letters.) On the other hand, if the bad thing is certain or very likely, it would be odd to call measures intended to prevent it precautionary. We may thus add the second necessary criterion for precaution:

> An action *a* is precautionary with respect to something undesirable U, only if the agent does not believe it to be certain or very likely that U will occur if *a* is not performed.

This is the *Uncertainty Criterion*. It should be kept in mind that 'uncertainty' here is used in a rather loose sense, without the decision-theoretic connotations of the term.

Epistemic reasonableness

Thirdly, there has to be a way of distinguishing between precautionary actions and actions which are merely thought to be precautionary for no good reason. Consider the following example: A factory worker in an industrialised country is well informed about the dangers of being exposed to a hazardous chemical X in his work. However, as a precautionary measure, he performs a ritualistic dance every morning at the factory gates, believing that this will keep the evil spirits residing in the chemical X happy and, consequently, protect him from harm.

Here it would be strange to say that his action is precautionary. In this case, he lacks good epistemic reasons for believing that his action will reduce the probability of harm. By 'good' epistemic reasons I mean reasons that are somehow externally good, external to the agent, that is. I do not think it is necessary to stipulate that the reasons be 'objectively good'. They may be thought of as relative to the state of modern science, a particular cultural sphere, or the like. The point is that the mere fact that an agent believes that he or she performs a precautionary action does not imply that the action is precautionary (though the converse relation holds). We should thus add a third necessary criterion, containing three sub-criteria (a)–(c), demanding that the agent has externally good epistemic reasons for certain beliefs:

> An action *a* is precautionary with respect to something undesirable U, only if the agent has externally good epistemic reasons (a) for believing that U might occur, (b) for believing that *a* will in fact at least contribute to the prevention of U and (c) for not believing it to be certain or very likely that U will occur if *a* is not performed.

This third criterion we term the *Reasonableness Criterion*. Put together the three criteria state that:

an action *a* is precautionary with respect to something undesirable U if and only if:

1 *a* is performed with the intention of preventing U,
2 the agent does not believe it to be very likely that U will occur if *a* is not performed, and
3 the agent has externally good epistemic reasons (a) for believing that U might occur, (b) for believing that *a* will in fact at least contribute to the prevention of U, and (c) for not believing it to be certain or very likely that U will occur if *a* is not performed.

I believe that with the criteria of intentionality, uncertainty, and reasonableness we have stated necessary and sufficient conditions for calling an action precautionary, and that the definition proposed is a reasonable explication of the concept of precaution, or at least, a precautionary action.

Once again, this applies to actions that are precautionary *with respect to* something undesirable. That, I believe, is as far as we will get. If we are looking for actions that are precautionary *sans phrase*, we will be looking in vain. This means that precaution essentially is a relative concept.

Conclusion

As the analysis above showed, a precautionary action can be seen as precautionary only with respect to something, and it needs to satisfy the criteria of intentionality, uncertainty, and epistemic reasonableness. I therefore propose the following maxim:

> When presenting a course of action (for instance, the introduction of certain regulation) as precautionary, it should be explicitly and precisely stated with respect to what undesirable outcome(s) that course of action is meant to be precautionary. Furthermore, it should be explicitly and precisely stated how the three criteria of intentionality, uncertainty, and epistemic reasonableness are fulfilled by the course of action.

Applied to the precautionary principle, this maxim could be formulated:

> When presenting a precautionary principle, it should be explicitly and precisely stated with respect to what undesirable outcome(s) that principle is meant to be precautionary, and it should be explicitly and precisely stated how the three criteria of intentionality, uncertainty, and epistemic reasonableness are addressed by the principle.

This does not solve the problem entirely, of course. But applying the maxim would have some advantages.

First, it is consistent with the observation that a universal precautionary principle is difficult to conceive. If one tries to construct a principle stating that one should be precautionary with respect to everything, it is hard to see how it could address the criteria of intentionality, uncertainty, and reasonableness.

Second, it would facilitate evaluation of measures that are presented as being prescribed by or at least in accordance with the precautionary principle. If it can be shown that these measures are not precautionary in the everyday sense of the term, there might be reason to discuss their legitimacy, or at least the way in which they are justified. Conversely, if they can be shown to be precautionary in the everyday sense of the term, someone who appeals to the precautionary principle arguably has a stronger case for the proposed measures.

A related point is that some criticisms of measures introduced with reference to the precautionary principle amount to questioning, though not necessarily explicitly, whether these measures are precautionary in the everyday sense. I will sketch but one example. Consider the case of hormones in beef. The EU's ban of growth hormones in beef production in the 1980s was regarded by the US as lacking scientific basis, and it was claimed that use of growth hormones in beef does not present a risk to human health (Wiener and Rogers 2002: 326). The discussion in this case focused around the available scientific evidence and whether it justified the precautionary measure of banning the use of hormones. If we transfer this reasoning to the analysis of the everyday concept of precaution discussed above, we see that it is criterion (3), epistemic reasonableness, that is under discussion. More specifically, it is the (a) part of the reasonableness criterion – that the agent have externally good reasons for believing that U might occur – that is called into question in this case. Thus it can be said that the US critique, albeit not explicitly, questions whether the measures are precautionary in the everyday sense. Another way of criticising a proposed measure would be to deny that sub-criterion (3b) is fulfilled – that the agent have externally good reasons for believing that a will in fact at least contribute to the prevention of U. This would simply be to question whether there are good reasons for believing in the efficacy of the proposed precautionary measure. A third way would be to focus upon sub-criterion (3c), that the agent have externally good reasons for not believing it to be certain or highly probable that U will occur if a is not performed. This is not uncommon. One example can be found in Santillo et al. (2002). Discussing the problem of TBT antifoulants, they note:

> It would be difficult to argue, therefore, that any of the actions to address TBT to date have been precautionary, resulting as they have from extensive documentation of ecological impacts. Actions have undoubtedly contributed towards remediating the most severe problems, *but this is not precaution.*
>
> (Santillo et al. 2002: 159, emphasis added)

Other criticisms are focused upon another of the three criteria, namely (1), the criterion of intentionality. An explicit example can be found in Miller and Conko (2000), who are highly critical of the precautionary principle in the context of biotechnology. They call the precautionary principle 'a neologism coined by opponents of technology who wish to rationalize banning or over-regulating things they don't like' (Miller and Conko 2000: 95). A few pages later, they claim that regulators are acting in their own interest and that ' "erring on the side of caution" is a convenient rationale for excessive, anti-innovative regulation' (Miller and Conko 2000: 101). Here Miller and Conko are calling the intention of precautionary measures into question. Rather than being intended to prevent the undesirable thing that they are claimed to be intended to prevent (typically, environmental or health effects), the precautionary measures discussed by Miller and Conko are intended to increase regulations and, presumably, regulators' budgets. It is of course possible that an action might be performed with several objectives. It is also possible that regulators' actions may be precautionary with respect to their own budgets, but that need not concern us here.

The third and final advantage of applying the maxim is that it would require proponents of the precautionary principle to be clear about what is at stake. I believe that in many situations, when faced with objections such as 'precautionary rejection of GM foods in developing countries may have the consequence of famine', proponents of the precautionary principle would respond along the lines that the measures proposed are not intended to be precautionary with respect to famine. Once that is admitted, however, the solution to the famine problem is open to discussion.

Thus, while not solving the problem, it would put the framing of the decision, or decision horizon, into focus. This is something that is not seldom overlooked in the debate on the precautionary principle.[14]

Notes

1 The latter example is from Glannon (2002).
2 Cf. Peterson (2006).
3 See references in Sandin et al. (2002).
4 See Manson (2002).
5 A related argument, which I will disregard here, says that precautionary measures make people more worried and thus reduce well-being. See Wiedemann and Schütz (2005).
6 Cf. Chisholm and Clarke (1993).
7 For a discussion along these lines, see Harris and Holm (2002), Holm (2006) and Sandin (2006).
8 For a proposal of the precautionary principle as belief-guiding, see Peterson (forthcoming).
9 Fisher (2002), cf. Fisher (2005).
10 Cf. Arcuri (2004).
11 Cf. Fisher (2002: 14).

12 An earlier version of the ensuing sections appeared in Sandin (2004).
13 One example is Martin (1997).
14 Tim Lewens, Sven Ove Hansson, Martin Peterson and Stephen John provided helpful comments on earlier versions of this chapter. The views expressed and the errors remaining are mine.

References

Arcuri, A. (2004) *The Case for a Procedural Version of the Precautionary Principle Erring on the Side of Environmental Preservation*, Hauser Global Law School Program, Global Law Working Paper 09/04.

Bodansky, D. (1991) 'Scientific uncertainty and the precautionary principle,' *Environment*, 33(7): 4–5, 43–4.

Brody, H., Rip, M.R., Vinten-Johansen, P., Paneth, N. and Rachman, S. (2000) 'Map-making and myth-making in Broad Street: the London cholera epidemic, 1854', *The Lancet*, 356: 64–8.

Chisholm, A.H. and Clarke, H.R. (1993) 'Natural resource management and the precautionary principle', in Dommen, E. (ed.) *Fair Principles for Sustainable Development: essays on environmental policy and developing countries*, Aldershot: Edward Elgar.

Dommen, E. (1993) 'Introduction', in Dommen, E. (ed.) *Fair Principles for Sustainable Development: essays on environmental policy and developing countries*, Aldershot: Edward Elgar.

Dworkin, R. (1978) *Taking Rights Seriously*, London: Duckworth.

Fisher, E. (2002) 'Precaution, precaution everywhere: developing a "common understanding" of the precautionary principle in the European Union', *Maastricht Journal of European and Comparative Law*, 9(1): 7–28.

—— (2005) 'Precaution, law and principles of good administration', *Water Science and Technology*, 52(6): 19–24.

Glannon, W. (2002) 'Extending the human life span', *Journal of Medicine and Philosophy*, 27(3): 339–54.

Greenpeace (2000) *Safe or Sorry: precautionary principle in the biosafety protocol*, Online. Available: http://archive.greenpeace.org/geneng/reports/bio/bio011.htm (accessed 25 April 2006).

Haigh, N. (1994) 'The introduction of the precautionary principle into the UK', in O'Riordan, T. and Cameron, J. (eds) *Interpreting the Precautionary Principle*, London: Cameron.

Hansson, S.O. (1997) 'The limits of precaution', *Foundations of Science*, 2: 293–306.

Harremoës, P. et al. (eds) (2002) *The Precautionary Principle in the 20th Century: late lessons from early warnings*, London: Earthscan.

Harris, J. and Holm, S. (2002) 'Extending human lifespan and the precautionary paradox', *Journal of Medicine and Philosophy*, 27: 355–68.

Holm, S. (2006) 'Reply to Sandin: the paradox of precaution is not dispelled by attention to context', *Cambridge Quarterly of Healthcare Ethics*, 15: 184–87.

Manson, N.A. (2002) 'Formulating the precautionary principle', *Environmental Ethics*, 24: 263–64.

Martin, P.H. (1997) 'If you don't know how to fix it, please stop breaking it', *Foundations of Science*, 2: 263–92.

Miller, H.I. and Conko, G. (2000) 'Genetically modified fear and the international regulation of biotechnology', in Morris, J. (ed.) *Rethinking Risk and the Precautionary Principle*, Oxford: Butterworth–Heinemann.

Ozonoff, D. (1999) 'The precautionary principle as a screening device', in Raffensperger, C. and Tickner, J. (eds) *Protecting Public Health and the Environment: implementing the precautionary principle*, Washington, DC: Island Press.

Peterson, M. (2006) 'The precautionary principle is incoherent', *Risk Analysis* 26(3): 595–601.

—— (2007) 'Should the precautionary principle guide our actions or our beliefs?', *Journal of Medical Ethics*, 33: 5–10.

Raffensperger, C. and Tickner, J. (eds) (1999) *Protecting Public Health and the Environment: implementing the precautionary principle*, Washington, DC: Island Press.

Sandin, P. (1999) 'Dimensions of the precautionary principle', *Human and Ecological Risk Assessment*, 5(5): 889–907.

—— (2004) 'The precautionary principle and the concept of precaution', *Environmental Values*, 13: 461–75.

—— (2006) 'A paradox out of context: Harris and Holm on the precautionary principle', *Cambridge Quarterly of Healthcare Ethics*, 15: 175–83.

Sandin, P., Peterson, M., Hansson, S.O., Rudén, C. and Juthe, A. (2002) 'Five charges against the precautionary principle', *Journal of Risk Research*, 5(4): 287–99.

Sandin, P. *et al.* (2004) 'Precautionary defaults: a new strategy for chemical risk management', *Human and Ecological Risk Assessment*, 10(1): 1–18.

Santillo, D., Johnston, P. and Langston W.J. (2002) 'TBT antifoulants: a tale of ships, snails and imposex', in P. Harremoës *et al.* (eds) *The Precautionary Principle in the 20th Century: late lessons from early warnings*, London: Earthscan, 148–60.

Stich, S.P. (1978) 'The recombinant DNA debate', *Philosophy and Public Affairs* 7(3): 187–205.

Sunstein, C.R. (2005) *Laws of Fear: beyond the precautionary principle*, Cambridge: Cambridge University Press.

Turvey, C.G. and Mojduszka, E.M. (2005) 'The precautionary principle and the law of unintended consequences', *Food Policy*, 30: 145–61.

UNCED (1993) *The Earth Summit: the United Nations conference on environment and development* (1992: Rio De Janeiro), Introduction and commentary by S.P. Johnson, London: Graham and Trotman.

Wiedemann, P.M. and Schütz, Holger. (2005) 'The precautionary principle and risk perception: experimental studies in the MEF area', *Environmental Health Perspectives*, 113(4): 402–5.

Wiener, J.B. and Rogers, M.D. (2002) 'Comparing precaution in the United States and Europe', *Journal of Risk Research*, 5(4): 317–49.

7

ACTING UNDER RISK

D.H. Mellor

Ends and means

Although many actions, such as playing or listening to music, may be done just for their own sake, most are not. Most actions, like taking exercise to keep fit, are done partly or mainly as a means to an end, the end being an intended effect of the action. Many actions, indeed, are only done as means to ends, as when we pay money to buy goods. In these cases agents need to decide whether (they think) the end justifies the means, e.g. whether (they think) the goods are worth the price; and the job of decision theorists is to say on what grounds such decisions are or should be made. And so they do; but the grounds that most of them give are wrong, I shall argue, because they are *subjective*. Merely *thinking* that an end justifies a means, or fails to justify it, is not enough to justify our adopting, or declining to adopt, that means to that end. But to say this is easier than to say what more it takes to justify making such decisions, and what we should do when, as is often the case, we know too little to justify them. Those are the questions I set out to answer in this chapter.

Deciding whether to adopt an undesirable means to a desirable end, such as having painful dentistry to cure a toothache, is often easy enough in practice, even when, because 'the spirit is willing but the flesh is weak', mental or physical incapacity makes it hard or impossible to act on the decision. Here, however, we can mostly ignore complications raised by weakness of the will and other mental or bodily limitations. For present purposes, most questions of how we do or should act may be treated as questions of how we do or should *decide* to act.

Yet easy though it often is in practice to decide whether an end justifies a given means, these decisions are less easy to understand in theory. The first theoretical problem is to understand how to balance the utility of an end against the disutility of the means it needs to justify. This seems easy to understand in some cases, as when we pay money for goods, but not in all. How, for example, can we decide if the positive utility of keeping fit outweighs the negative utility of taking the necessary exercise? The usual answer is that these utilities are utilities *for us*, the agents, and can therefore be defined, or at least constrained, by what we actually decide to do. Thus deciding to exercise to keep fit shows that, for us at the time, the utility of keeping fit exceeds the utility of not exercising, while deciding not to exercise shows the opposite.

This inference does not make decision theory vacuous; it merely follows the common practice of measuring causes by their effects, as when we infer temperatures from thermometer readings. What saves that inference from vacuity is the assumption that things have real properties (temperatures) whose effects include the thermometer readings we use to measure them. Similarly, what stops inferences from decisions to utilities being vacuous is the substantial assumption that we have desires whose degrees (utilities) affect the actual or hypothetical decisions we can then use to measure those utilities.

If decisions are theoretically problematic when we know that some available means certainly *will* achieve our ends, they are even more so when we don't, as when we gamble. Or, to take a few other obvious examples: we know that medicines don't always work; that giving up smoking doesn't always stop us getting cancer; that trains, planes and cars sometimes crash; and so on. The theoretical problem such cases pose is not that decision theory cannot cope with them: on the contrary, its ability to do so is what makes it practically useful and conceptually interesting. The problem is how to read the *probabilities* that the theory uses in these cases to say when we should adopt such fallible means. That is the problem whose orthodox solution I think is wrong and to which I shall now propose an alternative.

First, however, I need to say how and why I think the problem arises, given that probabilities do not figure in *all* principles that tell us how to decide whether to use means that we don't think are effective. For example, they figure in neither the *dominance* principle (Jeffrey 1983: Ch. 1.5) nor the *maximin* principle (Luce *et al.* 1957: 278): principles which, if they always gave us credible answers, would enable us to dispense with probabilities altogether. But they don't, as the classic case of smoking and cancer shows.

Suppose I am wondering whether to quit smoking as a means M to the end E of escaping cancer. Here and hereafter I shall take M and E to be *states of affairs*, like my quitting smoking and escaping cancer, where E is the end and M the supposed means. Being states of affairs, M and E correspond to propositions, 'M' and 'E', that are true if and only if M and E 'obtain' or 'come about'. This lets me use the negation symbol '~' to represent the states of affairs (my going on smoking, and getting cancer) that will, in the circumstances, come about if M and E do not, as ~M and ~E. And in the simple two-option case, which is all we need consider, the four possible combinations of these states of affairs – M&E, M&~E, ~M&E, ~M&~E – are all we need take into account.

Suppose, then, that, despite knowing that ~E may come about (I may get cancer) whether or not I 'do M', i.e. bring M about (by quitting smoking), I don't want my decision, to do M or not to do it, to depend on E's relative probabilities given M, $p(E|M)$, and given ~M, $p(E|\sim M)$. I may resist this dependency for various reasons – I may not know what $p(E|M)$ and $p(E|\sim M)$

are, I may not believe in such probabilities or I may deny that they apply to individuals – it doesn't matter. What matters is that, for whatever reason, I want a principle that will tell me what to do given only the four relevant utilities, which are of the following states of affairs:

(a) smoking and avoiding cancer, ~M&E;
(b) quitting smoking and avoiding cancer, M&E;
(c) smoking and getting cancer, ~M&~E; and
(d) quitting smoking and getting cancer, M&~E.

Then since I know that, while I would rather smoke whether I get cancer or not, getting cancer will, for me, be even worse than being deprived of tobacco, I prefer (a) to (b) to (c) to (d). In symbols, if the relevant utilities U(...) are governed by these preferences, then

(1) U(~M&E) > U(M&E) > U(~M&~E) > U(M&~E),

where ' > ' means 'greater than'. What, then, given (1), do the dominance and maximin principles tell me to do?

The simplest way to show what these principles say in cases of this simple kind is to display the relevant utilities in the matrix shown in Table 7.1.

The *dominance* principle, then, comes in two versions. The weak one says that one decision *dominates* if and only if, whatever the outcome (E or ~E), it has a greater utility than every alternative; the strong one only requires the dominant decision's utility to be no less than any alternative, and greater than at least one. In either version the dominant decision, if any, is the one the principle prescribes. In my case, therefore, both versions of the principle tell me to *go on smoking* (~M) because, since I will prefer to smoke whether I get cancer or not, going on dominates quitting. In general and in symbols, (1) implies that ~M dominates M because, in each column of Table 7.1, it makes the utility in the ~M row exceed the utility in the M row.

The *maximin* principle tells us to choose the course of action with the least bad worst outcome, i.e. to maximise the minimum utility (hence the name). In my case, therefore, maximin also tells me to *go on smoking* (~M) because, given (1), the lowest utility in the ~M row of Table 7.1, U(~M&~E), is greater than the lowest utility in the M row, U(M&~E). So in this case maximin agrees with dominance, as indeed it will whenever both principles apply. For

Table 7.1

	E	~E
M	U(M&E)	U(M&~E)
~M	U(~M&E)	U(~M&~E)

one decision can only have a greater utility than every alternative *whatever* the outcome if, in particular, its *minimum* utility exceeds that of every alternative.

Why, then, if these two principles, neither of which invokes probabilities, always agree in their prescriptions, should our decisions depend on probabilities at all? There are two main reasons. One is that neither dominance nor maximin applies to all credible combinations of utilities. If, for example, I know I'll prefer to smoke if I get cancer, but will prefer not to if I don't, so that

$$U(\sim M\&E) < U(M\&E) \text{ and } U(M\&\sim E) > U(\sim M\&\sim E),$$

then neither M nor ~M will dominate, and dominance will not apply. While if I know that cancer would leave me not caring whether I smoked or not, so that

$$U(\sim M\&\sim E) = U(M\&\sim E),$$

then the lowest utilities in the M and ~M rows of Table 7.1 will be equal, and maximin will also not tell me what to do.

The other, more serious, reason for rejecting dominance and maximin, even when they do apply, is their inability to distinguish relevantly different situations. Thus, in the smoking case, given (1), dominance tells me to go on smoking, and maximin tells me to quit, whatever the probabilities, $p(E|M)$ and $p(E|\sim M)$, of my avoiding cancer (E) if I quit (M) and if I don't. This implies that it neither would nor should affect my decision if I learned either that

$$p(E|M) = p(E|\sim M),$$

i.e. that I have the same probability of escaping cancer whether I quit smoking or not, or that

$$p(E|M) > p(E|\sim M),$$

i.e. that quitting smoking actually reduces my probability of escaping cancer. Yet it is clearly irrational to do something as a means to an end when we know that the end will be at least as probable if we don't do it. That is why the decision theories of Jeffrey (1983) and others take account of the relevant probabilities, which in our simple case they do as follows.

First, they define the so-called *expected* utilities of the supposed means M and its alternative, ~M. M's expected utility EU(M) is the sum of the utilities of M's two possible outcomes, M&E and M&~E, weighted by the probabilities, $p(E|M)$ and $p(\sim E|M)$, that they *are* the outcomes, where

(2a) $p(\sim E|M) = 1 - p(E|M),$

(2b) $p(\sim E|\sim M) = 1 - p(E|\sim M)$;

and similarly for $\sim M$. That is:

(3a) $EU(M) = U(M\&E).p(E|M) + U(M\&\sim E).p(\sim E|M)$;

(3b) $EU(\sim M) = U(\sim M\&E).p(E|\sim M) + U(\sim M\&\sim E).p(\sim E|\sim M)$.

Then the '*maximise expected utility*' principle, or MEUP for short, tells us to do M if M's expected utility $EU(M)$ exceeds $\sim$M's, to do $\sim$M if $EU(\sim M)$ exceeds $EU(M)$, and tells us nothing if the two are equal.[1]

MEUP does not, however, imply that what makes M a means to E is that $EU(M) > EU(\sim M)$. I have remarked already that an end E can *fail* to justify a means M if its utility fails to outweigh M's disutility, i.e. – according to MEUP – if $EU(M)$ does *not* exceed $EU(\sim M)$. That can happen because whether E justifies M depends on the relevant utilities, which M's being a means to E does not. Yet we can still use MEUP to tell us what makes M a means to E, as the following argument, taken from Mellor (1995: Ch. 7.4), shows.

First, if M's being a means to E is independent of the utilities of M&E, M&$\sim$E, $\sim$M&E and $\sim$M&$\sim$E, we can take these utilities to be whatever they need to be in order to let MEUP tell us what makes M a means to E. The utilities that do this are those that make M what I shall call a *pure* means to the end E. By this I mean that it makes no difference to E's utility, or to $\sim$E's, whether we do M or $\sim$M, so that

(4a) $U(M\&E) = U(\sim M\&E) = U(E)$ and

(4b) $U(M\&\sim E) = U(\sim M\&\sim E) = U(\sim E)$,

and, by definition, since E and not $\sim$E is the end, $U(E) > U(\sim E)$. Thus if, for example, quitting smoking *is* a means of escaping cancer, then it will be a *pure* means to that end if I know that, whether or not I escape cancer, I won't care whether I smoke or whether I don't.

The point of supposing M to be a pure means to E is that, by definition, it will then make no difference to E's utility whether M is brought about or not. This makes M's value to me purely instrumental, which means that MEUP should tell me to do M only if M *is* a means to E. In other words, MEUP should imply that M *is a means to E only if, were it to be a* pure *means to E, $EU(M)$ would exceed* $EU(\sim M)$.

To see how this condition requires M and E to be related, we modify (3a) by replacing $U(M\&E)$ and $U(\sim M\&E)$ with $U(E)$ – from (4a) – and $p(\sim E|M)$ with $1 - p(E|M)$ – from (2a) – and similarly for (3b). This gives us

(5a) $EU(M) = U(E).p(E|M) + U(\sim E).(1-p(E|M))$ and

(5b) $EU(\sim M) = U(E).p(E|\sim M) + U(\sim E).(1-p(E|\sim M))$;

which in turn, given that $U(E) > U(\sim E)$, entails that

(6) $EU(M) > EU(\sim M)$ if and only if $p(E|M) > p(E|\sim M)$,

and hence that, according to MEUP,

(7) M is a means to E only if $p(E|M) > p(E|\sim M)$.

In other words, MEUP implies the independently plausible condition that M *is a means to E only if E will be more probable if M is done than if it isn't.*

Risk and uncertainty

Note that the 'if and only if' in (6) has, in (7), been weakened to 'only if'. This is because at least three other conditions, besides M's raising E's probability, must be met if M is to be a means to E.

First, for M to be worth calling a means to E, it must raise E's probability by more than an infinitesimal amount. How much more is a moot but secondary question, like asking how hot is hot or how much hair a man must lose before he becomes bald: questions whose answers raise Sorites questions, and depend on context in various ways, that for present purposes we may set aside.

Second, doing M must be *feasible*, since nothing can be a useful means to an end E that is harder to bring about than E itself. If, for example, we could simply *will* our recovery from illness as easily as we can take medicine, there would be no point in taking medicine as a pure means to recovery even if the expected utility of doing so exceeded that of not doing so.

These two conditions may be vague, and perhaps debatable, but they are certainly less contentious that the third, which is the one I shall now argue for, namely that M *is a means to E only if it raises E's* objective *probability*.

What makes this condition contentious is the unorthodox reading of decision theory it requires, a reading I must therefore now explain and defend. To do so I start with the distinction between *risk* and *uncertainty* drawn by Luce and Raiffa (1957: 13) in their classic introduction to the theory of games and decision-making:

> As to the certainty–risk–uncertainty classification, let us suppose that a choice must be made between two actions. We shall say that we are in the realm of decision making under:

(a) *Certainty* if each action is known to lead invariably to a specific outcome ...

(b) *Risk* if each action leads to one of a set of possible specific outcomes, each outcome occurring with a known probability. The probabilities are assumed to be known to the decision maker. For example, an action might lead to this risky outcome: a reward of $10 if a 'fair' coin comes up heads, and a loss of $5 if it comes up tails. Of course, certainty is a degenerate case of risk where the probabilities are 0 and 1.

(c) *Uncertainty* if either action or both has as its consequence a set of possible specific outcomes, but where the probabilities of these outcomes are completely unknown or are not even meaningful.

In this quotation 'probability' clearly means a probability, e.g. of a coin toss landing heads, or of my escaping cancer, that is both objective and empirical. In what follows I shall, for brevity, call such probabilities 'chances' and write them '$ch(\ldots)$' but without, however, committing myself to any particular analysis of them.

Thus, for example, if E is my escaping cancer, $ch(E)$ is my objective chance of doing so, whether this chance be identified with the relative frequency with which people relevantly like me (in age, sex, diet, etc.) escape cancer, or with a propensity to escape it, i.e. with a probabilistic disposition to escape cancer that I share with other such people (Mellor 2005a: Chs 3–4).

But however they are analysed, objective chances must be distinguished from probabilities of at least one other kind, i.e. from a different application of the mathematical calculus of probability (Mellor 2005a: Chs 1, 5–6). These are the so-called *subjective* probabilities, which for short I shall call *credences* and write '$cr(\ldots)$', that measure our degrees of belief in possible states of affairs, e.g. that a coin toss will land heads or that I will escape cancer.

The difference between my credence $cr(E)$ that I will escape cancer and the chance $ch(E)$ of my doing so is, therefore, that while my $cr(E)$ measures how strongly I *believe* I will escape cancer, $ch(E)$ measures how likely I am to escape it *in fact*, whatever I or anyone else believes. This means that my $cr(E)$ may well differ from $ch(E)$, perhaps being lower if I am a confirmed hypochondriac or higher if I smoke but am, like all too many smokers, convinced that the statistics on smoking and cancer don't apply to me.

I take this difference between chances and credences to correspond to Luce and Raiffa's distinction between risk and uncertainty. That is, I take the *risk* of a means M failing to bring about an end E to be the *chance* $ch(\sim E|M)$ that it will fail to do so. *Acting under risk* I shall therefore take to be basing a decision, on whether to do M as a means to E, on the known value of $ch(\sim E|M)$ and hence – since $ch(\sim E|M) = 1-ch(E|M)$ – of $ch(E|M)$, the chance that M *will* bring E about. In other words, my decision will be made using what I shall call the *objective* reading of MEUP, on which (3a) becomes

$$EU(M) = U(M\&E).ch(E|M) + U(M\&\sim E).(1{-}ch(E|M)),$$

and similarly for (3b).

Just as I take the chance $ch(\sim E|M)$ to measure the risk of M's failing to bring E about, so I take my credence $cr(\sim E|M)$ to measure my degree of belief that M will fail to bring E about, and thus how *uncertain* I am that it *will* bring E about. *Acting under uncertainty* I shall therefore take to be basing a decision, on whether to do M as a means to E, on $cr(\sim E|M)$ and hence on $cr(E|M)$, my credence that M will bring E about. In other words, my decision will be made using what I shall call the *subjective* reading of MEUP, or 'subjective MEUP', on which (3a) becomes

$$EU(M) = U(M\&E).cr(E|M) + U(M\&\sim E).(1{-}cr(E|M)),$$

and similarly for (3b).

In short, I take Luce and Raiffa's two concepts, of acting under risk and under uncertainty, to make MEUP provide two quite different decision theories, theories whose prescriptions may well differ when, and because, our credences differ from the corresponding chances. When they do so differ, which should we follow?

Description and prescription

The question just posed has a deceptively simple two-part answer. The first part says that when there is no such thing as the objective chance $ch(E|M)$, or there is but we don't know what it is, we cannot use an objective MEUP and must therefore use a subjective one. The second part says that, when $ch(E|M)$ does exist and we do know what it is, then since our credence $cr(E|M)$ should generally equal it (Lewis 1980), the subjective and objective theories will generally prescribe the same decision anyway. So either way the question of which theory to choose need not arise: since we always can, and often must, use a subjective MEUP, which is therefore the one to follow.

The error here lies in the assumption, usually taken for granted, that a subjective decision theory gives us a good enough reason to do what it tells us to do. To see the error, we must now distinguish two readings of MEUP, whether they be objective or subjective: a *prescriptive* reading and a *descriptive* one. Read prescriptively, MEUP says that we *should* do M if EU(M) exceeds EU(~M), and *should* do ~M if EU(~M) exceeds EU(M). (If EU(M) equals EU(~M), it says nothing either way.) Read descriptively, MEUP says that we *will* follow these prescriptions if EU(M) and EU(~M) differ (and it says nothing if they don't).

This distinction gives us four possible MEUPs: a prescriptive one, using either chances or credences; and a descriptive one, again using either chances or credences. Which of the four should we use?

The answer is that we can use two of them: a prescriptive MEUP to tell us what we *should* do, and a descriptive one to tell us what determines what we *will* do. The latter will be a causal theory, i.e. one that tells us, rightly or wrongly, how relevant utilities and probabilities cause us to (decide to) act as we do. And this at once rules out a descriptive reading of an objective MEUP. For the direct causes of, say, my decision to quit smoking, which are what a descriptive MEUP offers to tell us, can hardly include the objective *chance* $ch(E|M)$ of my escaping cancer if I quit. That chance may indeed be an indirect cause of my quitting, if my knowing its value causes me to have the corresponding credence $cr(E|M)$. But that is only because the chance affects the credence which, together with my subjective utilities, is what directly causes me to quit. And similarly in all other cases: chances can only affect our decisions indirectly, via their effects our knowledge of them has on our credences. So it is the latter, not the former, that must figure in a descriptive MEUP; which is why that theory can only be subjective.

But how, then, can a subjective MEUP be prescriptive? How can a theory that claims to tell us what we *will* do also tell us what we *should* do? The answer, all parties agree, is that it can't; which is why most advocates of a subjective MEUP (generally called Bayesians, because they trace their views back to the work of Thomas Bayes (1763)), deny that it tells us what we will do:

> [T]he subjectivistic theory of probability is not an empirical psychological theory of degrees of belief ... the object [of tests of it] is not to find out if the theory accurately describes the behaviour of people, but to find out whether people are rational according to the prescriptions of the theory.
>
> (Kyburg and Smokler 1964: 6)

That is the orthodox Bayesian view: a subjective MEUP is prescriptive, and only tells us what we will do *if we are rational*, which it is taken for granted that we should be. I think this is wrong, and that a prescriptive reading of MEUP can only be justified if it is objective. A merely subjective MEUP I follow Ramsey (1926) in taking to be a descriptive theory of the causes of our decisions. That claim I have argued elsewhere (Mellor 2005b); here I make the case for requiring a prescriptive MEUP to be objective. But as part of that case is the prescriptive inadequacy of a subjective MEUP, I must restate briefly why I think it is inadequate.

I start with a presupposition shared by both sides to the dispute. This is that doing M as a means to E may be justified even if it is neither certain nor thought to be certain that M will in fact bring E about. The greater probability, subjective or objective, of my escaping cancer if I quit smoking may justify my quitting even if I still get cancer in the end. But that is just bad luck: it does not show that my decision to quit was wrong. But what, then, if my decision *was* right, made it so: how can doing M's raising E's probability make it right to do M? We all agree that doing M will be right if it raises E's probability enough to make M's expected utility exceed ~M's. What we disagree about is the *kind* of probability of E that doing M must raise if M is to be the right thing to do. Bayesianism implies that M need only raise the agent's *credence* in E; I say it must raise E's *chance*.[2]

To see why I say this, suppose I think that, whether I escape cancer or not, the utility for me of smoking will always exceed that of not smoking. Suppose too that, being 'in denial' about the relevant statistics, my credence that I will escape cancer (E) will be the same whether I quit smoking (M) or not, so that my $cr(E|{\sim}M) = cr(E|M)$. Then, however much E's utilities for me with and without M exceed ~E's, a subjective MEUP will always tell me to go on smoking.

To me and many others this prescription seems absurd, given the evidence for an objective if indeterministic causal link between smoking and cancer. (See the references to 'Fisher's problem' in Jeffrey 1983: 15, 25.) This is why I think that MEUP can only tell me whether to quit smoking if it is *objective*, i.e. if, for given utilities, EU(M) and EU(~M) are fixed not by my credences, $cr(E|M)$ and $cr(E|{\sim}M)$, but by the objective chances, $ch(E|M)$ and $ch(E|{\sim}M)$, of my escaping cancer if I quit smoking and if I don't. All a subjective MEUP can do is tell us what would make me *think* that quitting smoking is the right thing for me to do, whether it is or not.

Another way of putting the same point is to ask what makes my quitting smoking, M, a *means* to my end E of escaping cancer. I argued in the first section that a prescriptive MEUP will credit M with being a means to E only if it would tell us to do M when

(4a) $U(M\&E) = U({\sim}M\&E) = U(E)$ and

(4b) $U(M\&{\sim}E) = U({\sim}M\&{\sim}E) = U({\sim}E)$,

i.e. when, if M *is* a means to E, it is a *pure* means. This test, as we saw, makes a prescriptive MEUP say that if E is an end, i.e. if $U(E) > U({\sim}E)$, then whatever the relevant utilities,

(7) M is a means to E only if $p(E|M) > p(E|{\sim}M)$.

So here again the question is: should the probabilities in (7) be objective or subjective; should (7) require doing M to raise E's *chance* or my *credence* in E? And again the answer seems obvious: my quitting smoking is only a means of escaping cancer if it raises my *chance* of escaping cancer, not merely my *credence* that I will escape it. My $cr(E|M)$ exceeding my $cr(E|{\sim}M)$ may be what makes me *think* that M is a means to E. But thinking that will only make it so if raising my credence in E also raises E's chance – as indeed the so-called 'placebo effect' in medicine shows that it might.

The placebo effect is the benefit referred to in the medical definition of a placebo as 'a chemically inert substance given instead of a drug. Benefit may be gained from a placebo because the person taking it believes it will have a positive effect'. (British Medical Association 2002: 451). This definition implies that when the placebo effect occurs, i.e. when taking a placebo *is* in fact a means to the medical end E, what makes it so is the fact that, by raising a patient's credence in E, it thereby raises E's chance. Only by accepting that this is what a means to E must do that we can explain how placebos that work (i.e. produce the placebo effect) differ both from placebos that don't work and from 'non-placebo' medicines, i.e. medicines that need not raise the patient's credence in E in order to raise E's chance. (This is not to deny that patients may only take non-placebo medicines if they believe that doing so *will* raise their credence in E, merely that this effect on patients' credences has to be what makes the medicines work.)

In short, put in terms of the distinction between risk and uncertainty drawn in the second section of this chapter, M can only be a means to E if doing M reduces the *risk* of E's not coming about. It is not enough for doing M to reduce our *uncertainty* that E will come about, thereby making us *think* that M is a means to E. That thought cannot be self-verifying, as the contingency of the placebo effect shows. Yet that is what a prescriptive MUEP that is merely subjective must take it to be, by insisting that in reality uncertainty is all there to risk, and therefore that no one who thinks that M is – or is not – a means to E can be mistaken.

Subjective prescriptions

Bayesians may reply in three ways to the arguments of the third section of this chapter. First, those who, like de Finetti (1937), deny the very existence of objective chances, may therefore deny that in reality there *is* any more to risk than uncertainty. The objection to this is that the probabilities that all sciences, from microphysics to epidemiology, take to explain observed frequencies, can only do so if they are as objective as the frequencies they explain, i.e. are chances (Mellor 2005a: Ch. 10). My high credence in non-smokers escaping cancer may explain why I *expect* most of them to escape it: it cannot explain why most of them *do* escape it.

Second, most Bayesians who do admit chances will also admit that, as we noted on page 120, the values of $ch(E|M)$ and $ch(E|{\sim}M)$, when we know them, should usually also be the values of our $cr(E|M)$ and $cr(E|{\sim}M)$, and hence the values we should use in deciding whether to do M. Thus if all I know about a coin toss is that its chance of landing heads is p, then p is the credence I should use in deciding whether to accept a bet at any given odds that it *will* land heads. And this principle, which I shall here follow Lewis (1980: 87) in calling the 'principal principle', arguably exhausts chance's prescriptive role in MEUP. This lets Bayesians claim that a prescriptive MEUP, since it need not use chances, but only credences derived from them by the principal principle, can itself be purely subjective. That claim, however, begs the question against an objective MEUP, since the case for the principal principle presupposes, rather than proves, that we should base our decisions on known chances when we can: since that is *why* our credences – which, like our subjective utilities, are *measured* by the decisions they cause us to make (Ramsey 1926) – should equal those chances in the first place.

The third and strongest Bayesian reply is to ask how we can apply an objective MEUP when the relevant chances are unknown. It seems obvious that we can't, which is why, in the quotation on page 119, Luce and Raiffa limit 'the realm of decisions under ... risk' to situations where the relevant objective 'probabilities are assumed to be known to the decision maker'. If so, then when we must make decisions without knowing the relevant chances, as we often must, why should we not follow the prescriptions of a subjective MEUP, if only *faute de mieux*? How else can MEUP tell us how to act under uncertainty?

An objectivist response to this rhetorical question needs to make several points. First, it can and should insist that, as a descriptive theory of how our credences and subjective utilities make us act, a subjective MEUP is, if flawed, still

> a useful approximation to the truth particularly in the case of our self-conscious or professional life, and it is presupposed in a great deal of our thought. It is a simple theory and one which many psychologists would like to preserve by introducing unconscious desires and unconscious opinions in order to bring it more into harmony with the facts.
> (Ramsey 1926: 69)

This is what enables a subjective MEUP to explain many of our decisions, by giving our reasons for making them: as when it says that my reasons for quitting smoking are that I want to escape cancer and believe that quitting smoking is a means to that end.

However, the fact that a decision theory gives mental reasons (desires and beliefs) for our decisions makes some physicalists and others, who think all causes are physical, insist that since the theory cannot explain our decisions causally, it can only *rationalise* them, i.e. say how our beliefs and desires make them *rational*. Hence the temptation to think that since subjective MEUP tells us 'what we will do *if we are rational*, which ... we should be' (page 121), it tells us not how we will but how we should act under uncertainty.

The temptation should be resisted. For however our reasons for a decision are related to its physical causes (see e.g. Davidson 1963: Ch. 1, Crane *et al.* 1990), they can only make the decision rational if *they* are rational, and they may not be. For example, as I noted on page 122, it would be as irrational on present evidence for my quitting smoking not to raise my credence that I will escape cancer as it would for me positively to desire cancer. Whatever such credences and subjective utilities made me decide to do, they could not make that decision rational, and a prescriptive MEUP should not, as a subjective MEUP does, imply that they could.

Bayesians may reply to this by invoking an analogy between a rational decision and a deductively valid inference, i.e. one whose conclusion follows logically from its premises, and so cannot be false if they are true. For since an inference's validity does not depend on its premises' truth, false conclusions may well be validly inferred from false premises, as when, thinking on Sunday that today is Monday, I infer validly but falsely that today is a weekday. Yet the falsity of this conclusion is clearly no reflection on the inference itself, whose validity makes it equally rational whether or not its premises are true.

Similarly with inductive inferences (e.g. from 'X is copper' to 'X conducts electricity') that depend on laws of nature, which cannot be known *a priori*, to make their conclusions true when their premises are. Our knowledge of the laws that make these inferences truth-preserving may then make them as rational as deductive inferences, even when their conclusions ('This conducts electricity') are false because their premises ('This is copper') are.

And as with these deductive or inductive 'theoretical' inferences, so with the 'practical inferences', from credences and subjective utilities (the 'premises') to decisions (the 'conclusions'), that a subjective MEUP provides. Here too the inference may be rational even when the credences in its premises are so far from the relevant chances that its conclusion (e.g. to go on smoking) is objectively wrong, i.e. differs from that of an objective MEUP. Hence, Bayesians may say, the prescriptive force of a subjective MEUP when the relevant chances are unknown. Using it to derive decisions from credences and subjective utilities that may or may not match their objective counterparts is just as rational as using truth-preserving theoretical inferences to draw conclusions from beliefs that may or may not be true.

Some of this argument we may accept. No objectivist need deny that always using a subjective MEUP to make decisions is as rational as always using truth-preserving inferences to derive new beliefs from old, and for the same reason. For just as the latter is the only way to ensure that *if* the premises are true, they will yield true conclusions, so the former, objectivists will say, is the only way to ensure that, *if* our credences and subjective utilities match their objective counterparts, they will yield objectively right decisions. Moreover, if the conditions stated by these if-clauses are *not* met, no alternative principles of theoretical or practical inference can be relied on to do any better, if only because no principles of inference can then be relied on to do any good at all. So the weak dominance principle mentioned in the first section of this chapter, if nothing else, tells us to use the present principles of inference always, whether or not we know that their if-clauses are true. All objectivists can therefore admit that requiring practical inferences to conform to a subjective MEUP is as rational as requiring theoretical inferences to be truth-preserving.

So far so good for a prescriptive reading of a subjective MEUP. But that is as far as it goes, and it is not far enough for Bayesians. The trouble is that an inference's rationality, so understood, is not inherited by its conclusion when Bayesians need it to be. That is because, as we have seen, the merit of this kind of rationality is *conditional*: the condition in a theoretical inference being that its premises be true; and in a practical one that its credences and subjective utilities yield the same decision as their objective counterparts. In both cases, therefore, an inference's rationality only makes it rational to accept its conclusion when these conditions are met. When any of a theoretical inference's premises are false, the fact that the inference is truth-preserving is no reason to believe its conclusion. Similarly, objectivists will say, with decisions derived from our credences and subjective utilities. When those credences differ from the corresponding chances, the fact that the decision is prescribed by a subjective MEUP is no reason to think that it is right, i.e. that an objective MEUP would prescribe it.

This distinction, between the rationality of inferences and that of their conclusions, is unfortunately obscured in English by our calling the latter 'inferences' too, as when we call an inference false, meaning that its conclusion is. The ambiguity is especially unfortunate here because it encourages the false belief that an inference's being rational is enough to make its conclusion rational, which we have just seen that it isn't. That error is then reinforced by another ambiguity in claiming that inferences (and hence their conclusions) are justified *given their premises*. For this to be true, 'given the premises' needs to mean 'given that the premises are *justified*', whereas all it usually means is 'given that these *are* the premises', which is not enough to justify the conclusion of any inference, theoretical or practical. My believing that quitting smoking will lower rather than raise my chance of escaping cancer may partly *explain* my decision to remain a smoker; but given that this belief is neither true nor justified, it cannot *justify* that decision. That is why a merely subjective MEUP cannot tell us what we should do; only an objective MEUP can do that.

Acting under uncertainty

What, then, can tell us how to act under uncertainty as opposed to risk, i.e. when we don't know what the relevant chances are? Assuming with Ramsey that a subjective MEUP, read descriptively, is 'a useful approximation to the truth', it can tell us what we *will* do in that situation; but that will not tell us what we *should* do. Yet nor, it seems, can an objective MEUP tell us this when we don't know the chances it invokes to tell us what decisions to make. How, then, can any probabilistic decision theory tell us how to act under uncertainty?

To answer that question we must first ask if there *is* a right way of deciding whether an end E justifies a prospective means M when we have no idea what difference, if any, doing M will make to E's chance of coming about. We certainly want there to be a right way, since we quite often have to make decisions in this situation, decisions that may be serious, as when people who know no first aid must decide how to keep someone going after a sudden heart attack (say) until they can get medical advice. How can they tell what to do, when even doing nothing is only one of the potentially fatal (but also potentially life-saving) options open to us? The answer, I'm afraid, is that they can't, if they really know *nothing* about which option gives the patient his or her best chance of survival. (This is why we should all learn something about first aid.) For here, if not in the Big Bang, *ex nihilo nihil fit*: nothing comes of nothing. When we know none of the relevant empirical facts, theories of decision-making can no more tell us how to act than theories of inference can tell us what to believe; in neither case can any amount of rationality compensate for empirical ignorance. In epistemology, in short, there is no such thing as a fact-free lunch, which is why it is no objection to an objective MEUP that it fails to offer one.

An objective MEUP can, however, offer a useful *low*-fact diet, if not a no-fact one. For it rarely if ever requires us to know precise values of either utilities or chances for it to be able to tell us how to act. All it requires us to know is that their values lie in intervals, which are often quite long, within which all values will prescribe the same decision; and that much we often do know, as two examples will serve to show.

First, suppose you offer to bet me at 2:1 that a coin toss won't land heads. That is, you offer to pay me twice as much if it does land heads as I agree to pay you if it doesn't. Suppose too that, being neither averse nor attracted to the bet for its own sake, I will take the bet, if I do, purely as a means to winning it. Then if the ratio of the amounts to be won or lost measures the relative utilities for me of those outcomes, all I need to know, for an objective MEUP to tell me to take the bet, is that the coin toss's chance of landing heads is greater than 1/3, a fact I can easily know without knowing its precise value.

Now take the more serious case of smoking and cancer. Nearly all cancer patients will agree that, even if treatment stops cancer shortening their lives, the pain and anxiety it causes them and their families makes getting it more than twice as bad as quitting smoking, whatever many as-yet healthy smokers think. This, and the overwhelming statistical evidence that quitting reduces smokers' chances of getting cancer by over 50 per cent, is all an objective MEUP needs in order to advise them to quit smoking, however imprecise their knowledge of the relevant chances and utilities may be.

(Many smokers will, of course, fail to heed this advice, for one of two reasons. First, they may reject it by denying that, for them, quitting smoking will reduce their chance of getting cancer, or that getting it will be so much worse for them than quitting; in short, a smoker's relevant credences and/or subjective utilities may differ so much from the corresponding chances and objective utilities that they decide to go on smoking – a decision whose conformity to a subjective MEUP makes neither right nor rational. And second, smokers who apparently decide to quit may still not do so, because they can't: their addiction stops them. These, however, I take to be cases where 'the spirit is willing but the flesh is weak' and hence covered by the proposal in the first section to 'ignore complications raised by weakness of the will and other mental or bodily limitations'. We may therefore credit these addicted smokers with decisions, if not actions, that conform to both subjective and objective MEUPs.)

So far so good, but the 'reliabilist' view of knowledge (see, e.g., Armstrong 1973: Chs 11–13; Goldman 1986) that naturally accompanies an objective MEUP lets the latter do even better. For on a reliabilist view, what justifies our beliefs is our acquiring them by processes (e.g. those of our senses) that have a high enough chance of giving us true beliefs. (How high is high enough will vary with context, and doesn't matter for present purposes, provided it can be less than 1.) So in particular, if we acquire beliefs in *chances* by processes that give those beliefs a high enough chance of being true, then on this view they will be justified, even if they are false. And that is how our rules of inference from observed frequencies (e.g. of coin tosses landing heads or of smokers getting cancer) to chances work: by giving their conclusions a high chance of being true.[3]

Moreover, as the conclusions these inferences justify are always that a given chance lies in a given interval, they are, as we have just seen, precisely what an objective MEUP needs. And the wider the intervals the chances can lie in for this MEUP to prescribe a decision, the less frequency evidence it takes to give those intervals a high enough chance of containing those chances. Thus, in the coin-tossing example above, I need far less evidence to give the chance of heads a high chance of being greater than 1/3 than of being greater than 2/3. The evidence may still, of course, be less than I need; and then not even an objective MEUP will justify whatever decision I make. But, then, nor, I have argued, will anything else; in particular, a subjective MEUP will not justify it.

My coin-tossing bet shows too how reliabilism enables an objective MEUP to let decisions be justified which it also says are wrong. For suppose, in the example, that I accept your bet because a freak run of heads makes me infer, justifiably but falsely, that the coin's chance of landing heads when tossed is greater than 1/3. An objective MEUP can now admit that my decision, although made wrong by the falsity of my belief that the coin toss's chance of landing heads is greater than 1/3, was nevertheless justified by the statistical inference from the frequency data that gave this false belief of mine a high chance of being true. Similarly in the smoking and cancer case. An improbably low frequency of cancer in a population of smokers might justify their false belief, that quitting would not raise their chance of escaping cancer, and hence their objectively wrong decision to go on smoking.

That, in brief, is how an objective MEUP can prescribe and/or justify many, although of course not all, of the decisions we make under uncertainty about the relevant chances. But what, then, of the decisions under uncertainty that it *cannot* justify, let alone prescribe? What, for example, can an objective MEUP tell the people above who know too little first aid to justify any decision about how to keep a heart attack victim alive until they can get medical advice? I say it can tell them nothing, for the reasons I have given, except, as I have also said, that anyone who is likely to have to cope unaided with such situations *should* learn enough first aid beforehand. And similarly for all decisions made in situations of such uncertainty: all an objective MEUP can tell us is not to let these situations arise. Yet that is perhaps its most valuable prescription: to learn enough about the risks we are likely to encounter to enable us, if and when we encounter them, to make decisions that are objectively right, or at least objectively justified.[4]

Notes

1 Note that I do not mean 'doing M' to imply that it takes *action*, as opposed to inaction, to bring about M rather than ~M. It does not, since MEUP ignores the action–inaction distinction, which often does not apply or does not matter, as indeed it does not in the case of quitting or going on smoking. Where it does matter, as in the distinction between killing and letting die, MEUP can allow for it by letting it affect the relevant utilities.

2 In Mellor (2005b) I argue that a prescriptive MEUP also needs objective utilities, which may differ from what we *think* they are, i.e. from subjective utilities. But as this essay is chiefly about the kinds of probability, chances and credences that distinguish risk from uncertainty, I shall not repeat that argument here. Readers need only bear in mind that by 'utilities' in what follows I shall, unless I say otherwise, mean *objective* utilities, however, if at all, these differ from subjective ones. In particular, I shall now use the phrase 'utilities for us' introduced in the first section to mean utilities which, despite being objective (since they may differ from what we think they are), may be different for different people.

3 This statement is too simple as it stands; for a more detailed and accurate statement of how reliabilism can justify beliefs about chances, see Mellor (2005a: Ch. 8.III). The statement is also made contentious by its appeal to reliabilism and the existence of chances; but that is no objection to it as a statement of how reliabilism can assist an objective MEUP which takes chances for granted.

4 I am indebted to the editor Tim Lewens and to Wlodek Rabinowicz for invaluable comments on and corrections to earlier drafts of this essay.

References

Armstrong, D.M. (1973) *Belief, Truth and Knowledge*, Cambridge: Cambridge University Press.

Bayes, T. (1763) 'An essay towards solving a problem in the doctrine of chances', in Swinburne, R.G. (ed.) *Bayes's Theorem*, Oxford: Oxford University Press.

British Medical Association (2002) *Illustrated Medical Dictionary*, London: Dorling Kindersley.

Crane, T. and Mellor, D.H. (1990) 'There is no question of physicalism', *Mind*, 99: 185–206.

Davidson, D. (1963) 'Actions, reasons, and causes', *Journal of Philosophy*, 60: 685–99.

de Finetti, B. (1937) 'Foresight: its logical laws, its subjective sources', in Kyburg, H.E. Jr and Smokler, H.E. (eds) *Studies in Subjective Probability*, New York: Wiley.

Goldman, A.I. (1986) *Epistemology and Cognition*, Cambridge, MA: Harvard University Press.

Jeffrey, R.C. (1983) *The Logic of Decision*, Chicago: University of Chicago Press.

Kyburg, H.E. Jr and Smokler, H.E. (eds) (1964) *Studies in Subjective Probability*, New York: Wiley.

Lewis, D.K. (1980) 'A subjectivist's guide to objective chance', in his *Philosophical Papers, Volume II*, Oxford: Oxford University Press.

Luce, R.D. and Raiffa, H. (1957) *Games and Decisions*, New York: Wiley.

Mellor, D.H. (1995) *The Facts of Causation*, London: Routledge.

—— (2005a) *Probability: a philosophical introduction, London: Routledge.*

—— (2005b) 'What does subjective decision theory tell us?', in Lillehammer, H. and Mellor, D.H. (eds) *Ramsey's Legacy*, Oxford: Oxford University Press.

Ramsey, F.P. (1926) 'Truth and probability', in his *Philosophical Papers*, Cambridge: Cambridge University Press.

8

TOWARDS A POLITICAL PHILOSOPHY OF RISK

Experts and publics in deliberative democracy

Martin Kusch

Introduction

All societies need to make decisions concerning risks. Some of these decisions are substantive (e.g. should we rely on nuclear power?) others are procedural (e.g. who should decide on energy policy?). Procedural decisions are second-order: they are decisions on how to make substantive choices concerning risks. Political philosophies of risk should have something to say on both substantive and procedural issues, though the balance of the intellectual effort will usually and naturally lie on the second problem.[1] Obviously, political philosophies of risk cannot be free-standing; typically they will be offshoots of more general positions in political philosophy. Liberals and communitarians, multiculturalists and anarchists are likely to propose very different procedures for the collective handling of risk – after all, their radically different overall conceptions of what is a desirable political order are bound to make themselves felt also when it comes to deciding on risks. It is striking and perhaps surprising to note that very few contemporary strands of political philosophy contain explicit pre-scriptions on how to deal with risk and uncertainty. The exception to this rule is the direction committed to 'deliberative democracy'. In this chapter I shall review, and critically discuss, the two most important proposals for a political philosophy of risk within this broad school of thought.

The first set of suggestions comes from Cass Sunstein, the distinguished legal scholar and political scientist. In three recent books, Sunstein has defended the view that deliberative democracies should give experts in cost–benefit analysis a central role in decision-making on risk assessment and risk management (Sunstein 2002a, 2002b, 2005). Sunstein insists on separating questions of fact and value; he defends a realist view of risk; and he is deeply pessimistic con-cerning lay people's and politicians' abilities to correctly identify and weigh up risks and uncertainties.[2]

The second proposal has been developed over the past three decades within the field of 'Science and Technology Studies', or 'STS' for short. Although numerous scholars have contributed to the development of this position, I shall focus exclusively on the writings of Sheila Jasanoff and Brian Wynne. Jasanoff and Wynne are widely acknowledged to be the most influential and original writers on the politics of risk within recent STS. Although their sociological and historical investigations concern substantially different empirical materials, when it comes to their political philosophy, Jasanoffs and Wynne's views are close and in many ways complementary. Moreover, they frequently endorse, and never publicly criticise, each other's work. For the limited – and polemical – purposes of this chapter, these are reasons enough to treat Jasanoff and Wynne as contributors to one and the same position, and thereby largely suppress the differences that do exist between them. Jasanoff and Wynne are highly critical of cost–benefit analysis; they are deeply sceptical of the role of scientific experts in modern societies, especially in the assessment and management of risk; they regard risks as socially constructed; and they call for fundamental public debate over the future direction and role of science and technology.

Jasanoff, Sunstein and Wynne do not deserve our attention just because they have put forward relatively clear programmes for philosophies of risk from a deliberative perspective. Three further reasons are important, too. First and foremost, the two proposals are highly influential in both the US and the UK. Sunstein has repeatedly testified on Capitol Hill, advised President Clinton on legislation regarding new media, and counselled various countries – from Albania to Ukraine, China to South Africa – on law reform and constitution-making. Jasanoff is a professor in Harvard's Kennedy School of Government, the number-one training-ground for top-level public administrators in the US. She has been on various panels of the National Academy of Sciences, and on the Board of Directors of the American Association of the Advancement of Science. And Wynne has acted as a special adviser on risk for the UK government, the OECD, the EU, the UN and Greenpeace. These authors do not try just to interpret the world; their point is to change it. And they have the influence and power to do so.

Second, as will emerge in what follows, the two conflicting sets of ideas are uncompromising and radical, perhaps even extreme. As far as their normative positions go, the three authors make little attempt to occupy, or search for, a theoretical middle-ground. There is some merit to such one-sidedness in a nascent field like the political philosophy of risk. If one aims too quickly for a position that does justice to all considerations, then one runs the danger of ending up with a diffuse and unprincipled stance. Of course, such one-sidedness had better not be the endpoint of our reflections. Indeed, having seen where the two radical proposals lead us, we will be in a good position to formulate – towards the end of this chapter – *desiderata* for a middle ground that is itself principled, and thus not merely cobbled together from diverse and incompatible elements.

Third, and finally, it is surprising to note that to date there has been no real debate between Sunstein and STS. Jasanoff (2006: 749–50) refers only once, and then very briefly, to Sunstein's work.[3] Sunstein discusses some of the authors who have influenced STS, but not Jasanoff or Wynne. My essay will have achieved its main purpose if it helps to change this situation of non-communication.

The structure of this chapter is as follows. The first two sections will be brief summaries of Sunstein's and the STS-scholars' proposals. The following two sections will be dedicated to criticism: I shall scrutinise Sunstein's suggestions from perspectives provided primarily, though not exclusively, by Jasanoff and Wynne, before turning around and challenging the STS proposal from a 'Sunsteinian' viewpoint, broadly construed. The final section will sketch a 'synthesis' with respect to Sunstein's 'paternalist' 'thesis' and STS's 'participatory' 'antithesis'.

Sunstein's paternalist philosophy of risk

Sunstein's political philosophy of risk is naturally divided into descriptive–explanatory and normative components. Much of the descriptive–explanatory side is an attempt to account for the ways in which so-called 'ordinary people' make judgements concerning risks. Here Sunstein draws extensively on results in behavioural economics, as well as cognitive and social psychology. He claims these fields to have established that ordinary people's judgements concerning risks are frequently false. This is because ordinary people make such judgements on the basis of 'intuition' rather than scientific 'expertise' (Sunstein 2002a: 152). For instance, ordinary people err in: (a) assessing the probability of a given type of event on the basis of how many instances of the type they are able to recall ('availability heuristic') (2002a: 33; 2005: 35, 96); (b) concentrating their attention on worst-case scenarios ('probability neglect', 'alarmist bias') (2002a: 45; 2005: 35); (c) focusing on losses at the expense of gains ('loss aversion') (2002a: 42; 2005: 35); (d) ignoring the ways in which risks are interconnected ('system neglect') (2005: 35); (e) judging risks on the basis of emotional responses ('affect heuristic') (2002a: 43); (f) relying too much on information provided by others and thus opening the door to 'availability cascades' – events are deemed highly probable because they are often mentioned (2002a: 37–8, 48; 2005: 96); and (g) moving to extreme views when engaging in group discussions ('group polarisation') (2002a: 39; 2005: 99–103).

When Sunstein speaks of 'ordinary people' he includes legislators (2002a: 113). In assessing risks, ordinary people and legislators compare unfavourably with experts who evaluate risks and risk-management measures on the basis of cost–benefit analysis. Sunstein does not deny that experts too can make mistakes; indeed, they might even fall prey to some of the same biases, especially when they are insufficiently insulated from prevailing public fears (2005: 126). Experts can also have their own types of bias; for instance, they tend to believe what their paymasters would want them to believe ('affiliation bias') (2002a: 36). And they are prone to forget that regulatory systems dealing with risks 'need one thing above all – public support and confidence' (2002a: 294). Nevertheless, the fact remains: 'When they disagree, experts are generally right, and ordinary people generally wrong' (2002a: 55).

Sunstein rejects the idea – associated primarily with the psychologist Paul Slovic (2000) – that when it comes to risk perception, ordinary people and experts use 'rival rationalities'. As Sunstein sees it, differences in risk perception between ordinary people and experts can all be accounted for in terms of differences in values on the one hand, and mistakes by the non-experts, on the other hand (2002a: Ch. 3). A more general explanation of the differences, according to Sunstein, is the recently popular 'dual process' approach to cognition. It distinguishes between a 'System I' that is 'rapid, intuitive, and error prone' and a 'System II' that is 'more deliberative, calculative, slower, and more likely to be error free'. In the case of risk perception, System I is used by ordinary people, System II by experts (2002a: 68–9).

Sunstein's descriptive–explanatory work also has a historical component. He offers a number of case studies in recent risk regulation in the US, and describes the rise of the 'cost–benefit state' out of the ashes of '1970s environmentalism' (2002a, 2002b). The recurring theme of these case studies is that often US regulators have neglected to base their decisions on cost–benefit analysis, thereby wasting billions of dollars and – at least indirectly – causing many fatalities. As Sunstein reminds his readers, every $15 million wasted creates one statistical death (2002a: 138).

Sunstein's descriptive–explanatory results are meant to motivate his normative–prescriptive proposals. The most important of these is the demand to base – wherever possible – regulatory protection on cost–benefit analysis. Sunstein defends the use of cost–benefit analysis on the grounds that it is good for deliberative democracy, and that it is needed in order to correct our cognitive biases. The first reason rests on the second. Whatever improves the quality of reasoning about risks and uncertainties is beneficial for deliberative democracy. This is true especially since interest groups and politicians are eager to exploit the public's cognitive shortcomings (2002a: 7, 29, 35; 2002b: 27; 2005: 31).

Sunstein's advocacy of cost–benefit analysis comes with detailed recommendations on how to apply and institutionalise it. Overall his plea is for 'a large role' for 'experts', 'technocrats' or 'specialists' in the process of assessing and reducing risks (2002a: 7; 2005: 126). The most important specific proposals are: (1) that experts should be, as much as possible, insulated from public fears and debates (2002a: 22; 2005: 126); (2) that considerations of values and risks should be separated, with citizens debating the former and experts assessing the latter (2005: 128; 158); (3) that the public should be informed and educated about risks, for instance via a 'publicly available website' (2002a: ix, 118; 2005: 127); (4) that government has the right and the duty to manipulate the public when the latter's fears concerning low-probability risks are unfounded but difficult to alleviate by further information – 'The best approach might be this: *Change the subject* ... discuss something else and ... let time do the rest ... ' (2005: 125); (5) that governments should, wherever possible, determine the magnitudes of problems based on 'a quantitative analysis of risks' (2002a: 7); (6) that governments should assess trade-offs, and use effective and inexpensive tools (2002a: 5); (7) that governments should allow political issues such as the fair distribution of risks to play a role in cost–benefit analysis (2005: 158–74); and (8) that 'agencies should attempt to convert non-monetary values (involving, for example, lives saved, health gains, and aesthetic values) into dollar equivalents' (2002a: 111).

Some of the central ideas of Sunstein's prescriptive project concerning risk regulation are based on his previous work on 'legal reasoning and political conflict' (cf. the title of Sunstein 1996). Particularly important here is the concept of 'incompletely theorised agreements'. In the legal realm this is, first and foremost, the idea that judges should abstain from justifying their decisions in the light of general and fundamental theories. This recommendation is based on the observation that a focus on general theories 'often prevents people from getting along at all' since it 'forces people to contend, unnecessarily, over their deepest and most defining moral commitments' (1996: 50). Judges do better when they stick to 'mid-level principles' and the specifics of concrete cases. Sunstein uses the same idea also in his analysis of the role of constitutions. Constitutions are incompletely theorised agreements in so far as they are high-level abstractions on which people from diverse ethnic, religious or other backgrounds can agree even when they otherwise have very different visions of the good life (cf. Dickson 2001).[4] Applied to the context of risk regulation, Sunstein seems to suggest that cost–benefit analysis and related quantitative methods provide deliberative democracy with badly needed non-contentious 'mid-level principles'. When people disagree over the risk management concerning the 'genetic modification of food, or terrorism, or pesticides, or global warming', they do so in part because they cannot agree on 'the nature and meaning of human life'. A focus on cost–benefit analysis allows us to avoid these divisive issues (2005: 2–3).

Finally, it is important to mention that Sunstein believes risks to be real – rather than socially constructed. Risks 'exist "out there"' (2002a: 54), and 'whether a risk is serious, in the sense that many people will be hurt or die, is a question of fact'. Risks are 'socially constructed' only insofar as 'the categories that we use to perceive them are our own' (2002a: 109–10).

Jasanoff's and Wynne's participatory philosophy of risk

Jasanoff's and Wynne's more general claims on the politics of risk are often embedded in detailed sociological and historical investigations – for example, on the 'Windscale Public Inquiry' in the UK held in 1977 and meant to advise the government on the risks of building a reprocessing plant for spent nuclear fuels (Wynne 1982); on the conflicts between Cumbrian sheep farmers and (radiation and agricultural) scientists in the aftermath of the Chernobyl disaster (Wynne 1996a, 1996b); on the use of science by regulatory agencies in the US (Jasanoff 1990); on risk management after Bhopal (Jasanoff 1994); on the role played by science and technology in US courts (Jasanoff 1995); or on the ways in which the United States, Great Britain and Germany have responded to the challenges of risks associated with new biotechnologies (Jasanoff 2005). I cannot summarise all this detailed and long-term empirical work here; I confine myself to listing some of its central themes and theses.

First, Jasanoff contends that the ways in which different countries respond to technological risks can best be understood in light of these countries' respective 'political cultures', 'national styles of regulation' or 'civic epistemologies'. The latter are 'shared understandings about what credible claims should look like and how they ought to be articulated, represented, and defended', or 'culturally specific, historically and politically grounded, public knowledge-ways'. Because of the plurality of its civic epistemologies, Western democracy is fundamentally heterogeneous in the ways it constructs public reason (Jasanoff 2005: 18, 21, 249).

Second, according to Jasanoff, one of the most important developments in many political cultures – both Western and non-Western – over the past twenty-odd years has been the increasing call for the public's participation in decision-making on issues to do with technological change: 'we live in a time when knowledgeable citizens are more than ever demanding meaningful control over the technological changes that affect their welfare and prosperity' (Jasanoff 2005: 14). Political philosophy has so far ignored this development.

Third, both Jasanoff and Wynne maintain that the biggest hurdle for this development is the fact that 'science ... misunderstands both the public and itself' (Irwin and Wynne 1996b: 10). Scientists' dismissive and patronising attitudes towards the public are crystallised in the programme of 'Public Understanding of Science' (PUS), advocated and supported by many scientific institutions. One aspect of this programme is to document the public's lack of scientific understanding. For instance, a study for the 'Eurobarometer' in 2002 claimed that 36 per cent of European citizens believed that 'ordinary tomatoes do not contain genes, while genetically modified ones do' (Jasanoff 2005: 86). Or in 1991 a US *Science Indicators* report noted that only 6 per cent of the population could give a 'scientifically correct' answer to the question what causes acid rain (Wynne 1995: 366). On Jasanoff's and Wynne's reading of PUS, its advocates insist that science must have a 'privileged place in forming, and informing, an educated citizenry' (Jasanoff 2005: 252). Related scientists' prejudices concerning the public include the beliefs that the public 'passively takes up [and] fearfully rejects all scientific advances' (Jasanoff 2005: 255); that the public is unable to discuss fundamental questions such as the social vision and value of science (Wilsdon *et al.* 2005: 19); that 'lay knowledge [is] effectively worthless' (Wynne 1996b: 20); that "the public" is ... an aggregate of atomised individuals'; that its 'ignorance' is 'a function of intellectual vacuum or incapacity'; that its values must be those of science; and that the public has the same social opportunities for using available scientific knowledge as have scientists (Irwin and Wynne 1996a: 215).

Fourth, Jasanoff and Wynne hold that scientists' beliefs about the public – that is, scientists' 'deficit models of the public' (Wynne 1995) – are largely false. For instance, there is no reason to see the above-cited answer to the genes-in-tomatoes-question as a mistake: 'the public may correctly believe that genes in tomatoes do not matter for either consumption or policy (hence, for pragmatic purposes, do not "exist") unless they have been artificially imported into the tomatoes for specific purposes through technological means' (Jasanoff 2005: 88). In the same spirit, Wynne suggests that the public's ignorance of the causes of acid rain should not count against it; after all, scientists themselves are divided on the question (Wynne 1995: 366). Moreover, work by social scientists has shown that the European public is 'reflective, actively questioning and politically engaged' (Jasanoff 2005: 88); that 'the lay citizen is … a cultur-ally knowledgeable figure, able to master a more complex phenomenology in some respects than that of science' (Jasanoff 2005: 254); that the lay citizen '(as real publics are doing all over the world) shapes, crafts, reflects on, writes about, experiments and plays with, tests, and resists science and technology' (Jasanoff 2005: 255); that lay publics are 'capable of sophisticated and reflec-tive institutional analysis, and possibly better able than acknowledged experts to evaluate the implications of technological design for democratic governance' (Jasanoff 2006: 751); that lay people are often 'more ready than the scientific experts to reflect upon the status of their own knowledge' (Wynne 1996b: 40); that lay people frequently have 'vernacular, informal knowledge … about the validity of expert assumptions about real-world conditions' (Wynne 1996a: 59); that public groups are diverse (Irwin and Wynne 1996b: 9); that – for instance in the dispute between Cumbrian sheep farmers and radiation scientists – the lay knowledge (concerning the migration of radiation) of the former was in several ways superior to the expert knowledge of the latter (Wynne 1989, 1996a, 1996b); and that the ignorance of lay people of scientific knowledge is not 'a cognitive vacuum, or a deficit by default of knowledge, but an active construct': 'Technical ignorance … is a function of social *intelligence*, indeed of an *understanding* of science in the sense of its institutional dimensions'. Thus for instance radiation workers at nuclear plants may choose to remain ignorant of radiation risks on the grounds that knowledge of these risks might be unsettling (Wynne 1995: 380).

Fifth, Wynne in particular does not just contend that science is wrong about the public, he is also convinced that science is lacking in self-critical reflection. The reasons for this lack lie squarely with scientists' 'ideologies and training':

> As a result of their professional ideologies and training, scientists and lawyers find it very difficult to recognise the limitations of their concepts

and cognitive structures. They tend systematically to exalt their one
way of seeing into a superior – even unique – account.

(Wynne 1982: 144–45)

Scientists do not reflect on the nature of their work unless they are forced to
do so by outside criticism (Wynne 1996b: 43). If scientists were to engage in
such reflection, they would find, Wynne suggests, that modern science is
obsessed with control, prediction, standardisation and the belief that uncertainties can be contained (Wynne 1996b: 18–20); they would admit 'a deep
flaw in the very nature of science which drives it towards unrealism, insensitivity to uncertainty and variability, and incapability of admitting its own
limits' (Wynne 1996b: 35). Moreover, 'existing scientific culture seeks to
"colonise"' all questions about knowledge and its proper human purposes,
thereby effectively striving for "decisionism" and "*scientistic* cultural hegemony"'
(Wynne 2003: 408, 411). One expression of this tendency is science's practice
of 'framing' humans and their relations in 'objectivist language' (Wynne 1996a:
59): science 'tacitly imports and imposes particular and problematic versions of
social relationships and identities' (Wynne 1996b: 21); and 'scientific expert
knowledge itself embodies a particular culture – that is, it disseminates and
imposes particular and problematic normative versions of the human and the
social ... ' (Wynne 1996a: 75).

Sixth, Wynne stresses that these problematic features of science are clearly
in evidence in the realm of risk perception and management. Wynne speaks of
'the dominant scientistic cultural reification of risk as if it were an independently existing object ... ' (2005: 70). Scientific experts frame risks narrowly
by aiming for a 'quantifiable and systematic picture of risk ... [that] reduces the
whole topic to a single dimension: average magnitudes' (Wynne 1982: 144).
This procedure suppresses questions about the *meaning* of the figures; and it
ignores that risks are 'actually intellectual constructs which artificially reduce
larger uncertainties to ostensibly calculable probabilities of specific harm'
(Wynne 1996a: 57). The public is thus right to contest this framing of risks
and to focus instead on issues to do with trust, institutions, morality and
metaphysics: given the magnitudes of uncertainty, the public attends less to the
numbers than to the trustworthiness of institutions which produce the calculations and which present themselves as being able to protect the public
(Wynne 1996a: 58); and given the public's ability to ask fundamental questions, it is more likely to be concerned about the moral and metaphysical
character of the worlds imposed upon us by new technologies (Jasanoff 2006:
751).

In Jasanoff's and Wynne's writings layers of description are often interwoven
with layers of evaluation and prescription – and, no doubt, for good reasons. This
is reflected in my summary above. Nevertheless, the following key demands of
their political philosophy of risk are worth stating explicitly. From political
philosophy, our two authors demand a systematic re-thinking of core-concepts

like 'citizenship' or 'deliberation': in modern technological and scientific societies, citizenship and deliberation have to be constructed to include the right and duty to reflect on the values of science and the desirability of new technologies. Put differently, political scientists – and indeed all of us – need to envision and realise 'new political orders' that give citizens control over technological changes (Jasanoff 2005: 6, 14, 88). The central element of all such new political orders must be the creation of forums for 'upstream engagement' between scientists, engineers and the public. Upstream engagement takes place before or during the process of developing new technologies. Questions central to upstream engagement are: 'Why this technology? Why not another? Who needs it? Who is controlling it? Who benefits from it? Can they be trusted? What will it mean for me and my family? Will it improve the environment? What will it mean for people in the developing world?' (Wilsdon et al. 2005: 32–3). Upstream engagement can and also should scrutinise the 'codes, values, and norms that govern scientific practice' (Wilsdon et al. 2005: 19). In so doing, upstream engagement enables scientists to overcome their lack of critical self-reflection. This development should be encouraged further by providing incentives for scientists to become 'citizen scientists'; these are scientists who treat reflection – carried out jointly with the public – on upstream questions as 'part of their everyday work and responsibility' (Wilsdon et al. 2005: 47). Finally, these changes will make it possible to shift from 'technologies of hubris' (like cost–benefit analysis) to 'technologies of humility': acknowledging the effects of framing; giving room to the articulation of vulnerability; considering questions concerning fair distribution; and creating 'avenues through which societies can collectively reflect on the ambiguity of their experiences, and ... assess the strengths and weaknesses of alternative explanations' (Jasanoff 2003b: 240–42).

Against Sunstein's paternalism

Jasanoff's and Wynne's picture of PUS captures, in almost uncanny fashion, many central elements of Sunstein's position. Although Sunstein does not use the term 'Public Understanding of Science', his work on risk perception fits PUS hand-in-glove: he lists and analyses alleged deficits in the public's knowledge and reasoning; he issues stark warnings about the political consequences of listening to an ignorant public; and he discusses the pros and cons of educating the public. Indeed, Sunstein goes further than other PUS advocates in proposing that (risk) scientists should be kept away from the public and its contagious biases. Moreover, like Wynne's stereotypical scientific expert, Sunstein treats the public – that is, 'ordinary people' – as an aggregate of individuals, and he shows no interest in understanding diversity and multitude within the public. Predictably, Sunstein's public is neither reflective nor actively questioning: its main source of judgement is intuition, not deliberation. Little surprise then that the public is said to easily fall prey to 'availability entrepreneurs' – special interest groups and politicians who exploit the public's intellectual shortcomings. Fortunately though, there are experts in cost–benefit analysis, and they can rescue democracy. They do so by putting a check on the public's 'misfearing' (Sunstein 2006). And yet, Sunstein's experts remain as elusive and undifferentiated a group as does the public. Nor do we learn much about what kind of democracy the experts are defending. Although Sunstein claims to speak in the name of 'deliberative democracy', it seems that – at least as far as risk assessment is concerned – the technocrats and the politicians are the only real deliberators. For Sunstein deliberative democracy regarding risks does not involve the creation of new public forums for debating fundamental political questions. For Sunstein deliberative democracy means the creation of institutions designed to guarantee that the best scientific opinions win the day – even if this involves state agencies in paternalist manipulation of an ignorant and fearful public.

To show that Sunstein's position fits Jasanoff's and Wynne's picture of PUS is one thing; to argue that Sunstein is wrong is of course quite another. I now turn to the latter task. Sunstein's claim according to which his analysis is based on existing work in cognitive psychology and behavioural economics has to be taken with a large pinch of salt. This is because his diet of psychological and economic results is strangely one-sided. For instance, although he frequently aligns himself with the well-known 'heuristics-and-biases' programme of Daniel Kahneman and Amos Tversky, he fails to give proper heed to one of the most striking and pertinent insights of the large body of empirical work generated within this tradition: to wit, that 'the reliance on heuristics and the prevalence of biases are not restricted to laymen. Experienced researchers are also prone to the same biases' (Tversky and Kahneman 1982: 18). Indeed, experimental evidence suggests that, when no frequency data is available, 'experts are just as likely as laypeople to err in evaluating risk, even when experts have Ph.D.s in probability and statistics and have been warned previously about the same errors' (Shrader-Frechette 2003; cf. Gigerenzer 2002).

It is true that the just-cited passage from Tversky and Kahneman continues with the words: ' – when they think intuitively' (1982: 18). In full, the second sentence says: 'Experienced researchers are also prone to the same biases – when they think intuitively.' Sunstein might regard this qualification as grist to his mill. After all, he claims that experts do better than ordinary people precisely because they rely on the reflective 'System II' rather than the intuitive 'System I'. Let us ignore for the moment the patronising and dismissive implication that the reasoning of lay people is confined to unreflective intuition. Here it is more to the point to emphasise that some leading authorities from within the heuristics-and-biases programme disagree with Sunstein's optimistic assertions regarding System II (Kahan et al. 2006). To begin with, they point out that, in many of the public 'risk panics' deplored by Sunstein, experts can be found on all sides of the argument. Examples are 'panics' over nuclear power, arsenic in drinking water or mad cow disease. The experts involved in these 'panics' do not just put forward intuitive judgements; they usually offer detailed and reflective arguments in favour of their views. Moreover, a number of psychological studies have demonstrated that the same sorts of social and cultural factors that can be used to predict differences in lay perceptions of risk also explain the distribution of patterns of opinion amongst disagreeing risk experts. Such factors include gender, political ideology and institutional affiliation. Alas, Sunstein shows no interest in differences in judgements *within* his two main groups of ordinary people and experts. And finally, the superiority of System II relative to System I is not as clear-cut an issue as Sunstein believes. There are cases where 'risk as feeling may outperform risk as analysis'. And there is plenty of evidence that System II is vulnerable to biasing influences (Kahan et al. 2006).

It is striking and surprising that Sunstein pays so little attention to research on experts' biases. His stated aim is to improve societal risk perception and risk management, and to lessen the waste of money and lives. He believes that to achieve these goals we have to give a greater role to science in general and cost–benefit analysts in particular. Given this starting point, he is right to try to assemble a case against relying on the public's judgements. He can even insist with some (initial) plausibility that his cost–benefit analysts need to be protected from the public. But for all that, he surely should be *equally* worried by the possibility that his experts fall prey to their own biases. If correct and unbiased cost–benefit analysis is the goal, then obviously *all* serious impediments need to be identified and, if possible, rooted out. Sunstein does occasionally mention the 'affiliation bias' – experts' tendency to find in favour of their paymasters. However, he never spends more than a couple of lines on this problem. This contrasts sharply with the chapter-long treatments of the public's alleged main biases.

In the context of Sunstein's programme, a detailed investigation of the affiliation bias should be important not only as a guide to institutional reform. It might also be helpful for understanding why ordinary people are not irrational when responding with some scepticism to expert risk assessments. Remember some well-documented cases from the realm of medical research. It has been shown, for instance, that the conclusions of review articles on second-hand smoking – whether second-hand smoking is harmful or not – vary systematically with whether or not the author of the review article is affiliated with the tobacco industry (Barnes and Beto 1998: 1599). And studies of published papers on drug testing, papers in which rival drugs were compared, found that almost always the drug produced by the sponsor of the research was found superior (Davidson 1986; Stelfox *et al.* 1998; Friedberg *et al.* 1999; cf. Brown 2004).

Similar conclusions can be reached by challenging Sunstein's characterisation of risk assessments as objective and – at least potentially – value-free. Consider the risk associated with living near a waste dump. The level of risk of living near a waste dump depends of course on the various hazardous materials stored at the site. But few hazardous materials have been studied in any detail, and our knowledge of their interaction is little understood. Accordingly, risk assessment involves mathematical models that determine the relevant risk probabilities. Such models are needed because no frequency data are available. Indeed, it is precisely the *lack* of frequency data that is usually taken to be definitive of formal risk analysis. Put differently, the events modelled in risk analysis fall under the concept of 'Bayesian uncertainty'. And this brings us to the crucial point: 'given this Bayesian uncertainty, virtually all risk experts accept the fact that risk analyses typically err by 4 to 6 orders of magnitude' (Shrader-Frechette 2003). In other words, and to stick to the above example, most risk experts accept that the likelihood of harm associated with living near a waste dump may well be between 10,000 and 1,000,000 times higher than their best – or their more optimistic – estimates predict. It is hard to resist two conclusions from this uncertainty: first, that the public will often be right to be cautious and incredulous when confronted with optimistic risk assessments about, say, nuclear power or eating British beef. And second, it is reasonable to assume that experts' own values and normative commitments play a substantial role in whether they prefer to err on the side of caution or the side of optimism.

Let us return to the idea of deliberative democracy. It is customary to speak of a 'deliberative turn' in theories of democracies, a turn that is said to have occurred during the 1980s and 1990s (Fishkin 1995; Bohman and Rehg 1997; Kymlicka 2002; Ackerman and Fishkin 2004). Put in a nutshell, the main point of this turn was a change from 'vote-centric' to 'talk-centric' conceptions of democracy. Political theorists realised that modern mass democracies do not provide citizens with public spaces in which they can collectively test and debate their preferences; no public forums in which minorities can make themselves heard and thereby influence political decisions; and no incentives for citizens to get informed about the pressing political issues of the present and the future. Advocates of deliberative democracy therefore set themselves the task of developing and justifying new forms of institutional arrangements in which such new forms of political discussion might take place. Prominent amongst such new forms are 'consensus conferences', 'citizen juries', 'deliberative polling', or 'deliberation days'. The details need not concern us here; what is important is that theorists of deliberative democracy aim to broaden and widen political debate on all levels, and amongst all groups of citizens.

Sunstein repeatedly represents himself as a champion of deliberative democracy (2002a: 7, 8, 256, 257, 294; 2002b: 27; 2005: 1, 158) – indeed he even writes a back-cover endorsement for Bruce Ackerman and James S. Fishkin's *Deliberation Day* (2004). But it is hard to see how his largely tacit democratic theory fits with the sketch provided in the last paragraph. Sunstein's democratic theory is first and foremost about securing more deliberative space for 'technocrats', a deliberative space that, as he insists, is best cordoned off from the public.[5] The distance from the goals of writers like Ackerman and Fishkin is obvious. It is equally clear in the following passage: 'America was supposed to be a deliberative democracy, in which representatives, accountable to the people, would make decisions through a process of deliberation uncontrolled by private factions. Without better information, neither deliberation nor democracy is possible' (Sunstein 2002a: 257). Note: it is not 'the people' who are doing the deliberating; it is only their representatives. People vote, their representatives deliberate. This is the 'vote-centric' democracy of old, the very form of democracy that proponents of the 'deliberative turn' seek to overcome.

At one time Sunstein seems to have believed that he had a theoretical ground for being sceptical about public deliberation. In *Risk and Reason* (2002a) he suggests that deliberation inevitably leads to group polarisation: 'Group polarization is the typical result of deliberation, which moves people toward a more extreme point in the direction that they were already heading' (2002a: 30). If that were true, then of course little good could come of any deliberation – regardless of whether the deliberators are ordinary people or experts. But here too the Sunstein of *Risk and Reason* gives the available evidence a one-sided gloss. Group-communication research has identified various arrangements that can lessen group polarisation and indeed eliminate it altogether. This is now acknowledged by Sunstein himself: 'Group polarisation can be heightened, diminished and possibly even eliminated with seemingly small alterations in institutional arrangements' (quoted from Ackerman and Fishkin 2004: 63; cf. Kahan *et al.* 2006: 1101–2). While this acknowledgement is a step in the right direction, it does not, on its own, constitute a recognition that a deliberative democracy worth its name must involve broad public deliberations.

Finally, Sunstein does not seem to recognise that two of his central recommendations concerning the expert–public interaction are an instance of the very ignorance that he laments in the concluding section of *Risk and Reason*: 'technocrats tend to ignore the fact that to work well, a regulatory system needs one thing above all – public support and confidence' (2002a: 294). The recommendations I have in mind are, first, the recommendation to insulate technocrats from the public, and, second, to actively manipulate the public's fear about low-level risks: 'The best approach may well be this: *Change the subject*. . . . Perhaps the most effective way of reducing fear of a low-probability risk is simply to discuss something else and to let time do the rest' (2005: 125). As concerns the latter proposal, one feels inclined to ask: does Sunstein really believe that the public would have confidence in a paternalist regulatory system that is permitted to treat the public as a child? Does he really believe the public would vote for such a proposal? As regards the former suggestion – insulate the technocrats – Sunstein could have learnt a lot from Jasanoff's and Wynne's wealth of empirical work. Jasanoff and Wynne document time and time again that public scepticism and distrust towards experts increases in direct proportion to the degree of invisibility of the process resulting in expert advice.

Against Jasanoff's and Wynne's participatory politics

When Jasanoff and Wynne criticise other positions in science policy and the political philosophy of risk, three accusations are usually paramount: first, that their opponents pay insufficient attention to the diversity of scientific practices, publics, civic epistemologies, political settlements or forms of democracy; second, that their rivals fail to treat science and the public symmetrically, that is, that their rivals disregard 'lay expertise'; and third, that their competitors are technocratic in failing to make room for fundamental political debate over the framing, value and direction of science and technology (see, e.g., Jasanoff 2003a, 2004b; Wynne 2003, 2005). In what follows, I shall speak of the 'diversity', 'symmetry' and 'fundamental debate' points.

Jasanoff and Wynne are often right when making these accusations, and I have taken them as my guides when identifying problems with Sunstein's paternalist philosophy of risk. Nevertheless, I cannot resist the thought that Jasanoff and Wynne routinely commit some of the very sins that they so passionately and justifiably deplore in others.

Consider first the issue of diversity. No doubt, Jasanoff has done much valuable work in identifying the differences in political culture and civic epistemology in India and in three leading Western industrial nations. Jasanoff also deserves praise for reminding us that science cannot simply be divided into 'pure' and 'applied'; her study of 'regulatory science' in the US is a landmark investigation into a form of science to which previous research had given scant attention. And yet this high regard for detail and diversity is thrown overboard the moment Jasanoff and Wynne begin discussing the relationship between the public and science, and start to argue for their agenda in normative political philosophy. At that moment their renditions of 'the public' and 'science' become strangely flat and unyielding. Two sections back I have quoted extensively from their work precisely to be able to make this point here. The 'public' is 'culturally knowledgeable', 'capable of sophisticated ... institutional analysis', more willing to reflect on its limitations than are scientists; it possesses lay knowledge that can compete with science; and it has means to validate expert judgements. Do *all* publics have and do that? Are these forms of knowledge and ability distributed evenly over publics? What makes 'a public' in the first place? These questions are not even posed.[6] Jasanoff and Wynne are keenly attuned to the ways in which scientists and technocrats 'frame' the public. But for all that, their own 'framing' of the public is oddly coarse and undifferentiated. Things get worse – especially in Wynne's writings – when we come to science: unless they are challenged, scientists do not reflect on their practices; they are trapped in 'ideologies' of their own superiority; they are unable to see the 'deep flaw in the very nature of science which drives it towards unrealism, insensitivity to uncertainty and variability'; they are striving for '*scientistic* cultural hegemony'; and they are defending a narrow 'decisionism'. Again, what justifies these sweeping claims, and where is the attention to detail and diversity? How can such essentialism come from the pens of scholars who swear by Shakespeare's 'I'll teach you differences!' (*King Lear*, 1.4)?

Jasanoff's and Wynne's failure to meet their own 'diversity point' is of course connected to their unbalanced evaluation of the public and science. In other words, their violation of the diversity requirement is linked to their missing the 'symmetry point'. This is ironic given how central a demand 'symmetry' is for signed-up students of the 'Sociology of Scientific Knowledge' (cf. Bloor 1976) – and both Jasanoff and Wynne wish to be members of the club (e.g. Jasanoff 2004a; Wynne 2003). The public is always actively constructing, reflective and savvy in cultural and political matters; the scientific experts are biased, trapped in ideology, unreflective and politically naïve. Even when members of the public seem by all (sensible) counts to simply hold mistaken beliefs, Jasanoff and Wynne argue for a 'no-guilty' verdict in at least two respects: the ignorance of the public is no 'lack' but an 'active construct', and what seems like a false belief about one thing is actually a true belief about another. Thus someone who falsely denies that tomatoes have genes is claimed to actually and truly believe that the unmodified genes of tomatoes need not worry the consumer. This level of charity borders on the humorous, especially when it is spiced with opaque references to lay citizens' 'complex phenomenology'. But humorous or not, the question remains why scientific experts should not be treated with the same charity. The vocabulary used – 'ideology', 'reification', 'hegemony', 'decisionism', 'subversion' – hints that the reasons might have something to do with a new form of, or an analogue of, the good-old class-struggle. Alas, it remains obscure how the potpourri of terms from Marx, Lukács, Gramsci, Foucault and Habermas can illuminate the differences between publics and experts.

I do not of course mean to deny that the 'ignorance' of ordinary people concerning many technical issues may often be an 'active construct'; it is easy to see, for instance, why workers in a nuclear power station may choose not to learn about the dangers of their profession. Or, to pick another case cited by Wynne, it is not difficult to understand that some women reject dominant medical views of menstruation when these views are based on the interpretation of menstruation as 'failed reproduction' (Martin 1989; Wynne 1995: 376). No doubt, such 'active constructions' of ignorance are far from rare. Nevertheless, here as everywhere it is important not to overstate a correct insight. Not every form of ignorance is an active construction – at least my own (honest) introspection of my own ignorance tells me that most of it is not actively constructed at all. Moreover, actively constructed or not, in some crucial respects at least, ignorance just is ignorance: when it comes to making decisions, say, regarding the correct medication for my child's breathing problems, I want to hear the views of those in the know, not the views of those who are ignorant – never mind that their 'technical ignorance' may be 'a function of *social intelligence*'.[7]

In the last section I criticised Sunstein for the one-sided use he makes of the psychological literature on risk perception, heuristics and biases. Jasanoff and Wynne make no use of this literature at all. Even studies on the *cultural* and *social* variables of risk perception by the anthropologist Mary Douglas and the political scientist Aaron Wildavsky receive scant attention in Jasanoff's and Wynne's work (Douglas and Wildavsky 1982).[8] I hazard the guess that this is because, for Jasanoff and Wynne, any research that finds the public making mistakes, or any investigation that identifies limits in the public's political imagination, is principally suspect. To my mind at least, this stance is indefensible for many reasons – but first and foremost it is indefensible on the grounds that it contradicts the aims and purposes of deliberative democracy itself. Disregarding the facts about our cognitive limitations we make ourselves unable to correct for them. The project of deliberative democracy includes, at least in the understanding of its leading theoreticians (Ackerman and Fishkin 2004), the search for institutional arrangements that help us – ordinary people and experts alike – to overcome or at least restrict the scope of these limitations. To pretend they are not there is not to advance deliberative democracy, it is to perpetuate our blunders.

In the above I have suggested that Jasanoff and Wynne do not live up to two of the three standards by which they measure the success or failure of proposals on how to deal with risk: the demands of diversity and symmetry. This leaves the third standard: the requirement to be committed to debate over the value and direction of science and democracy, and ultimately about the good life itself. My concern regarding this third issue is not that Jasanoff and Wynne fail to meet it; my worry is rather that in advocating this ideal, the two authors bypass far too quickly a number of important worries.

First of all, Jasanoff and Wynne need to do more to justify and motivate the demand for such a principled debate of ultimate values. Usually their argument in favour of such discussion is no more than the empirical observation that in various, primarily European, countries many politically powerful bodies – like the UK government, the European Commission, the House of Lords, or various Royal Commissions – have called for, and have organised, various events in which the public was and is 'engaged'. This would be a good argument if Hegel was right and 'what is reasonable is actual, and what is actual is reasonable'. But is it? Should not authors who allude to Marx and Foucault as important resources in their political philosophy be much more sceptical of such newly found openness in some of our most powerful institutions? Indeed, should not such authors seek a greater political distance from such institutions?[9]

Second, Jasanoff and Wynne are highly critical of authors who propose types of participant or modes of decision-making for negotiations over risk-related questions like 'should you eat British beef, prefer nuclear power to coal-fired power stations, [or] want a quarry in your village'? (Collins and Evans 2002: 236). Indeed, Jasanoff and Wynne are hostile towards such authors even when their proposals include the demand to let some members of the public, namely members of the public with relevant 'non-certified' expertise, participate in the technical decision-making. For Jasanoff and Wynne such suggestions are forms of 'decisionism' since they reduce public participation to the answering of 'propositional [yes–no] questions', and fail to pay attention to the ways in which such questions are always already 'scientistically' framed (Jasanoff 2003a; Wynne 2003). And in order to properly address the 'framing' issue, Jasanoff and Wynne insist, we have to move to a much more fundamental debate over what kind of science and technology we collectively want. Now, I have no quarrel with the demand for conversations over our ultimate values and aspirations, including our ultimate values and aspirations for science and technology. My worry is rather that our modern socially, politically, ethnically, religiously diverse and divided societies will not be able to come up with a consensus or even a lasting compromise concerning such ultimate commitments (cf. Rawls 1993; Mouffe 2000; Geuss 2001a, 2005). And thus I am doubtful that we can achieve a 'framing' of technological questions that remains uncontested for longer than a moment. This is the point, it seems to me, where Sunstein's idea of 'incompletely theorized agreements' proves to be a real insight and help. Given the enormous diversity of our ultimate values and aspirations, we cannot, and maybe we should not, aim for a consensus concerning them. But it might well be possible that even from our diverse ultimate commitments we are able to agree on 'mid-level principles', principles that define procedures to be followed,[10] and types of (certified and uncertified) expertise to be consulted.

Third, and finally, Jasanoff and Wynne do not seem to realise that there is a basic tension in their overall political position.[11] On the one hand, their demand for an all-inclusive fundamental debate between cognitive equals places them firmly in the tradition of *liberalism* with its emphasis on anti-paternalism, consensus-oriented deliberation and the common good. On the other hand, their demand for diversity and their use of terms like 'ideology', 'hegemony', 'reification' or 'subversion' are naturally seen as elements of a neo-Marxist multiculturalism that sees society *sub specie belli*, that is, as characterised by irresolvable conflict and disagreement – at least this side of the revolution. On the latter view, every real debate must be local, contingent, partial and ideological. Invoking both traditions at the same time guarantees the applause from most positions of the political spectrum: from the Left, the Centre and even the moderate Right. Successful this combination of traditions might be, coherent it is not.[12]

Conclusions

The main title of this chapter is 'Towards a political philosophy of risk'. The 'towards' is meant to signal that, although we already have important first stabs at the problem, much work of development, critical scrutiny and synthesis remains to be done. I have tried to contribute to this endeavour by testing two existing radical, and diametrically opposed, proposals. I conclude by indicating – wherever possible – where I see 'syntheses' out of Sunstein's 'theses' and the STS scholars' 'antitheses'.

(1) The metaphysics of risk

The thesis is Sunstein's claim that risks are real; the antithesis is Jasanoff's and Wynne's contention that risks are, in good part, socially constructed. I have not said much on this issue in the above, hoping that it receives extensive attention in other contributions to this volume. I here only register my view that neither Sunstein nor the STS authors have made a convincing case for their respective positions on the metaphysics of risk and that much more work is required to work out a satisfactory synthesis of realist and constructivist intuitions and insights. We need a much better understanding of what is socially constructed about risks, and what this social construction entails for their reality and objectivity.

(2) Relevant empirical work

It is one of the many strengths of both proposals discussed here that they pay extensive attention – indeed are based upon – empirical work. Sunstein's thesis insists that the most important work for the study of risk comes from cognitive psychology and behavioural economics; the STS scholars' antithesis stresses the unique significance of work in social history and the sociology of scientific knowledge. In my criticism of both positions I have argued that it is important to use the results of both fields of inquiry. Formulated thus abstractly, synthesis comes cheap. Of course, in many cases the results of cognitive psychology and behavioural economics may not be easy to combine with the sociological findings. This is where a lot more work is needed.

(3) Background political theory

The two positions borrow at least some of their central ideas from different political traditions and schools of thought. Sunstein's (largely implicit) thesis is that the most relevant background theory for the political philosophy of risk is the philosophy of vote-centric liberal democracy.[13] Jasanoff's and Wynne's antithesis is to invoke theoretical defences of talk-centric deliberative democracy as well as neo-Marxism and multiculturalism. My suggestion for an improvement over both positions does not qualify as a 'synthesis', but here it is anyway. It seems to me that political philosophies of risk had better be explicit about the more general political philosophies upon which they seek to build. After all, decisions about risks are related to many other issues central to political philosophy, issues like justice, citizenship or democracy.

(4) Deficit models

Sunstein's thesis is a deficit model of 'ordinary people'; Jasanoff's and Wynne's antithesis is a deficit model of scientists and experts. The synthesis – in good-old Hegelian fashion – destroys both thesis and antithesis, and yet preserves them on a higher level: we need to recognise the heuristics and biases involved in the thinking of all of us, experts and non-experts alike. There is no justification for denying our shortcomings, and every reason for seeking institutional arrangements that help us to overcome, or at least contain, our blunders.

(5) Symmetries and asymmetries

The thesis is Sunstein's attempt to use an epistemic asymmetry (between experts and the public) as an argument for a political asymmetry. The STS antithesis is not always clear. Sometimes it sounds like Jasanoff and Wynne wish to argue from an epistemic symmetry (between experts and publics) to a political symmetry. In other places, they can be read as basing epistemic symmetry upon political symmetry. The synthesis seems to be to accept that our problem is more difficult than what Sunstein or the STS scholars envisage: we want political symmetry despite epistemic asymmetries. To make sense of this conundrum is the real challenge for political philosophies of risk.

(6) Key yardstick

While Sunstein is happy to admit that other measures are important too, he puts special emphasis on dollars and lives saved (= thesis). Jasanoff and Wynne would hardly deny the desirability of saving lives, but their key yardstick is nevertheless the inclusiveness of debates over the fundamental orientation of science and technology (= antithesis). The goal must surely be a 'reflective equilibrium' that brings both goals into coherence with one another (= synthesis).

(7) Fundamental normative commitments

Sunstein's thesis of 'incompletely theorised agreements' is based on the idea that we cannot hope to achieve consensus on many of our most fundamental values or conceptions of the good life. Jasanoff's and Wynne's antithesis emphasises that an adequate public deliberation over science and technology must include explicit consideration of such fundamentals. Here my position is closer to Sunstein than to the STS scholars. Given the diversity of modern societies – often stressed by Jasanoff and Wynne themselves – it is unrealistic, and perhaps even morally wrong, to expect consensus on our conceptions of the good life. It might therefore be more advisable to aim for 'mid-level principles' when it comes to the assessment and regulation of risks.

(8) Understanding of deliberative democracy

Should our understanding of democracy be vote-centric (= Sunstein's thesis) or talk-centric (= Jasanoff's and Wynne's antithesis)?[14] This is precisely one of the key questions where a political philosophy of risk must turn into a general political philosophy. Sunstein's commitment to deliberative democracy is somewhat half-hearted – it seems that for him a democracy is deliberative if the decisions reached would match an 'ideal' deliberation amongst perfectly informed and un-biased 'ideal deliberators' (i.e. cost–benefit analysts). This model of deliberation is well-familiar from the early John Rawls (1971) and recent work by Philip Kitcher on the philosophy of science policy (Kitcher 2001; cf. Lewontin 2002; Brown 2004, Jasanoff 2004).[15] Jasanoff's and Wynne's sympathies lie with those who insist that political deliberations must be 'real' and involve 'real' actors (e.g. Ackerman and Fishkin 2004). Clearly, our intuitions about deliberation pull us in both directions. A critical synthesis of models of ideal and real deliberation remains a key challenge for political philosophy.

(9) Key demand

Sunstein's key demand – thesis – is for more space for experts in decision-making over risks. Jasanoff's and Wynne's antithesis calls for less space for (credentialed) experts, especially when it comes to re-evaluating the purposes of science and technology. The natural synthesis may be a political theory of expertise: such theory would work out who can lay claim to what kind of expertise in which domains, and which issues are best addressed by what kinds of expertise. There may then be issues in which we all are (almost) equally expert – questions, say, about the good life for ourselves; questions regarding which we wish to have input from both credentialed and un-credentialed experts; and questions concerning which we would only trust a certified expert, trained in the most exclusive institutions.[16] We have some tentative first steps towards such theories of expertise (Collins and Evans 2002; Turner 2003) but much work remains to be done.

(10) Norm subjects

Sunstein's 'norm subjects' are politicians and the public: the former are told to create institutions in which objective cost–benefit analysis can flourish, the latter are requested to leave all questions of fact to technocrats. This is the thesis. Jasanoff and Wynne address politicians and scientists: the former are asked to construct new forms of political order, the latter are called upon to turn themselves into 'citizen scientists'. This is the antithesis. My synthesis is simplicity itself: developing new political arrangements for dealing with the risks of the twenty-first century will confront all of us – experts and non-experts alike – with fundamental and new challenges. We will all have to change in their wake.[17]

Notes

1 I am using the term 'political philosophy of risk' very broadly so that it includes positions that reject our contemporary preoccupation with risks, and that insist instead that our focus should be on, say, the unjust distributions of technological means, or the role of capitalism in shaping modern technologies, etc. In other words, I am using 'philosophy of risk' in analogy to 'philosophy of religion': like atheism is a position in the philosophy of religion, so a critique of the focus on risk is a position in the philosophy of risk.

2 Sunstein's views are very similar to those of US Supreme Court Justice Stephen G. Breyer (1993).

3 But see Jasanoff (1994), a review of Breyer (1993). While Breyer's position is more radical than Sunstein's, his proposals are similar.

4 This position is similar in some respects to that of the later Rawls (1993: 133–72).

5 Sunstein does of course support the idea of the public debating questions of value. But not only does he – falsely – believe that these questions of value can be separated from questions of fact, he also insists that deliberation on questions of fact should be confined to the experts. It is this later deliberation I am referring to in the text.

6 At least not as far as Jasanoff's and Wynne's own concept of the public is concerned. Jasanoff (2005: Ch. 3) skilfully analyses how Europe is producing the very public it is seeking to govern. Here too though one could go much further and investigate the genealogy of our very concept of 'the public'. See Geuss (2001b) for a first impressive stab at the problem.

7 The existence of alternative medicine is no objection to my point: practitioners of alternative medicine are experts, too.

8 But could not Jasanoff and Wynne insist that this work is simply irrelevant to their projects? After all, what would the heuristics-and-biases literature or the study by Douglas and Wildavsky contribute to, say, Jasanoff's detailed historical study of the governance of biotechnology in the UK, Germany and the US (Jasanoff 2005)? First, as far as the heuristics-and-biases literature is concerned, it seems to me that it is irrelevant only as long as Jasanoff and Wynne do (primarily descriptive) sociology or social history of science and technology. But the moment they begin pronouncing on normative political philosophy, that is, the moment they propose institutional arrangements for political debate over risk, science and technology, the heuristics-and-biases literature should be relevant for the reasons given in the main text. Second, regarding the work by Douglas and Wildavsky, I strongly disagree with the view (popular amongst recent writers on risk in STS), that it is outdated and discredited. I believe that a critical engagement with Douglas and Wildavsky (1982) can still be enormously fruitful. Take, for instance, Jasanoff's suggestion that the different civic epistemologies of the US, Britain, and Germany can be summed up in three models, labelled 'contentious', 'communitarian' and 'consensus-seeking' (Jasanoff 2005: 259). A perspective informed by Douglas and Wildavsky would lead one to ask a set of important further questions: to what extent are these civic epistemologies those of the centre or the peripheries of these nations? Are there rival civic epistemologies within nations or national cultures? How do these civic epistemologies relate to the social structures of these nations? And so on. (In passing I

note that Douglas and Wildavsky (1982) continue to stimulate empirical work in social and cognitive psychology. See Kahan et al. 2006.)

9 I am aware of the fact that Jasanoff and Wynne sometimes criticise the limited ways in which these institutions 'frame' openness. What I am missing in both Jasanoff and Wynne is a self-reflective worry about the enormous success they have in and with these very institutions.

10 Lest I be misunderstood, I am not here endorsing Sunstein's suggestion that cost–benefit analysis is the needed mid-level principle.

11 Here I am influenced by Geuss (2001a, 2001b, 2005). I am grateful to Jeff Kochan for having impressed upon me the importance of Geuss's work for my project.

12 It has been suggested to me that in the above I am doing Jasanoff an injustice by linking her views to Wynne's 'deficit model of the scientist'. According to this objection, Jasanoff does not deny that scientists use a deficit model of the public, but she insists that, in so doing, scientists themselves are victims of political elites, capitalism, various institutional forces and late modernity. Moreover, so the objection continues, Jasanoff would be unhappy with the label 'philosophy of risk'; for her, the focus on risk – rather than, say, injustice – is itself part of the problem. These are of course weighty considerations, and if they had been developed clearly and at length in Jasanoff's published work, they would no doubt have left a mark on this paper. (Despite careful searching, I have been unable to find discussions of justice and capitalism in Jasanoff's extensive oeuvre.) Be this as it may, as far as (much of) my criticism is concerned, the mentioned considerations do not justify separating Jasanoff's from Wynne's views. My criticism focuses on the way in which Jasanoff and Wynne 'frame' scientific experts and the public. The question to what degree scientists – and their views of the public – are themselves victims of others powers, be it capital, be it late modernity, is not my concern here. I acknowledge that in some ways it may be odd to call Jasanoff and Wynne 'political philosophers of risk'. But I here construe 'political philosophy of risk' broadly enough for it to include forms of political philosophy that challenge the very focus on risk (cf. note 1 above).

13 Of course, Sunstein's paternalism does not fit well with classical liberalism. For the latter, see, e.g., Geuss (2001b: 92).

14 Of course, I do not mean to suggest that Jasanoff and Wynne are not paying a lot of attention to materiality and visual culture. My point is that their's is a deliberative democracy in which deliberations on facts and values are not confined to elected representatives.

15 I do not mean to suggest here that Sunstein's overall political philosophy is Rawlsian. But he shares with Rawls the idea of ideal deliberation. Cf. also note 11 above.

16 Given what I have said in my criticism of Sunstein above, I hope it is clear that in my view his cost–benefit analysts do not fall into the last-mentioned category.

17 For extensive comments on a first draft, I am grateful to Ipek Demir, Rob Doubleday, Sarah Gore, Bill Grundy, Sheila Jasanoff, Stephen John, Jeff Kochan, Tim Lewens and Peter Lipton. Jasanoff's comments were naturally of special significance.

References

Ackerman, B. and Fishkin, J.S. (2004) *Deliberation Day*, New Haven and London: Yale University Press.

Barnes D. and Beto, L.A. (1998) 'Why review articles on the health effects of passive smoking reach different conclusions', *Journal of the American Medical Association*, 279: 1566–70.

Bloor, D. (1976) *Knowledge and Social Imagery*, London: Routledge & Kegan Paul.

Bohman, J. and Rehg, W. (eds) (1997) *Deliberative Democracy: essays on reason and politics*, Cambridge, MA: MIT Press.

Breyer, S.G. (1993), *Breaking the Vicious Circle: toward effective risk regulation*, Cambridge, MA: Harvard University Press.

Brown, J. (2004) 'Money, method and medical research', *Episteme*, 1: 49–59.

Brown, M.B. (2004) 'The political philosophy of science policy', *Minerva*, 42: 77–95.

Collins, H.M. and Evans, R. (2002) 'The third wave of science studies: studies of expertise and experience', *Social Studies of Science*, 32: 235–96.

Davidson, R. (1986) 'Source of funding and outcome of clinical trials', *Journal of General Internal Medicine*, 12: 155–58.

Dickson, J. (2001) 'Interpretation and coherence in legal reasoning', *Stanford Encyclopedia of Philosophy*. Online. Available: http://www.seop.leeds.ac.uk/archives/sum2003/entries/legal-reas-interpret (accessed 1 May 2006).

Douglas, M. and Wildavsky, A. (1982) *Risk and Culture: an essay on the selection of technical and environmental dangers*, London: Routledge.

Fishkin, J.S. (1995) *The Voice of the People: public opinion and democracy*, New Haven and London: Yale University Press.

Friedberg, M., Saffran, B., Stinson, T., Nelson, W. and Bennett, C.L. (1999) 'Evaluation of conflict of interest in economic analyses of new drugs used on oncology', *Journal of the American Medical Association*, 282: 1453–57.

Geuss, R. (2001a), *History and Illusion in Politics*, Cambridge: Cambridge University Press.

—— (2001b) *Public Goods, Private Goods*, 2nd edn, Princeton, NJ and Oxford: Princeton University Press.

—— (2005) *Outside Ethics*, Princeton, NJ and Oxford: Princeton University Press.

Gigerenzer, G. (2002) *Reckoning with Risk: learning to live with uncertainty*, London: Allen Lane.

Irwin, A. and Wynne, B. (1996a) 'Conclusions', in Irwin, A. and Wynne, B. (eds) *Misunderstanding Science? The public reconstruction of science and technology*, Cambridge: Cambridge University Press.

—— (1996b), 'Introduction', Irwin, A. and Wynne, B. (eds) *Misunderstanding Science? The public reconstruction of science and technology*, Cambridge: Cambridge University Press.

Jasanoff, S. (1990) *The Fifth Branch: science advisers and policymakers*, Cambridge, Mass.: Harvard University Press.

—— (ed.) (1994) *Learning from Disaster: risk management after Bhopal*, Philadelphia: University of Pennsylvania Press.

—— (1995) *Science at the Bar: law, science, and technology in America*, Cambridge, Mass.: Harvard University Press.

—— (1996), 'The dilemmas of environmental democracy', *Issues in Science and Technology*. Online. Available: http://www.issues.org/13.1/jasano.htm (accessed 14 May 2006).

—— (2003a) 'Breaking the waves in science studies', *Social Studies of Science*, 33: 389–400.

—— (2003b) 'Technologies of humility: citizen participation in governing science', *Minerva*, 41: 223–44.

—— (2004a) 'The idiom of co-production', in Jasanoff, S. (ed.) *States of Knowledge: the co-production of science and social order*, London: Routledge, 1–12.

—— (2004b) 'What inquiring minds should want to know' (Review of *Science, Truth, and Democracy* by P. Kitcher), *Studies in History and Philosophy of Science*, 35: 149–57.

—— (2005) *Designs on Nature: science and democracy in Europe and the United States*, Princeton, NJ and Oxford: Princeton University Press.

—— (2006) 'Technology as a site and object of politics', in R.E. Goodin (ed.) *The Oxford Handbook of Work of Contextual Political Analysis*, Oxford and New York: Oxford University Press.

Kahan, D.M., Slovic, P., Braman, D. and Gastil, J. (2006) 'Fear of democracy: a cultural evaluation of Sunstein on risk', *Harvard Law Review*, 119: 1071–9.

Kitcher, P. (2001) *Science, Truth, and Democracy*, Oxford: Oxford University Press.

Kymlicka, W. (2002) *Contemporary Political Philosophy: an introduction*, 2nd edn, Oxford and New York: Oxford University Press.

Lewontin, R. (2002) 'The politics of science', *New York Review of Books*, 49(8), 9 May: 28–31.

Martin, E. (1989) *The Woman in the Body*, Milton Keynes: Open University Press.

Mouffe, C. (2000) *Deliberative Democracy or Agonistic Pluralism*, Vienna: Institut für Höhere Studien, Reihe Politikwissenschaft 72.

Rawls, J. (1971) *A Theory of Justice*, Cambridge, Mass.: Harvard University Press.

—— (1993) *Political Liberalism*, New York: Columbia University Press.

Shrader-Frechette, K. (2003) Review of Sunstein (2002a), *Notre Dame Philosophical Reviews*. Online. Available: http://ndpr.nd.edu/review.cfm?id = 1252.

Slovic, P. (2000) *The Perception of Risk*, London: Earthscan Publications.

Stelfox, H.T., Chua G., O'Rourke, K. and Detsky, A.S. (1998) 'Conflict of interest in the debate over calcium-channel antagonists', *New England Journal of Medicine*, 338: 101–6.

Sunstein, C.R. (1996) *Legal Reasoning and Political Conflict*, Oxford and New York: Oxford University Press.

—— (2002a) *Risk and Reason: safety, law, and the environment*, Cambridge: Cambridge University Press.

—— (2002b) *The Cost–Benefit State: the future of regulatory protection*, Chicago: ABA Publishing.

—— (2005) *Laws of Fear: beyond the precautionary principle*, Cambridge: Cambridge University Press.

—— (2006) *Misfearing: a reply*, The Law School, University of Chicago: John M. Olin Law & Economics Working Paper No. 274 (2nd series).

Turner, S.P. (2003) *Liberal Democracy 3.0*, London: Sage.

Tversky, A. and Kahneman, D. (1982) 'Judgment under uncertainty: Heuristics and biases', in D. Kahneman, P. Slovic and A. Tversky, *Judgment Under Uncertainty: heuristics and biases*, Cambridge: Cambridge University Press.

Wilsdon, J., Wynne, B. and Stilgoe, J. (2005) *The Public Value of Science: or how to ensure that science really matters*, London: Demos.

Wynne, B. (1982) *Rationality and Ritual: the Windscale Inquiry and nuclear decisions in Britain*, Chalfont St. Giles: The British Society for the History of Science.

—— (1989) 'Sheep farming after Chernobyl: a case study in communicating scientific information', *Environment Magazine*, 31(2): 10–15, 33–9.

—— (1995) 'Public understanding of science', in S. Jasanoff, G.E. Markle, J.C. Petersen and T. Pinch (eds) *Handbook of Science and Technology Studies*, London: Sage.

—— (1996a) 'May the sheep safely graze? A reflexive view of the expert–lay knowledge divide', in S. Lash, B. Szerszynski and B. Wynne (eds) *Risk, Environment & Modernity*, London: Sage.

—— (1996b) 'Misunderstood misunderstandings: social identities and public uptake of science', in A. Irwin and B. Wynne (eds) *Misunderstanding Science? The public reconstruction of science and technology*, Cambridge: Cambridge University Press.

—— (2003) 'Seasick on the third wave? Subverting the hegemony of propositionalism', *Social Studies of Science*, 33: 401–18.

—— (2005) 'Risk as globalizing "democratic" discourse? Framing subjects and citizens', in M. Leach, I. Scoones and B. Wynne (eds) *Science and Citizens: globalization and the challenge of engagement*, London and New York: Zone Books.

9

MORAL HEURISTICS AND RISK

Cass R. Sunstein

Introduction

Pioneering the modern literature on heuristics in cognition, Amos Tversky and Daniel Kahneman contended that 'people rely on a limited number of heuristic principles which reduce the complex tasks of assessing probabilities and pre-dicting values to simpler judgmental operations' (Tversky and Kahneman 1974: 1124). Intense controversy has developed over the virtues and vices of the heuristics, most of them 'fast and frugal', that play a role in many areas (Gigerenzer and Todd 1999; Gilovich *et al.* 2002). But the relevant literature has only started to investigate the possibility that in the moral and political domain, people also rely on simple rules of thumb that often work well but that sometimes misfire (Baron 1994). In fact the central point seems obvious. Much of everyday morality consists of simple, highly intuitive rules that generally make sense but that fail in certain cases. It is wrong to lie or steal, but if a lie or a theft would save a human life, lying or stealing is probably obligatory. Not all promises should be kept.

One of my major goals in this essay is to identify a set of heuristics that now influences not only factual but also moral judgments in the domain of risk, and to try to make plausible the claim that some widely held practices and beliefs are a product of those heuristics. Often risk-related heuristics represent gen-eralizations from a range of problems for which they are indeed well-suited (Baron 1994), and hence most of the time, such heuristics work well. The problem comes when the generalizations are wrenched out of context and treated as freestanding or universal principles, applicable to situations in which their justifications no longer operate. Because the generalizations are treated as freestanding or universal, their application seems obvious, and those who reject them appear morally obtuse, possibly even monstrous. I want to urge that the appearance is misleading and even productive of moral mistakes. There is nothing obtuse, or monstrous, about refusing to apply a generalization in con-texts in which its rationale is absent.

To the extent that Kahneman and Tversky were dealing with probability judgments, they could demonstrate that the heuristics sometimes lead to errors.

Unfortunately, that cannot easily be demonstrated here. In the moral and political domains, it is hard to come up with unambiguous cases where the error is both highly intuitive and on reflection uncontroversial – where people can ultimately be embarrassed about their own intuitions. Nonetheless, I hope to show that whatever one's moral commitments, moral heuristics exist and indeed are omnipresent, adversely affecting both individual and social reactions to risks.

Ordinary heuristics, probability, and an insistent homunculus

The classic work on heuristics and biases deals not with moral questions but with issues of fact, usually in the domain of probability judgments. In answering hard factual questions, those who lack accurate information use simple rules of thumb. How many words, in four pages of a novel, will have 'ing' as the last three letters? How many words, in the same four pages, will have 'n' as the second-to-last letter? Most people will give a higher number in response to the first question than in response to the second (Tversky and Kahneman 1984) – even though a moment's reflection shows that this is a mistake. People err because they use an identifiable heuristic – the availability heuristic – to answer difficult risk-related questions. When people use this heuristic, they answer a question of probability by asking whether examples come readily to mind. How likely is a flood, an airplane crash, a traffic jam, a terrorist attack, or a disaster at a nuclear power plant? Lacking statistical knowledge, people try to think of illustrations. For people without statistical knowledge, it is far from irrational to use the availability heuristic; the problem is that this heuristic can lead to serious errors of fact, in the form of excessive fear of small risks and neglect of large ones.

Or consider the representativeness heuristic, in accordance with which judgments of probability are influenced by assessments of resemblance (the extent to which A 'looks like' B). The representativeness heuristic is famously exemplified by people's answers to questions about the likely career of a hypothetical woman named Linda, described as follows: 'Linda is 31 years old, single, outspoken, and very bright. She majored in philosophy. As a student, she was deeply concerned with issues of discrimination and social justice and also participated in antinuclear demonstrations' (Kahneman and Frederick 2002). People were asked to rank, in order of probability, eight possible futures for Linda. Six of these were fillers (such as psychiatric social worker, elementary school teacher); the two crucial ones were 'bank teller' and 'bank teller and active in the feminist movement'.

More people said that Linda was less likely to be a bank teller than to be a bank teller and active in the feminist movement. This is an obvious mistake, a conjunction error, in which characteristics A and B are thought to be more likely than characteristic A alone. The error stems from the representativeness heuristic: Linda's description seems to match 'bank teller and active in the feminist movement' far better than 'bank teller'. In an illuminating reflection on the example, Stephen Jay Gould observes that 'I know [the right answer], yet a little homunculus in my head continues to jump up and down, shouting at me – "but she can't just be a bank teller; read the description"' (Gould 1991: 469). Because Gould's homunculus is especially inclined to squawk in the moral domain, I shall return to him.

The principal heuristics should be seen in light of dual-process theories of cognition (Kahneman and Frederick 2002). Those theories distinguish between two families of cognitive operations, sometimes labeled System I and System II. System I is intuitive; it is rapid, automatic, and effortless (and it features Gould's homunculus). System II, by contrast, is reflective; it is slower, self-aware, calculative, and deductive. System I proposes quick answers to problems of judgment and System II operates as a monitor, confirming or overriding those judgments. Consider, for example, someone who is flying from New York to London in the month after an airplane crash. This person might make a rapid, barely conscious judgment, rooted in System I, that the flight is quite risky; but there might well be a System II override, bringing a more realistic assessment to bear. System I often has an affective component, but it need not; for example, a probability judgment might be made quite rapidly and without much affect at all.

There is growing evidence that people often make automatic, largely unreflective moral judgments, for which they are sometimes unable to give good reasons (see Haidt 2001; Greene and Haidt 2002). System I is operative here as well, and it may or may not be subject to System II override. Consider the incest taboo. People have moral revulsion against incest even in circumstances in which the grounds for that taboo seem to be absent; they are subject to 'moral dumbfounding' (Haidt et al. 2004), that is, an inability to give an account for a firmly held intuition. It is plausible, at least, to think that System I is driving their judgments, without System II correction. The same is true in legal and political contexts relating to risk as well.

Heuristics and morality

To show that heuristics operate in the moral domain, we have to specify some benchmark by which we can measure moral truth. On these questions I want to avoid any especially controversial claims. Whatever one's view of the foundations of moral and political judgments, I suggest that moral heuristics are likely to be at work in practice.

Many utilitarians, including John Stuart Mill and Henry Sidgwick, argue that ordinary morality is based on simple rules of thumb that generally promote utility but that sometimes misfire (Mill 1971: 28–9; Sidgwick 1981: 199–216). For example, Mill emphasizes that human beings 'have been learning by experience the tendencies of experience', so that the 'corollaries from the principle of utility' are being progressively captured by ordinary morality (Mill 1971: 29). Is ordinary morality a series of heuristics for what really matters, which is utility?

These large debates are not easy to resolve, simply because utilitarians and deontologists are most unlikely to be convinced by the suggestion that their defining commitments are mere heuristics. Here there is a large difference between moral heuristics and the heuristics uncovered in the relevant psychological work, where the facts or simple logic provides a good test whether people have erred. If people tend to think that more words, in a given space, end with the letters 'ing' than have 'n' in the next-to-last position, something has clearly gone wrong. If people think that some person Linda is more likely to be 'a bank teller who is active in the feminist movement' than a 'bank teller', there is an evident problem. In the moral domain, factual blunders and simple logic do not provide such a simple test.

My goal here is therefore not to say anything controversial about the correct general theory with respect to risks, but more cautiously that in many particular cases, moral heuristics are at work – and that this point can be accepted by people with diverse general theories, or with grave uncertainty about which general theory is correct. In the cases catalogued below, I contend that it is possible to conclude that a moral heuristic is at work without accepting any especially controversial normative claims. In several of the examples, that claim can be accepted without accepting any contestable normative theory at all. Other examples will require acceptance of what I shall call 'weak consequentialism', in accordance with which the social consequences of the legal system are relevant, other things being equal, to what law ought to be doing.

Of course some deontologists will reject any form of consequentialism altogether. But weak consequentialism seems to me sufficiently nonsectarian, and attractive to sufficiently diverse people, to make plausible the idea that in the cases at hand, moral heuristics are playing a significant role. And for those who reject weak consequentialism, it might nonetheless be productive to ask whether, from their own point of view, certain moral judgments about risks are reflective of heuristics that sometimes produce serious errors.

The Asian disease problem and moral framing

In a finding closely related to their work on heuristics, Kahneman and Tversky themselves find 'moral framing' in the context of what has become known as 'the Asian disease problem' (Kahneman and Tversky 1974). Framing effects do not involve heuristics, but because they raise obvious questions about the rationality of moral intuitions, they provide a valuable backdrop. Here is the first component of the problem:

> Imagine that the USA is preparing for the outbreak of an unusual Asian disease, which is expected to kill 600 people. Two alternative programs to

combat the disease have been proposed. Assume that the exact scientific estimates of the consequences are as follows:

If Program A is adopted, 200 people will be saved.

If Program B is adopted, there is a one-third probability that 600 people will be saved and a two-thirds probability that no people will be saved.

Which of the two programs would you favor?

Most people choose Program A. But now consider the second component of the problem, in which the same situation is given but followed by this description of the alternative programs:

If Program C is adopted, 400 people will die.

If Program D is adopted, there is a one-third probability that nobody will die and a two-thirds probability that 600 people will die.

Most people choose Problem D. But a moment's reflection should be sufficient to show that Program A and Program C are identical, and so too are Program B and Program D. These are merely different descriptions of the same programs. The purely semantic shift in framing is sufficient to produce different outcomes. Apparently people's moral judgments about appropriate programs depend on whether the results are described in terms of 'lives saved' or instead 'lives lost'. What accounts for the difference? The most sensible answer begins with the fact that human beings are pervasively averse to losses (hence the robust cognitive finding of loss aversion) (Thaler 1991). With respect to either self-interested gambles or fundamental moral judgments, loss aversion plays a large role in people's decisions. But what counts as a gain or a loss depends on the baseline from which measurements are made. Purely semantic reframing can alter the baseline and hence alter moral intuitions (for many examples involving fairness, see Kahneman *et al.* 1986).

Moral framing has been demonstrated in the important context of obligations to future generations (Frederick 2003), a much-disputed question of morality, politics, and law. To say the least, the appropriate discount rate for those yet to be born is not a question that most people have pondered, and hence their judgments are highly susceptible to different frames. From a series of surveys, Maureen Cropper *et al.* (1994) suggest that people are indifferent between saving one life today and saving 45 lives in 100 years. They make this suggestion on the basis of questions asking people whether they would choose a program that saves '100 lives now' or a program that saves a substantially larger number '100 years from now'. It is possible, however, that the responses depend on uncertainty about whether people in the future will otherwise die (perhaps technological improvements will save them?); and other ways of framing the same problem yield radically different results (Frederick 2003). For example, most people consider 'equally bad' a single death from pollution next year and a single death from pollution in 100 years. This finding implies no preference for members of the current generation. The simplest conclusion is that people's moral judgments about obligations to future generations are very much a product of framing effects.

Of course it is possible to question whether people actually err when they make different judgments in response to logically identical descriptions of risk-related problems. Perhaps the manipulation from one logical form to another equivalent one serves to alter the subject's understanding of the substance of the problem, in a way that does introduce ethical differences. Certainly this is possible if the manipulation trades on various assumptions about the pragmatics of communication; we might distinguish here between truth-value and speech-act. If a doctor says that five years after a certain operation, '90 per cent of patients are alive', the speech-act is different from if the doctor had said that after a certain operation, '10 per cent of patients have died' – even though the truth-value remains the same. While strongly suspecting that these explanations are not adequate to account for framing effects (Frederick 2003), I mean not to reject them, but only to suggest the susceptibility of moral intuitions to frames.

As a further example, consider the question whether government should consider not only the number of 'lives' but also the number of 'life years' saved by regulatory interventions. If the government focuses on life years, a program that saves children would be worth far more attention that a similar program that saves senior citizens. Is this immoral? People's moral intuitions depend on how the question is framed (Sunstein 2004). People will predictably reject an approach that would count every old person as worth 'significantly less' than what every young person is worth. But if people are asked whether they would favor a policy that saves 105 old people or 100 young people, many will favor the latter, in a way that suggests a willingness to pay considerable attention to the number of life years at stake.

At least for unfamiliar questions of morality, politics and law, people's intuitions are very much affected by framing. In the domain of risk, it is effective to frame certain consequences as 'losses' from a status quo; when so framed, moral concern becomes significantly elevated. It is for this reason that political actors often describe one or another proposal as 'turning back the clock' on some social advance. The problem is that for many social changes, the framing does not reflect social reality, but is simply a verbal manipulation.

Let us now turn to examples that are more controversial.

Morality and risk regulation

Cost–benefit analysis

An automobile company is deciding whether to take certain safety precautions for its cars. In deciding whether to do so, it conducts a cost–benefit analysis, in which it concludes that certain precautions are not justified – because, say, they would cost $100 million and save only four lives, and because the company has a 'ceiling' of $10 million per life saved (a ceiling that is, by the way, significantly higher than the amount the United States Environmental Protection Agency uses for a statistical life). How will ordinary people react to this decision? The answer is that they will not react favorably (Viscusi 2000: 547, 558). In fact they tend to punish companies that base their decisions on cost–benefit analysis, even if a high valuation is placed on human life. By contrast, they impose less severe punishment on companies that are willing to impose a 'risk' on people but that do not produce a formal risk analysis that measures lives lost and dollars, and trades one against another (Tetlock 2000; Viscusi 2000). The oddity here is that under tort law, it is unclear that a company should be liable at all if it has acted on the basis of a competent cost–benefit analysis; such an analysis might even insulate a company from a claim of negligence. What underlies people's moral judgments, which are replicated in actual jury decisions (Viscusi 2000)?

It is possible that when people disapprove of trading money for lives, they are generalizing from a set of moral principles that are generally sound, and even useful, but that work poorly in some cases. Consider the following moral principle: *Do not knowingly cause a human death*. In ordinary life, you should not engage in conduct with the knowledge that several people will die as a result. If you are playing a sport or working on your yard, you ought not to continue if you believe that your actions will kill others. Invoking that idea, people disapprove of companies that fail to improve safety when they are fully aware that deaths will result. By contrast, people do not disapprove of those who fail to improve safety while believing that there is a 'risk', but appear not to know, for certain, that deaths will ensue. When people object to risky action taken after cost–benefit analysis, it seems to be partly because that very analysis puts the number of expected deaths squarely 'on-screen' (Tetlock 2000).

Companies that fail to do such analysis, but that are aware that a 'risk' exists, do not make clear, to themselves or to anyone else, that they caused deaths with full knowledge that this was what they were going to do. People disapprove, above all, of companies that cause death knowingly. There may be a kind of 'cold-heart heuristic' here: those who know that they will cause a death, and do so anyway, are regarded as cold-hearted monsters.[1] On this view, critics of cost–benefit analysis should be seen as appealing to System I and as speaking directly to the homunculus: 'Is a corporation or public agency that endangers us to be pardoned for its sins once it has spent $6.1

million per statistical life on risk reduction?' (Ackerman and Heinzerling 2004).

Note that it is easy to reframe a probability as a certainty and vice-versa; if I am correct, the reframing is likely to have large effects. Consider two cases:

(a) Company A knows that its product will kill ten people. It markets the product to its ten million customers with that knowledge. The cost of eliminating the risk would have been $100 million.
(b) Company B knows that its product creates a one in one million risk of death. Its product is used by ten million people. The cost of eliminating the risk would have been $100 million.

I have not collected data, but I am willing to predict that Company A would be punished more severely than Company B, even though there is no difference between the two.

I suggest, then, that a moral heuristic is at work, one that imposes moral condemnation on those who knowingly engage in acts that will result in human deaths. And of course this heuristic does a great deal of good. The problem is that it is not always unacceptable to cause death knowingly, at least if the deaths are relatively few and an unintended byproduct of generally desirable activity. When government allows new highways to be built, it knows that people will die on those highways; when government allows new coal-fired power plants to be built, it knows that some people will die from the resulting pollution; when companies produce tobacco products, and when government does not ban those products, it knows that hundreds of thousands of people will die; and the same is true for alcohol. Of course it would make sense, in all of these domains, to take extra steps to reduce risks. But that proposition does not support the implausible claim that we should disapprove, from the moral point of view, of every action taken when deaths are foreseeable.

I believe that it is impossible to vindicate, in principle, the widespread social antipathy to cost–benefit balancing.[2] But here too, 'a little homunculus in my head continues to jump up and down, shouting at me' that corporate cost–benefit analysis, trading dollars for a known number of deaths, is morally unacceptable. The voice of the homunculus, I am suggesting, is not reflective, but is instead a product of System I and a crude but quite tenacious moral heuristic.

Betrayals and betrayal risk

To say the least, people do not like to be betrayed. A betrayal of trust is likely to produce a great deal of outrage. If a babysitter neglects a child or if a security guard steals from his employer, people will be angrier than if the identical acts are performed by someone in whom trust has not been reposed. So far, perhaps, so good: when trust is betrayed, the damage is worse than when an otherwise identical act was committed by someone who was not a beneficiary of trust. And it should not be surprising that people will favor greater punishment for betrayals than for otherwise identical crimes (Koehler and Gershoff 2003). Perhaps the disparity can be justified on the ground that the betrayal of trust is an independent harm, one that warrants greater deterrence and retribution – a point that draws strength from the fact that trust, once lost, is not easily regained. A family robbed by its babysitter might well be more seriously injured than a family robbed by a thief. The loss of money is compounded and possibly dwarfed by the violation of a trusting relationship. The consequence of the violation might also be more serious. Will the family ever feel entirely comfortable with babysitters? It is bad to have an unfaithful spouse, but it is even worse if the infidelity occurred with your best friend, because that kind of infidelity makes it harder to have trusting relationships with friends in the future.

In this light it is possible to understand why betrayals produce special moral opprobrium and (where the law has been violated) increased punishment. But consider a finding that is much harder to explain: *people are especially averse to risks of death that come from products (like airbags) designed to promote safety* (Koehler and Gershoff 2003). The aversion is so great that people have been found to prefer a higher chance of dying as the result of accidents from a crash to a significantly lower chance of dying in a crash as the result of a malfunctioning airbag. The relevant study involved two principal conditions. In the first, people were asked to choose between two equally priced cars, Car A and Car B. According to crash tests, there was a 2 per cent chance that drivers of Car A, with Air Bag A, would die in serious accidents as a result of the impact of the crash. With Car B and Air Bag B, there was a 1 per cent chance of death, but also an additional chance of one in 10,000 (0.01 per cent) of death as a result of deployment of the air bag. Similar studies have involved vaccines and smoke alarms.

The result was that most participants (over two-thirds) chose the higher-risk safety option when the less risky one carried a 'betrayal risk'. A control condition demonstrated that people were not confused about the numbers: when asked to choose between a 2 per cent risk and a 1.01 per cent risk, people selected the 1.01 per cent risk so long as betrayal was not involved. In other words, people's aversion to betrayals is so great that they will increase their own risks rather than subject themselves to a (small) hazard that comes from a device that is supposed to increase safety. 'Apparently, people are willing to incur greater risks of the very harm they seek protection from to avoid the mere possibility of betrayal' (Koehler and Gershoff 2003: 244). Remarkably, 'betrayal risks appear to be so psychologically intolerable that people are willing to double their risk of death from automobile crashes, fires, and diseases to avoid incurring a small possibility of death by safety device betrayal'.

What explains this seemingly bizarre and self-destructive preference? I suggest that a heuristic is at work: *punish, and do not reward, betrayals of trust*. The heuristic generally works well. But it misfires in some cases, as when those who deploy it end up increasing the risks they themselves face. An air bag is not a security guard or a babysitter, endangering those whom they had been hired to protect. It is a product, to be chosen if and only if it decreases aggregate risks. If an air bag makes people safer on balance, it should be used, even if in a tiny percentage of cases it will create a risk that would not otherwise exist. Of course it is true that some kinds of deaths are reasonably seen as worse than others. It is not absurd to prefer one kind of death to another. But betrayal aversion is not adequately explained in these terms; the experimental work suggests that people are generalizing from a heuristic.

In a sense, the special antipathy to betrayal risks might be seen to involve not a moral heuristic but a taste. In choosing products, people are not making pure moral judgments; they are choosing what they like best, and it just turns out that a moral judgment, involving antipathy to betrayals, is part of what they like best. It would be useful to design a purer test of moral judgments, one that would ask people not about their own safety but about that of others – for example, whether people are averse to betrayal risks when they are purchasing safety devices for their friends or family members. There is every reason to expect that it would produce substantially identical results to those in the experiments just described. Closely related experiments support that expectation (Ritov and Baron 2002: 168). In deciding whether to vaccinate their children from risks of serious diseases, people show a form of 'omission bias'. Many people are more sensitive to the risk of the vaccination than to the risk from diseases – so much so that they will expose their children to a greater risk from 'nature' than from the vaccine. (There is a clear connection between omission bias and trust in nature and antipathy to 'playing God', as discussed below.) The omission bias, I suggest, is closely related to people's special antipathy to betrayals. It leads to moral errors, in the form of vaccination judgments, and undoubtedly others, by which some parents increase the fatality risks faced by their own children.

Emissions trading

Through what mechanisms should regulators attempt to reduce social risks? In the last decades, those involved in enacting and implementing environmental law have experimented with systems of 'emissions trading'. In those systems, polluters are typically given a licence to pollute a certain amount, and the licences can be traded on the market. The advantage of emissions trading systems is that if they work well, they will ensure emissions reductions at the lowest possible cost.

Is emissions trading immoral? Is this a morally unacceptable means of reducing the risks associated with pollution? Many people believe so. Political theorist Michael Sandel, for example, urges that trading systems 'undermine the ethic we should be trying to foster on the environment' (Sandel 1997; see also Kelman 1981). Sandel contends:

[T]urning pollution into a commodity to be bought and sold removes the moral stigma that is properly associated with it. If a company or a country is fined for spewing excessive pollutants into the air, the community conveys its judgment that the polluter has done something wrong. A fee, on the other hand, makes pollution just another cost of doing business, like wages, benefits and rent.

(Sandel 1997)

In the same vein, Sandel objects to proposals to open carpool lanes to drivers without passengers who are willing to pay a fee. Here, as in the environmental context, it seems unacceptable to permit people to do something that is morally wrong so long as they are willing to pay for the privilege.

I suggest that like other critics of emissions trading programs, Sandel is using a moral heuristic; in fact he has been fooled by his homunculus. The heuristic is this: *people should not be permitted to engage in moral wrongdoing for a fee*. You are not allowed to assault someone so long as you are willing to pay for the right to do so; there are no tradable licences for rape, theft or battery. The reason is that the appropriate level of these forms of wrongdoing is zero (putting to one side the fact that enforcement resources are limited; if they were unlimited, we would want to eliminate, not merely to reduce, these forms of illegality). But pollution is an altogether different matter. At least some level of pollution is a byproduct of desirable social activities and products, including automobiles and power plants. Of course certain acts of pollution, including those that violate the law or are unconnected with desirable activities, are morally wrong; but the same cannot be said of pollution as such. When Sandel objects to emissions trading, he is treating pollution as equivalent to a crime in a way that overgeneralizes a moral intuition that makes sense in other contexts. There is no moral problem with emissions trading as such. The insistent objection to emissions trading systems stems from a moral heuristic.

Unfortunately, that objection has appeared compelling to many people, so much as to delay and to reduce the use of a pollution-reduction tool that is, in many contexts, the best available. Here, then, is a case in which a moral heuristic has led to political blunders, in the form of policies that impose high costs for no real gain.

The precautionary principle and loss aversion

In many nations, risk regulation is undertaken with close reference to the precautionary principle (Sunstein 2005). The precautionary principle has no canonical formulation, but in its strongest and most distinctive forms, it is designed to insert a 'margin of safety' into all decision-making, and to impose a burden of proof on proponents of activities or processes to establish that they are 'safe'. Thus understood, the precautionary principle is taken to have important consequences. For example, it is thought to raise serious questions about DDT, genetically modified organisms, nuclear power, electromagnetic fields, and the emission of greenhouse gases.

On reflection, however, it should be clear that in its strong forms, the precautionary principle is incoherent: it condemns the very measures that it requires. The reason is that risk regulation often introduces risks of its own. Sometimes it does so because it eliminates the risk-reduction benefits associated with the activity in question. Regulation of DDT, for example, can increase the risk of malaria – and thus violates the precautionary principle. In other contexts, precautionary steps give rise to substitute risks. For example, controls on nuclear power increase the likelihood that societies will depend on fossil fuels, which create air pollution and emit greenhouse gases. In any event, precautionary steps sometimes create risks merely by virtue of their expense. By its very nature, costly regulation threatens to increase unemployment and poverty, and both of these increase risks of mortality. If we are truly serious about the precautionary principle, we will condemn measures that increase such risks by virtue of their expense – and hence condemn the very measures that the precautionary principle requires. A vivid example involves the risks associated with pre-emptive war. President George W. Bush justified the war in Iraq on precautionary grounds, as a way of eliminating the danger from Saddam Hussein. The problem is that the war offered risks of its own. Whether or not the war was ultimately justified, no precautionary principle would suffice to support it.

Why, then, is the principle widely thought to give guidance? I suggest that two mechanisms are at work. The first is the availability heuristic. Sometimes a certain risk, said to call for precautions, is cognitively available, whereas other risks, including those associated with regulation itself, are not. In many cases where the precautionary principle seems to offer guidance, some of the relevant risks are available while others are barely visible. And if one nation is concerned with the risk of sunbathing and another is not, availability is likely to provide a large part of the reason. The second mechanism involves loss aversion. As I have noted, human beings are typically averse to losses, which they dislike more than they like corresponding gains (Sunstein 2005). When the precautionary principle seems coherent, it is often because the status quo is taken as the baseline for its operation; losses 'code' as especially troublesome, whereas foregone opportunities do not. This point helps explain intense disapproval, in some quarters, of genetically modified organisms and food. The potentially large social benefits of genetic modification, perhaps saving numerous lives, are not much on the public view screen.

I do not mean to deny the possibility that the precautionary principle can be reconstructed in coherent terms, nor do I contend that in all imaginable forms, the principle becomes operational only because of the availability heuristic and loss aversion. But most of the time, a senseless idea – that it is possible to be precautionary *in general* – appears sensible only because people operate with selective blinders, focusing on some but not all of the universe of relevant risks.

There is a much broader point in the background. Precautionary thinking often involves a form of the act–omission distinction, in a way that seems to reflect a moral heuristic, and a highly destructive one. Both regulators and ordinary people often worry that they will be blamed for licensing a potentially dangerous process or activity (such as a drug) that might cause deaths, while showing much less concern about the failure to prevent deaths through their refusal to license a process or activity that is potentially beneficial. At times, the result has been a precautionary stance that imposes undue barriers to life-saving processes or activities.

To be sure, the act–omission distinction might be plausibly defended on consequentialist or deontological grounds, at least in many contexts in ordinary life. But for risk regulators, the distinction seems to operate as a kind of heuristic, one that misfires in many cases. I believe that in the general context of risk reduction, intense concern about potentially harmful acts and relative indifference to the effects of relatively harmful omissions is best seen as the squawking of an internal homunculus on the part of regulators and their constituents – very much like Gould's in the context of the representativeness heuristic.

Rules and blunders

I have argued here that moral judgments about risks, no less than probability judgments, are often a product of heuristics, and that they often misfire. To the extent that moral heuristics operate as rules, they might be defended in the way that all rules are – as better than the alternatives even if productive of error in imaginable cases. Moral heuristics might show a kind of 'ecological rationality', working well in most real-world contexts (Gigerenzer 2000); recall the possibility that human beings live by simple heuristics that make us good. My suggestion is not that the moral heuristics, in their most rigid forms, are socially worse than the reasonable alternatives. It is hard to resolve that question in the abstract. I am claiming only that such heuristics lead to real errors and significant confusion in thinking about risk. Regulators, after all, are not in the position of ordinary people, with limited time and in need of a simple rule of thumb. They typically have significant resources, including significant time, and they can do far better than to rely on heuristics.

If it is harder to demonstrate that heuristics are at work in the domain of morality than in the domain of facts, this is largely because we are able to agree, in the relevant cases, about what constitutes factual error, and often less able to agree about what constitutes moral error. With respect to the largest disputes about what morality requires, it may be too contentious to argue that one side is operating under an heuristic, whereas another side has it basically right. But I hope that I have said enough to show that in particular cases, sensible rules of thumb lead to demonstrable errors not merely in probability judgments, but in moral assessments of risks as well.[3]

Notes

1 I am grateful to Jonathan Haidt for this suggestion.
2 I put to one side cases in which those who enjoy the benefits are wealthy and those who incur the costs are poor; in some situations, distributional considerations will justify a departure from what would otherwise be compelled by cost–benefit analysis.
3 I am grateful to Daniel Kahneman and Martha Nussbaum for valuable discussions. For helpful comments on a previous draft, I also thank Tim Lewens. A different version of this essay was published as 'Moral heuristics', *Behavioral and Brain Sciences*, 28: (2005); 531–46; this essay has been revised to focus more particularly on the issue of risk.

References

Ackerman, F. and Heinzerling, L. (2004) *Priceless: on knowing the price of everything and the value of nothing*, New York: The New Press.

Baron, J. (1993) 'Heuristics and biases in equity judgments: a utilitarian approach', in Mellers, B. and Baron, J. (eds) *Psychological Perspectives on Justice*, New York: Cambridge University Press.

Baron, J. (1994) 'Nonconsequentialist decisions', *Behavioral and Brain Sciences*, 17: 1–10.

Cropper, M.L., Aydede, S.K., and Portney, P.R. (1994) 'Preferences for life-saving programs: how the public discounts time and age', *Journal of Risk & Uncertainty*, 8: 243–65.

Frederick, S. (2003) 'Measuring intergenerational time preference: are future lives valued less?', *Journal of Risk and Uncertainty*, 26(1): 39–53.

Gigerenzer, G. (2000) *Adaptive Thinking: rationality in the real world*, New York: Oxford University Press.

Gigerenzer, G. and Todd, P. (1999) *Simple Heuristics that Make Us Smart*, New York: Oxford University Press.

Gilovich, T., Griffin, D., and Kahneman, D. (eds) (2002) *Heuristics and Biases: the psychology of intuitive judgment*, Cambridge: Cambridge University Press.

Gould, S.J. (1991) *Bully for Brontosaurus: reflections in natural history*, New York: W.W. Norton & Company.

Greene, J. and Haidt, J. (2002) 'How (and where) does moral judgment work?', *Trends in Cognitive Sciences*, 6: 517–23.

Haidt, J. (2001) 'The emotional dog and its rational tail: a social intuitionist approach to moral judgment', *Psychological Review*, 108(4): 814–34.

Haidt, J., Bjorklund, F., and Murphy, S. (2004) 'Moral dumbfounding: when intuition finds no reason', unpublished manuscript, University of Virginia.

Kahneman, D. and Frederick, S. (2002) 'Representativeness revisited: attribute substitution in intuitive judgment', in Gilovich, T., Griffin, D., and Kahneman, D. (eds) *Heuristics and Biases: the psychology of intuitive judgment*, Cambridge: Cambridge University Press.

Kahneman, D., Knetsch, J.L., and Thaler, R.H. (1986) 'Fairness as a constraint on profit-seeking: entitlements in the market', *American Economic Review*, 76: 728–41.

Kelman, S. (1981) *What Price Incentives? Economists and the environment*, Boston: Auburn House.

Koehler, J.J. and Gershoff, A.D. (2003) 'Betrayal aversion: when agents of protection become agents of harm', *Organizational Behavior and Human Decision Processes*, 90(2): 244–61.

Kuran, T. and Sunstein, C.R. (1999) 'Availability cascades and risk regulation', *Stanford Law Review*, 51: 683–768.

Mill, J.S. (1971) *Utilitarianism*, Indianapolis: Bobbs-Merrill Company.

Morrison, E.R. (1998) 'Comment: judicial review of discount rates used in regulatory cost–benefit analysis', *University of Chicago Law Review*, 65(4): 1333–370.

Ritov, I. and Baron, J. (2002) 'Reluctance to vaccinate: omission bias and ambiguity', in Sunstein, C.R. (ed.) *Behavioral Law and Economics*, New York: Cambridge University Press.

Sandel, M. (1997) 'It's immoral to buy the right to pollute', *New York Times*, 15 December: A23.

Sidgwick, H. (1981) *The Methods of Ethics*, Indianapolis: Hackett Publishing Company.

Slovic, P., Finuncane, M., Peters, E., and MacGregor, D.G. (2002) 'The affect heuristic', in Gilovich, T., Griffin, D., and Kahneman D. (eds) *Heuristics and Biases: the psychology of intuitive judgment*, Cambridge: Cambridge University Press.

Sunstein, C.R. (2004) 'Lives, life-years, and willingness to pay', *Columbia Law Review*, 104: 205–52.

Sunstein, C.R. (2005) *Laws of Fear: beyond the precautionary principle*, Cambridge: Cambridge University Press.

Tetlock, P. (2000) 'Coping with tradeoffs', in Lupia, A., Popkin, S. and McCubbins, M.D. (eds) *Elements of Reason: cognition, choice, and the bounds of rationality*, Cambridge: Cambridge University Press.

Thaler, R. (1991) *Quasi-Rational Economics*, New York: Russell Sage.

Tversky, A. and Kahneman, D. (1974) 'Judgment under uncertainty: heuristics and biases', *Science*, 185: 1124–131.

Viscusi, W.K. (2000) 'Corporate risk analysis: a reckless act?', *Stanford Law Review*, 52: 547–97.

10

RISK AND TERRORISM

Alan Ryan

Preamble

This essay is brief and artless. It is also slightly derivative from my own earlier work. Twenty years ago, I wrote an essay on terrorism, against the background of the troubles in Northern Ireland, but reaching back to the long tradition of revolutionary violence, which was what explained the essay's reference to Red and White terror (Ryan 1991). On this occasion, the background of recent terrorist attacks on the United States, Spain, and Britain is too obtrusive to be ignored; and the continued violence in Iraq, which may (or may not) have diminished by the time this volume appears in the bookstores, is also too obtrusive and too much to the purpose of this essay to be ignored. Many of the earlier essay's assumptions about the aims and methods of contemporary terrorism were based on the activities of the IRA and ETA, and have become irrelevant to present purposes; its view of how terrorism should be understood, however, is something on which I have not changed my mind. So, the first part of this essay contains some reflections on risk, and the second the direct and particular relevance of those reflections to the topic of terrorism.

Risk and the rational assessment of risk

The object of this part of the essay is to cast doubt on the so-called 'precautionary principle', and to make some sceptical observations about the difficulty that human beings have in making rational assessments of risk, both because of our difficulties with probabilistic reasoning and because of the difficulty of knowing how much we like (or dislike) an uncertain outcome. The starting point of any discussion of risk has to be the standard model on which all of Rational Choice Theory is based: the present value of an uncertain outcome to a rational agent is $p(v)$, which is to say the positive or negative utility that we attach to an outcome multiplied by the probability of its occurrence. The model is that of a bet on a desired outcome or insurance against an undesired outcome. 'Risk' strictly concerns only the numerical value of p, that is the probability of the event, whatever it is; 'risk assessment', however, invokes both, because the value of taking precautions against a risk plainly involves the potential cost of the undesired event and the cost of preventive measures. So, a business's risk assessment exercise distinguishes between how likely an event is – p – and how damaging it will be to the business – v – and by doing so arrives at a prioritised list of dangers worth attending to. Talk of 'risk' always refers to the probability of an undesired outcome; jokes about our 'risking' a spell in office by standing in an election depends on the thought that electoral success is evidently what we hope for, but that it may bring with it some unthought-of of problems too; and good and bad outcomes are a matter of perspective: the bookies see the victory of the wrong horse as a risk, whereas the punters see it as a hope. The present valuation of an uncertain future outcome is thus $p(v)$, where v represents its (dis)utility, or money values assumed to reflect (dis)utility; a one in two chance of £100 is worth £50. All insurance contracts reflect this underlying calculation, as well as much else.

The so-called 'precautionary principle' will not feature in the discussion of the real risks posed by terrorism when we reach it. This is because I believe that there is no distinctive and coherent account to be given of what the precautionary principle amounts to, in which I largely agree with Sunstein (2005). It is incontestable that there are many situations in which some variation on 'better safe than sorry' is a good rule of thumb; the minor inconvenience of fastening one's seat-belt is a small price for the added protection for which one will be very grateful in the event of an accident. Again, many people think it is worth insuring against bad things happening while it is not worth while gambling on good things happening, because there is an asymmetry in most people's minds between the prospect of gain and the prospect of loss; the fact that there is no such asymmetry in the mind of an insurance company is another element in the possibility of insurance. That asymmetry might be thought to represent an intuitive attachment to a 'better safe than sorry' principle. We are less elated by finding ourselves £100 better off than we are miserable at losing £100.

The interpretation of that fact is not simple. Consider the most obvious way of rationalising our reactions. According to the principle of diminishing marginal utility, the value of £100 increases as our total assets diminish, so losing £100 is a greater deduction from present utility than a gain of £100 is an addition to it. That does not appear to account for our psychological reactions as an empirical matter. The graphical representation of diminishing marginal utility is a smoothly flattening curve, as successive increments of a good yield slowly diminishing satisfaction per unit of the good. On such a curve the subtraction of one unit of a good occasions a greater loss of utility than the addition of one unit would provide on the positive side; but the difference at any given point is small. Our aversion to loss is not of that nature. It is hard to say what its nature is, because we are tempted to tidy up our description of the subjective phenomenon by adjusting it to the demands of rational choice theory, or to the demands of a less stringent theory of how reasonably to evaluate a situation or a choice. A person who asks herself 'what do I really feel about this?' is more usually described as *making up* her mind rather than discovering a pre-existent entity; the difference between 'how do I feel?' and 'how would I feel if I were being rational?' is often very small. This affects belief as much as desire; 'what do I think the odds are?' and 'what are the odds *really?*' are not generally questions about two different facts.

Nonetheless, many of us find ourselves almost immovably averse to risking the loss of particular goods – especially intangibles and such near-intangibles as income – even though we know that *before* we acquired what we are now unwilling to lose, we did without it quite painlessly, and that the gamble we are asked to make is on its face a safe bet. Whether we are following some variation of a 'maximin' rule is, again, not easy to say. Because we are prioritising the avoidance of losses over the making of gains, that appears to be a plausible reading; we may not strictly be maximising our minimum payoff or minimising our maximum loss, but we are being more conservative than is strictly rational in rational choice terms. Someone may claim that his underlying strategy is to maximise his average utility over the long run, just as rational choice theory requires, but that so far as he is concerned many goods yield utility asymmetrically. In particular, their enjoyment yields dramatically less utility than their loss yields pain. The thought, then, must be that the graphical representation of the way in which goods are related to utility should be stepped rather than smooth, or even that the shape of the function relating the enjoyment of a good to the utility it delivers is a smoothly diminishing curve on the ascent and a near-precipice on the descent. For some goods, this is unsurprising; political and other sorts of liberty, for instance, may not be greatly valued before they are enjoyed, but once enjoyed their loss is intolerable (Mill 2006: 238–40). Intangibles such as the affection of other people are not dissimilar; the familiarity of an environment might be another. For goods of this sort a high degree of risk-aversion is rational enough; if the precautionary principle is confined to such cases, it makes good sense.

If the precautionary principle is only a reminder that many of us weigh losses disproportionately against gains, that this makes good sense for some goods, and that balancing downside risks against upside benefits should reflect that fact, the discussion of the previous paragraph captures its essence. Defenders of the precautionary principle resist that thought, because they wish to make it a principle of more general application; conversely, its critics point out that an attempt to eliminate *all* risk would leave us unable to make any choices at all (Sunstein 2005: 13–34). In practice, the precautionary principle is employed to resist technological innovations, especially farming technologies which may have an untoward impact on the environment; the requirement to adopt a precautionary principle has been written into the regulatory regime of the United Kingdom and the European Union in the context of introducing genetically modified crops (Ryan 1999). Notice, however, that in that context, it is a principle employed to constrain the behaviour of governments rather than individuals. One might say that whether individuals choose to be cautious in matters that concern nobody else is their business and nobody else's; if they forgo gains to their welfare they might easily have had, but do not mind, then that is up to them. Governments are not in that position; a government – in a modern, liberal-democratic society at least – is obliged to do its best for the general welfare, and one cannot say that if it chooses to forgo gains that the public might easily have had, or to impose costs on the public out of irrational caution, it is 'up to it'. It is worth moving on to two other issues: first to draw a distinction between risks we take on our own behalf and those we take on behalf of others; and second to mention the importance of *irreversibility* as an element in inducing caution about environmental impacts.

Individuals are more or less risk-averse about their own choices; many are much less affected by what I have been representing as a near-universal trait. It is importantly true, but ignored here, that cultural factors make a great difference to both cognitive and evaluative factors: cultural pressures make people more or less risk-averse, and make them more or less likely to anticipate good, bad, or indifferent outcomes (Kahan *et al.* 2006). Not only different individuals, but different cultures see the glass as half full or half empty. It is very important in everyday life, and also ignored here, that age makes a lot of difference; whether teenagers underestimate the probability of killing themselves in risky activities or care less about the prospect is anyone's guess; but it is hardly an accident that war is a young man's game. Many individuals of any age enjoy gambling even when they lose, and offset their losses with happy thoughts of what might have been. It is arguable that a modern consumer economy could not survive unless most of us overestimated both the likelihood and the amount of the pleasure that increased consumption will give us. In the individual case, variations in risk aversion do not matter, short of a genuine addiction to gambling, so long as the gains and losses accrue only to the individual. When we are responsible for other people's welfare, however, risk aversion becomes a duty rather than a psychological option. We might think someone *foolish* to drive at high speed round a racetrack; we would think him *wicked* if he did it – without a convincing excuse – on a busy main road. In the one case, he hazards his own neck; in the other he hazards everyone else's. The fact that it is not his own neck only that he hazards makes all the difference.

It is important to observe the shift of reasoning from the prudential to the moral at this point. There is a difference between seeing the precautionary principle as a dictate of prudence for individuals and as a moral constraint on government. The temptation is to say that the difference is that there are more lives at stake; but this is not the right point. If I drive dangerously, I may put no more necks at risk in the high street than on the race track; but in the latter case it is *my* neck I hazard, in the former it is *yours*. In a Grand Prix there are sixteen racing cars hurtling round the track; but the sixteen necks at risk belong to sixteen persons who have each of them volunteered to take that risk. The point is that *I have no right* to take unconsented-to risks with other people's necks; when risk aversion is *required*, it is required as a moral matter.

We have a duty not to put other people at risk and they have a right not to have unconsented-to risks imposed on them. The rule that tells us not to take risks with other people's lives presupposes that we may do so with our own, and that there is an asymmetry between self-regarding and other-regarding considerations.

The topic becomes interesting and difficult when governments calculate $p(v)$. Governments have to distribute unconsented-to risks among their population; they are uniquely charged to do just that. Thus, a road improvement scheme may reduce overall death and injury but in the process make some people who were previously safer than average less safe, while making other people who were previously less safe than average safer. A government that does this puts me at greater or lesser risk for the sake of reducing risk overall. Because states are not individuals, there is no distinction between what they may risk for themselves and what they may not risk for others; the question whether they ought to apply a precautionary principle in formulating public policy is, in general, the question whether they should weigh the danger of aggregate losses disproportionately against aggregate gains forgone. It is important in this context not to confuse the *aggregative* issue with the *distributive*. My claim is that when we think, as we very often do, that a state should *not* behave in a way that maximizes total utility – which maximizes aggregate $P(V)$ – it is almost never because we are attached to the precautionary principle, and almost always because we are invoking considerations of justice (Rawls 1971 is the *locus classicus* of the attempt to connect rational choice theory and justice). The idea that the only thing a state needs compute is whether the gains of those who prosper outweigh the losses of those who lose out ignores the justice of the distribution between winners and losers. *Who loses*, however, is a quite different question from that of weighing losses disproportionately against gains, even though an unwillingness to impose those losses on a particular group of people might lead us to forgo gains we could otherwise have. To jump ahead, even if we could make ourselves marginally safer from terrorism by engaging in 'racial profiling', many of us would refuse to do it because it would burden one section of the community in ways we think unjust. In less contentious areas, the same thought is at work. For instance, the cheapness of land in run-down inner cities makes derelict inner-city sites a good place to put incinerators and waste-disposal facilities; but to many of us it seems unfair that the poor, who already do badly enough by being poor, should do even worse by having these facilities parked next to them. Efficiency points in one direction, distributive justice in another. The – heroic – presumption here is that we can bracket out issues of distributive justice, and focus on collective rationality; assuming that considerations of justice have been met, ought we to forgo potential gains to overall welfare by adopting the precautionary principle? It seems to me that the answer is no.

The precautionary principle encourages us to fear dangers to which we can attach no probabilities, and whose disvalue is impossible to compute. This is especially the case where risks to the environment are at stake. One reason for the attractiveness of the precautionary principle where environmental issues are at stake is that an undesired outcome is for most people more undesirable if it is irreversible; if I lose £100 at the races, I can work harder and make it up. The dead loss is the extra hours of work. If I bet a family heirloom on some outcome and the person to whom I lose it will not restore it to me for love or money, the loss is irremediable. Sometimes damage to the environment cannot be remedied; but this is not always true. Just as some goods are such that there is an asymmetry between losses and gains, but many are not of this sort, so the preservation of an environment in its present condition is sometimes overwhelmingly more important than improving it, but very often it is not.

The way the precautionary principle is appealed to in environmental debates encourages us to estimate downside risks as carefully as we have already agreed that we must, and then encourages us to be more frightened than we have reason to be. This was obvious both when working on Ryan (1999) and in responses to it. GM crops provoked not only a host of excitable press reports but lobbying from scientifically well-informed people that encouraged the public to think that *something* really dreadful might occur – though what the damage would be and what the chances of its occurrence were, were never spelled out, and could not be. It is certainly true that many disasters have occurred against which we wish we had taken precautions, but which were unpredictable given the extent of scientific knowledge *ex ante*. Industrial processes of all sorts did untold damage before their effects were well understood. Outside the realm of industrial diseases, smoking is the most obvious example: almost nobody had an inkling of the connection with lung cancer until Richard Doll's painstaking demonstration of the link (Doll and Hill 1954). But, impressive though that example is, both in terms of the quality of the science and the quantity of illness we now know how to prevent, it tells one nothing beyond the commonsensical; we ought to take seriously both the risks we know about and the second-order risk that we have missed something important; we should take the second-order risk the more seriously, the more damage a mistake will do.

Further than that, we enter the territory of Donald Rumsfeld's 'unknown unknowns, the ones we don't know we don't know' (Rumsfeld 2002), which is to say the reminder that we do not know everything, and do not know which portions of what we do not know will turn out to be the ones that we devoutly wish that we had known. That is not an argument for remaining paralysed by uncertainty, nor does it do anything to support the glib observation that 'absence of evidence is not evidence of absence'. That is at best a half-truth; under conditions where our procedures for detecting problems are well based, the absence of evidence really is evidence of absence. If you have *really* gone through *all* your pockets, you can be sure your keys are not there.

I have said that it is important to detach the estimation of risk from the question of how inclined we are to run the risk thus estimated; that is to reiterate the distinction between 'how likely?' and 'how bad?' It is also important to notice that our view of 'how bad' may, as a psychological fact, not be independent of our view of 'how likely', and conversely. It is clear that calculating probabilities is often beyond us; but attaching a determinate value to v may also tax an agent's resources. We may like tomatoes, but only when we eat them with fried bread; if we are offered the chance of a tomato, but under conditions where we are unsure whether it will be accompanied by fried bread, we may be hard put to it to calculate $p(v)$. We are also beset by what Kahneman and Tversky referred to as 'framing problems' (Tversky and Kahneman 1981 is the classic paper). Rational choice theory requires us to ignore irrelevant alternatives; but human agents do not ignore irrelevant alternatives. A person proposing to cross a river on a plank bridge ought to concentrate on two questions: the disagreeable consequences of falling in and the likelihood of falling in. These are separate issues. As a matter of fact, most people react to a heightened sense of the disvalue of v by exaggerating the risk of the disagreeable outcome. They also attach a higher (negative) value to v when they are provoked to consider other unpleasant possibilities not presently before them.

There is a plausible conjecture about why we behave like this that may be a scientific fairy-tale, but which accounts very well for familiar cognitive weaknesses to which most of us are prone; indeed, its own (non-epistemic) attractions as an explanation exploit the weaknesses it explains. That is, it is attractive because it is a *striking* theory. Human beings are good observers of their surroundings, though under-equipped in each of the senses compared with other animals; our hearing is not especially acute, nor our ability to pick up scents, nor our eyesight. We have offsetting advantages; our vertical stance allows us to see a long way without having to climb a tree for the purpose; we have good stereoscopic vision and can estimate distances better than most creatures. And we are not the natural prey of more than a few animals. Our earlier selves needed to pick up the signs of – for instance – a sabre-tooth tiger lurking in the bushes, and to have quick 'fight or flight' reflexes; we did not need to be able to calculate odds. It was *salience* that mattered; and given that these are matters of life and death, the irreversibility of death being too obvious to need dwelling on, the capacity to seize on small signs of great danger is what evolution should have designed our risk assessment capacities around.

Consider our ancestors' objective situation. Once nature had equipped them with a tolerably good ability to discriminate between food and non-food, and an eye for obvious dangers, there was no scope for risk assessment in the modern sense. Modern technology did not exist. There was no medical science, and no way of considering the results of a long run of blind testing with samples of a sufficient size to yield reliable results. In the absence of written language, there was no way of transmitting information beyond the few neighbours to whom we might talk. Not until the historian Herodotus do we find anyone in the Western world seriously suggesting that we should scrutinise stories we have been told for their intrinsic plausibility. Nor does Herodotus's own practice live up to the highest modern standards; his need for rhetorical effect was often at odds with his doubts about the veracity of informants and with his own inclination towards scepticism.

What Herodotus produced was the history of political good and ill fortune, and behind the flux of events he discerned the malice of the gods (Herodotus 1954). Medicine, like political theory, resembled Herodotus's style of history. Exemplary stories of successful and unsuccessful cures were offered in the hope that we might imitate the successful and avoid the unsuccessful cases; until the seventeenth century even simple inductive logic was pretty well foreign to these accounts. If the 'sabre-tooth theory' of cognitive history is even half-way correct, it is unsurprising that we are prone to seize on striking events and striking cases of good and evil outcomes and to attach to them an evidential significance they might not possess according to the best canons of inductive logic (Sutherland 1994). Even if rustling bushes only very rarely indicated that a large cat might be hoping to have us for lunch, the precautionary principle was properly in place. Over-confidence would be fatal, and the downside of reacting to a false alarm was only an unnecessary sprint.

What impact does the fact that our brains are attuned to sabre-tooth tigers have on our capacity for estimating the probability of an event? The most plausible view is that it reinforces our readiness to ignore background dangers and to exaggerate the dangerousness of striking and sudden events. The concept of 'background' here is subjective; it is the cognitive cupboard to which issues are consigned that an ordinarily busy human agent regards herself as having no time and no need to attend to. The data are the stuff of everyday life. When there was a rail accident at Hatfield in October 2000 that killed four people and injured a further seventy, the railway system was half-paralysed for several months while track was inspected and – as it happened – it was discovered that there were no more broken rails of the kind that had caused the accident (Economist 2000). The effect of the collapse of railway timetables was to drive more people onto the roads, where nine people a day are killed, ten times that number seriously injured, and forty times that number slightly injured. On the railways, the annual death toll of passengers is less than the daily death toll of road users. It seems just about certain that the effect of taking steps to make the railways even safer than before was to kill more people.

One asks, therefore, what aspect of $p(v)$ it is that we should focus on in cases like this. Does the public that clamours for greater safety on the railway network believe that p is vastly higher than it really is? Or is v – the disutility of being involved in a railway accident – vastly higher than the v of being involved in a road accident? If trains are inherently safer than cars, why does an occasional railway accident frighten people so much more than the slow drip of death and injury on the road? Our fundamental question is not yet answered; do we over-estimate p, have curious views about v, or both? My guess is that it is both in the following sense. Our nervous ancestors, on the watch-out for the sabre-tooth tiger, were not very anxious about dying in violent conflict with one another; they killed each other in large numbers. They were also less anxious than we are about catching incurable diseases, though they caught and died of them much more often than we do. The obvious thought is that illness was one of the background hazards of life, no more present to consciousness than the dangers of being run over or thrown through the windscreen are present to our consciousness when walking or driving. Moreover, death in fights with one another was something over which young men had some control; in this as in other contexts, the degree of control we have over events distorts the perception of risk. In a train, the passenger is passive; the driver and conductor are far distant; and the train itself unresponsive to anything beyond acceleration and braking. Steering round an obstacle is not in its repertoire and everyone knows it. A motor cycle is the paradigm case of a vehicle that is immediately responsive to the rider's wishes, and that is connected to the fearlessness of the rider – especially where the rider is middle-aged and his level of skill not what it used to be.

We might then expect that the fact that train accidents are violent, noisy, involve numerous people, and are thus spectacular and extraordinary, will exaggerate in the spectator's mind the likelihood of their occurrence. The same is true of accidents to large passenger aircraft; if something goes wrong, it usually goes spectacularly and disastrously wrong. The question is whether we are not merely so impressed that we over-estimate the likelihood of such events, but whether we attach an inexplicably high value to v. The thought might be as follows: v represents the value – disvalue – to the individual of her or his share of the outcome; rational choice theory assumes that an agent conducts herself or himself in the light of the expected value of an outcome to herself or himself only. Yet we are appalled at disasters in ways that do not quite match that assumption. If I am killed in a plane crash, the v in which I am rationally interested is, so to speak, my share of the v^* that represents the total disvalue of the deaths and injuries occasioned. But it seems psychologically implausible to suppose we in fact think like this.

The size of v^* is philosophically complicated to calculate. The obvious way of calculating it is to add up the disvalue of the death or injury of each victim and take that as the answer. That is how the insurance company does it; the damage to the company's accounts is the total amount insured under the policies on the insured lives. If there were negligence or deliberate malfeasance, then the families of victims might be tempted to sue for punitive damages, the size of which when they are awarded in American courts may be thought to reflect the incapacity that most of us have to balance the concept of punishment with the concept of damages. But many people seem to feel that the simple addition of one loss to another does not meet the case, as though there is an enormity about the size of the loss that should be added to the total of individual losses.

There is no obvious way of demonstrating the existence of this phenomenon other than pointing to our reactions as reported in the mass media; that is an unreliable source of evidence because the mass media is particularly interested in striking phenomena and the evidence is therefore skewed. A possible thought experiment is to consider what we might have felt if the attack on the World Trade Center in September 2001 had not been an attack but an accident resulting from a freak failure of air traffic control at JFK or La Guardia. There is a great deal of aircraft traffic above New York City along the Hudson River, and it is not hard to imagine that two aircraft might stray far enough off course to hit the World Trade Center; nervous air passengers have probably feared such an occurrence many times a day. The death toll resulting from a fire and subsequent building collapse would have been much the same, and so would the economic losses. The deaths of slightly under 3,000 people in one accident would have been horrifying; the added horror of their being brought about deliberately is plainly something to be taken into account in this instance, but the immediate question is whether the sheer size of the disaster adds to the horror in a non-cumulative fashion. I find the question unanswerable, other than in the sense that size is important in securing *salience* in our consciousness.

The toll would have been on a par with that of some recent major earthquakes, only one-tenth of the worst of them and one-hundredth of the tsunami of December 2004. It would have been on a par with one month's fatalities on American roads – which in 2001 were around 42,000 in the whole year. Murders ran at around 1200 a month, so it would have been on a par with ten weeks' murders, and five weeks of all deaths from gunshot wounds, whether homicide, suicide or accidents. Does the bare fact of all the deaths occurring in one spectacular event make a difference to v^* – the total negative value of the event? The analytical problem with the question is that it is impossible to attach a great deal of sense to the questions to which it presupposes an answer. Would we have been so shocked if 'only' one of the two World Trade Center towers had collapsed? Would we have been so shocked by a death toll of 2,000 rather than 3,000? Would we have been so shocked if it had been an accident in the middle of a storm, and not something that came literally out of a clear blue sky? It seems impossible to say. One thing we can say is that rational choice theory is not equipped to draw the categorical distinctions we habitually make. All the difficult work has been done by the time we assign a value to v. Importantly in this case, of course, we draw sharp distinctions between natural phenomena and human action; an effective enemy can increase the likelihood of something happening that we very much dislike, but that is a different matter from their affecting the nastiness of the event in itself. It seems clear enough that it makes a great difference; what is less clear is whether it affects the intrinsic nastiness of the event – that is, that the malicious origin of the disaster is additional to the disaster – or extrinsically – in inducing anxiety about future strikes.

We are moving towards the subject of the second half of this chapter, so I should content myself with saying that in my view the explanatory mechanism is *salience*; the size of an event, its proximity, and its surprisingness are all factors contributing to its ability to seize our attention. Road-safety campaigners sometimes place the photographs of all the people killed in the past month in an appropriate newspaper to rub in the fact that these are large numbers; sometimes, they place the photographs of a particular family in the newspaper to emphasise that each case counts. Either is a device to heighten salience. In the case of events depending on human ill-will, of which 9/11 was a paradigm case, the number of deaths our enemies bring about in one fell swoop adds a further dimension in pressing upon us the fact that they hate us a great deal and are effective in making the point. Sheer numbers may be almost less important than the ability to strike repeatedly; in the autumn of 2002, suburban Washington was terrified by a pair of snipers who killed six victims at random over a period of four weeks (Zernicke 2002). Many people interviewed at the time looked back to 9/11 in accounting for their heightened anxiety in the face of the sniper attacks, so one can safely presume that the malignity of human agency is a more powerful source of fear than the malignity of nature, and can plausibly guess that it is the prospective factor – fear of future attacks – that is the more important factor.

How terrorism takes advantage of 'framing problems'

Having thus lined up the second half of the topic, it is not difficult to pick out the main lines of inquiry. I have argued elsewhere that the *point* of employing terror tactics is to undermine the will to resist of the families, friends, allies, employers, and especially governments of the actual victims of terror. On this view, terror may be deployed by governments as readily as by non-official groups or by individuals. The carpet bombing of German cities by the RAF and USAF during the Second World War was, on my view, the employment of terror: its aim was to break the will of the German population by inspiring such fear that they would lose the will to continue the war (Grayling, 2006). It did not do so, but such was its object. As a topic for political theorists, terror has a long, if unattractive, history, but the thought that terror is 'special' is a very modern thought. Warfare in the ancient world spared nobody; the victors were uninhibited by moral considerations in their treatment of the defeated on the battlefield, and almost as uninhibited in their treatment of civilians. Massacring one's enemies to terrify all who heard of it was commonplace, as was the execution in disgusting ways of leaders who were captured alive; the Athenians were no nicer in these matters than anyone else (Herodotus 1954: 602–3). Nor was Christian Europe more squeamish than the ancient world; whether one contemplates the Albigensian Crusade when Europe was nominally united in the Catholic faith or the destructive aftermath of the Reformation, when Europe was anything but united, the objection to describing the methods of the winning parties to these conflicts as 'terrorist' is only that they were often devoted to simple extermination. On my analysis, the point of terror is to instil fear in spectators, survivors, and those who expect to be attacked in future, whereas the point of extermination is to empty the world of those who are exterminated. 'Terrorist' is so much a term of abuse in the modern world that it is worth observing that the violence of the ancient and mediaeval worlds did not attract a great deal of moral obloquy at the time and ought not to attract it in retrospect. 'Terror' is the Latin for 'fear'; making our enemies fear us sufficiently to keep the peace is the beginning of political wisdom. Instilling more fear than necessary is disgusting and inefficient in all sorts of ways, but instilling fear is a necessary part of politics, and the question of how much fear to instil and by what means is wholly discussable (Machiavelli 1988).

Uninhibition about brutality is, on this view, a precondition of talking sense about internal order as well as international relations. Joseph de Maistre wrote a memorable couple of pages about the role of the executioner, 'the horror and the bond of human society', in which he argued that the executioner, the man who breaks parricides and blasphemers on the wheel, is 'incomprehensible', but provides the foundation on which all glory and all authority are erected (de Maistre 1965: 202–4). To say, as I have just done, that it is disgusting and inefficient to instil more fear than is necessary cut little ice with de Maistre; the reality of Original Sin was always present to his mind, and he often thought that authority existed only because there were ways of terrifying us into obedience; God threatens the everlasting fire, and earthly rulers must threaten the stake and the gibbet. Peace and good order are possible, and societies can run for substantial periods on habits of cooperation and mutual affection; but the framework that allows voluntary cooperation to flourish requires a ruler's will to sustain it, and that requires that no other will can oppose it. Behind this thought lies a particularly fierce understanding of the Judeo-Christian religious tradition, in which the arbitrary and incomprehensible character of divine authority is much to the fore, and the terrifying character of divine wrath is emphasised. 'More fear than is necessary' is an almost empty concept.

The purpose of these prefatory remarks is not to suggest that a long historical investigation into the role of violence in politics is essential to a discussion of risk and terrorism, but the reverse. I want to pull the discussion away from such familiar topics as the contrast between Red Terror and White Terror – which, in the writings of Trotsky and others boils down to the distinction between violence used against the more-or-less innocent for progressive purposes and the same sort of violence used for reactionary purposes (Ryan 1991). I also want to pull the discussion away from the enthusiasms of late nineteenth-century anarchist dynamiters, whose purpose was to bring home to the capitalists and militarists of the day the unhappiness of those they oppressed. Some theorists of the propaganda of the deed were Situationists *avant la lettre*, who thought that the sheer surprisingness of violent *attentats* launched against the economic and political leaders of the day would liberate the insurrectionary energies of the oppressed (Most 1885). Still, in broad outline it seems plausible to think that it was neither the revolutionary spectacle nor the instilling of fear in others that was the object of such terrorism, but rather the punishment of the wicked. This motivation was yet another reason why orthodox Marxists very much disliked such activities; a Marxist was obliged to think that individuals are doomed – or at least constrained – by their position in the productive process to act as that position requires. Capitalists must do what capitalists must do; otherwise, they will go out of business. Some are benign, some malign; none are interesting candidates for moral judgement *qua* capitalist.

The terrorism practised by the IRA was not like that which was praised by some anarchists. The IRA waged asymmetrical warfare, though they were prone to broaden the notion of the agents of the British state rather widely to include building contractors and the like; ethnic (or confessional) cleansing was a feature of life on working-class housing estates as republicans and loyalists competed for territory both for its own sake and to provide safe havens for their paramilitaries. 'Punishment', as a feature of IRA and loyalist terrorism, and indeed of almost all terrorist movements, was directed against their own side, to keep their supporters in order and to prevent informers undermining their paramilitaries. Neither side was interested in *punishing* the other side, merely in killing its agents and leaders. The campaign against the British state was conceptualised as a war. There was a great deal of ancillary criminality both for fund-raising purposes and out of simple greed; but criminality was as a matter of logic not implicit in the campaign, and may in fact have undermined it.

The campaign of terrorism on the mainland and in Ulster itself was intended to render it impossible for the British government to govern the province of Ulster; the point of attacks on the mainland in particular was to raise the cost of the continued union of Great Britain and Northern Ireland to the point where the mainland government would abandon the Province. Among the oddities of the IRA campaign, one was the fact that the British government was deterred from abandoning the Province by the knowledge that there would have been civil war in Ulster, and possibly throughout the whole island; the former would have been catastrophic for the Catholic population in the North, and the latter for absolutely everyone in Eire and the United Kingdom. The coincidence of the Yugoslav civil war of the early 1990s and the beginning of the peace process in 1994 may not have been wholly coincidental; the horrors of the Balkans may have sobered the contending parties in Ulster.

The point of rehearsing these familiar points is to emphasise that IRA terrorism was amenable to conventional risk management. The fact that the IRA generally tried hard to give warnings of attacks on civilian targets shows well enough that it did not wish simply to kill as many people as possible; it was not an exterminationist organization. Nor was its intention even to turn the political and economic advantages of the Protestant population of the North into disadvantages. In intention, the object was to create a secular socialist republic in a united Ireland. It was therefore possible to plan on the basis that where the IRA was intent on a spectacular act of destruction, it would be economic destruction; 'v' would be a very large number in economic terms, but not necessarily in 'human' terms. Of course, all such claims need substantial qualification. Almost everyone caught up in the Manchester bombing that destroyed a large part of the city centre was rightly terrified at the time; many people found it hard to shake off the fear of a further occurrence for years afterwards. Still, in terms of risk management, the parameters were clear enough; it could be made very difficult for bombers to get through to economic targets. They did not intend to get killed during their operations, and that gave the forces of law and order advantages they lack when confronting suicide bombers or gunmen who are happy to be killed so long as they have a chance to carry out the assassinations they have in view.

The crucial point about contemporary terrorism is that it takes advantage of the weaknesses in risk assessment that the first half of this essay claimed that ordinary human beings suffer from. Some terrorist behaviour acts directly on v in the sense of doing things or threatening things that are particularly horrible; the suicide bombing of a wedding of one's fellow-religionists is especially nasty, as is the video-taped throat-cutting of a perfectly harmless elderly hostage. The negative value represented by v needs no elaboration. From the point of view of this essay, and that alone, the crucial features of terrorist behaviour bear on the difficulty of disentangling the assessment of probability and the assignment of value. What follows picks up the points made earlier to bring out their implications.

It was argued earlier that we have inherited a risk-assessment mechanism appropriate to a world in which the careful calculation of $p(v)$ would have done us less good than a quick eye for sudden disturbances in the environment. One implication is that life becomes difficult when we have to assess what is happening in the hitherto taken for granted background for clues to future danger, especially when we do not know what clues to look for. Sabre tooth tigers do not spend their time inventing new ways of sneaking up on their prey, or of deceiving their prey into taking precautions against non-threats the better to take them unawares. The contrast with the activities of human beings who wish us ill is too obvious to spell out. The impact of the contrast is worth spelling out. In the first instance, every risk pulled out of the background of the buried and ignored hazards of everyday life is one more thing that demands attention; that is a cost to the individual in time, attention, and anxiety. Rendering a danger more salient is an achievement in any campaign to instil fear; it will very probably lead us to overestimate p but even if it does not do so, it imposes a cost.

It may well achieve nothing else; the most obvious feature of terrorism is that its most common effect is to increase government authoritarianism. It has never advanced the cause of proletarian democracy, nor the prospects of a socialist or Islamist utopia. For our immediate purpose, however, which is to see a little further into the way in which terrifying events undermine our capacity for estimating risk – that is, our ability to estimate probability in a cool and rational fashion – the ineffectiveness of terrorism as a weapon of political construction is neither here nor there. We are trying to understand how terrorism can be effective as a force of political destruction, that is, how it makes the ordinary, everyday application of governmental authority to the tasks of running a country more difficult or even impossible.

The terrorist, then, is in the business of instilling fear, with the ultimate intention of inducing family, employers, and governments to succumb to whatever demands the terrorists may have. One oddity is that the terrorism of which we are most afraid has few demands for attainable political goals. This is not true of all terrorism; it is important to understand that, because there are cases where terrorists have goals which are limited, a-political, and successfully achieved, precisely because, as the previous paragraph insisted, *destructive* purposes are more readily achieved than *constructive*. Paramilitaries with a vested interest in the failure of eradication programmes in Colombia and Afghanistan have stopped farmers cooperating with these programmes and have ensured that the programmes are not vigorously pursued. This is not an articulate political programme, but it has no need to be, since all it requires for success is that ordinary law enforcement is made impossible. It is clear what will increase and what will decrease the levels of violence, and to the extent that what is intended is that the drugs trade continues unmolested, so-called 'narco-terrorism' is successful. This also suggests how narrow the line is between some activities described as 'terrorist' and those of violent criminal enterprises such as the Mafia and the Camorra, and reinforces the point made at the beginning of this section about the importance of not thinking that terrorism is 'special' in its use of violence.

There is one contemporary, and unequivocally terrorist, enterprise with genuinely political purposes, and purposes that terrorism has some, if only some, prospect of achieving. This is Palestinian suicide bombing; the maximalist aim of the organizations behind the bombings is the abolition of the state of Israel, and this is unattainable under any imaginable conditions. The goal of establishing a Palestinian state alongside a Jewish state is entirely attainable, and the tactic of wearing down Israeli determination to remain in occupation of Gaza and the West Bank by putting up the price of occupation in civilian casualties as well as military casualties and wasted economic resources is not irrational. The means chosen may be immoral, but that is not the issue. The point, to reiterate, is that destructive purposes can be achieved where constructive purposes cannot; and the pushing out of alien occupiers by making the cost of occupation too high is a straightforward destructive goal.

The plausibility of the tactics is not disputable; Israel came into existence when the British decided that sustaining the Palestine Mandate against Jewish terrorist gangs was not worth the price. Cyprus became independent at least partly because the British did not think continued custody of the island was worth the effort of combating EOKA. These examples also suggest something else that everyone observes, that in many cases there is a dispute about whether what we have is terrorism or 'national liberation', as witness Chechnya among other examples today. The employment of terrorist tactics by national liberation forces has some plausibility. Where we have unequivocal 'foreign occupation', making the costs of occupation too high is an obvious tactic for forces of national liberation to pursue; it will not work if the occupiers are willing to behave as savagely as the Germans behaved in occupied Europe, but events in Iraq suggest the possibilities where the occupiers are more squeamish. It is almost certain that the insurgency could be crushed by the familiar tactics of holding families hostage for the behaviour of their members, destroying whole villages when one of their inhabitants is involved in insurgency, and so on. Since this was how Saddam Hussein maintained order, and was just the sort of thing the invasion of Iraq was intended to prevent, it is not something the occupying forces can contemplate.

Drawing a line between national liberation and terrorism is impossible where there is no agreement on *whose* territory it is; the Russian government and the Chechnya insurgents are at odds over exactly that. Israelis and Palestinians are at odds about the rightful owners of Jerusalem and much of historical Palestine. Nationalist Iraqi insurgency in Iraq is different from Islamist terrorism in Britain, Spain, or the US. In the former case, it could be – though much obviously is not – a rational, if appalling, way of raising the costs of occupation; in the latter case, it is less likely to be that, though again that may be a secondary purpose. It was understood in that light by the Spanish government, though apparently not by the terrorists themselves, who proposed to continue their campaign after the government had decided to withdraw Spanish troops from Iraq. 9/11 seems to have been more nearly a punitive gesture than part of a campaign to induce a change of American policy in any particular area, and the same seems to have been true of the bombings in London in July 2005.

We should turn to something that commentators often notice without further analysis; the more terrorism resembles warfare in the usual sense – that is, the more a society believes that it is engaged in a war fought by unorthodox means, the more the inhabitants of a society adjust their anxieties to the real probability of death and injury. During the Second World War, civilian life in London continued without much increased apprehension of death and injury; no doubt there is some sort of tipping point beyond which everyone's attention is devoted to bare survival, but one effect of habitual exposure to danger is that people take precautions, such as sleeping in shelters, but do not generally suffer from heightened anxiety. Towards the end of the Second World War, V-2 rockets caused greater anxiety, because their arrival was completely unforeseeable, unlike that of the V-1, which was a pilotless jet aircraft that could be tracked, and shot down or knocked off course. The evidence is that Israelis have generally behaved much as Londoners behaved in the Second World War. This is not surprising; horrible though it is to live with the threat of being murdered at random, the cleverness with which terrorists plan their murders can be matched by the cleverness with which security forces foil them, and the risk of death and maiming can be assimilated into background cautiousness of the kind that prevents most of us from inadvertently stepping under a bus.

On this view terrorists are right to aim at producing 'spectaculars', events that kill a lot of people at once, and preferably when the deaths can play on pre-existing anxieties. The attacks of 9/11, and the abortive attempt to blow up a dozen 747s over the Pacific, fit this pattern, as did the bombings of the US embassies in Kenya and Tanzania. The London bombings of July 2005 fit the pattern all too well. Among the deaths that none of us wishes to contemplate, being blown to bits, asphyxiated, or left to die of one's injuries deep underground, in pitch darkness, and with no way to call for help come high on the list. Earlier accidents on the London Underground had given everyone a fore-taste of what a terrorist attack could do, and contriving three more or less simultaneously – followed by an attack on a bus – made the attacks a set-piece demonstration of the capacity of terrorism to create alarm and its ineffective-ness as a political weapon. The attacks unnerved the entire country, but because they were a 'one-off', and it soon emerged there was no real organisa-tion behind them, their effect was very temporary. From the terrorists' per-spective, 9/11 was many orders of magnitude more effective: not only was it much more spectacular and the death toll a great deal larger, but it came with alarming credentials. It self-evidently took much organizing; it spoke to a great deal of patience and years of planning; it came in the wake of terrifying truck-bombings elsewhere, and suggested that for all anyone knew, Al-Q'aida had half a dozen more such horrors primed and ready to go.

Given what was claimed earlier about our propensity to exaggerate the evi-dential value of spectacular occurrences, it is easy to see how 9/11 might induce real panic. Some commentators argued at the time that the conspirators had simply 'got lucky', as though there had been dozens of abortive attempts along the same lines of which this one had so to speak 'got through'. Whether that was so is impossible to guess in the absence of a reliable analysis of the organisation's history over the previous decade. Even if it was so, there was no likelihood of that being a popular view; although one man in a panel van had come close to destroying one of the World Trade Center towers in the early 1990s, the idea that the destruction of both was a lucky strike by a bunch of amateurs was impossible to embrace. At that point, all the human weaknesses in evaluating evidence and therefore in assessing $p(v)$ in a rational fashion showed themselves.

They were exacerbated by a weakness of modern governments. In a world where the threat of nuclear annihilation has diminished, and where in devel-oped countries at least, neither accidents nor disease pose much threat until old age, governments promise almost complete safety to their citizens; yet, where politics is based on party competition for office, governments must inculcate sufficient alarm to induce the citizenry to display their gratitude by voting for whatever party does or might ensure their safety. The temptation for a government is to praise itself for making the citizenry safe while playing up the dangers from which the citizenry is being protected. This temptation is exacerbated by the modern newspaper press and in the United States by local television, where the depiction of violent crime – or, more generally, the depiction of excited commentary on it – is a cheap way of filling airtime. One result has been that during a period when violent crime has dropped by a quarter, the public perception is that it has been increasing.

Given such a mismatch between perception and reality, one might have feared that 9/11 would have led to mass hysteria. How to characterise what it did lead to is beyond the scope of this essay; one might point to the relatively restrained and un-panic stricken behaviour of governments internally, or to the rather less restrained and more panicky attacks on Afghanistan and Iraq, as evidence either that the public at large rapidly recovered its poise and did not see dangers everywhere or that its attention was distracted to distant parts of the world, and that hysteria was globalised. The point of this essay has not been to take sides on contentious political issues but to illustrate one of the many ways in which our innate weaknesses in risk-assessment can be taken advantage of in a political context. To the degree that this essay has a moral, it is that governments could perform a service to the public by rowing *against* our tendency to miscalculate $p(v)$ in predictable ways, rather than exacerbating it; but this case has been argued at length by Professor Sunstein elsewhere, and I need here do no more than endorse it (Sunstein 2005).

References

de Maistre, J. (1965) *Works of Joseph de Maistre* (ed. and trans. Jack Lively), London, Macmillan.

Doll, R. and Hill, A. B. (1954) 'The mortality of doctors in relation to their smoking habits. A preliminary report', *British Medical Journal*, 4877: 1451–455.

Economist, The (2000) 'How not to run a railway', 23 November.

Grayling, A.C. (2006) *Among the Dead Cities*, London: Bloomsbury.

Herodotus (1954) *The Histories* (trans. A. de Selincourt), London: Penguin Books.

Kahan, D. M., Slovic, P., Braman, D. and Gastil, J. (2006) 'Fear of democracy: a cultural evaluation of Sunstein on risk', *Harvard Law Review*, 119: 1071–109.

Machiavelli, N. (1988 [1532]) *The Prince*, Cambridge: Cambridge University Press.

Mill, J.S. (2006) *On Liberty* and *The Subjection of Women*, London: Penguin Books.

Most, J. (1885) *The Science of Revolutionary Warfare*, New York.

Rawls, J. (1971) *A Theory of Justice*, Cambridge, MA: Harvard University Press.

Rumsfeld, D. (2002) *Department of Defense News Briefing*, 12 February. Quoted in H. Seely 'The poetry of D.H. Rumsfeld', *Slate*, 2 April 2003.

Ryan, A. (1991) 'State and individual, red and white', in R. Frey and C. Morris (eds) *Violence, Terrorism, and Justice*, New York: Cambridge University Press.

Ryan, A. (ed.) (1999) *Genetically Modified Crops: the ethical and social issues*, London: Nuffield Council on Bioethics.

Sunstein, C. (2005) *Laws of Fear: beyond the precautionary principle*, New York: Cambridge University Press.

Sutherland, S. (1994) *Why We Don't Think Straight*, New Brunswick, NJ: Rutgers University Press.

Tversky, A. and Kahneman, D. (1981) 'The framing of decisions and the psychology of choice', *Science*, 211(4481): 453–58.

Zernicke, K. (2002) 'The hunt for a sniper: the reaction. Losing its terror the mundane turned joyous', *New York Times*, 25 October.

11

RISK, HARM, INTERESTS, AND RIGHTS

Stephen Perry

Introduction

We often speak of an action of one person as imposing a risk of some kind on another person. In this chapter I argue that, contrary to what has sometimes been claimed, the imposition of a risk of, say, physical harm – or, in a different formulation, the deprivation of a chance of avoiding an adverse physical outcome – is not a form of harm in itself. One of the implications of the argument I shall present is that the concept of imposing risk is a complex and sometimes elusive one. On first examination one might think, for example, that the character and the magnitude of the risk that one person has imposed on another are matters that can be settled simply by appealing to ordinary facts or to scientific knowledge, but I argue that this is not so. For moral purposes, at least, we can only determine what risk A has imposed on B by making certain assumptions about the knowledge and beliefs that an actor in the position of A ought to have possessed at the time of acting, and the question of which assumptions are appropriate requires us to look to moral considerations. It fol-lows that, in the moral context, at least, the concept of risk imposition is itself a moral notion. A more general theme of the chapter concerns the importance of what I shall call morally determined epistemic perspectives in all moral and legal discourse about risk. In the final section of the chapter I refine the claim that risk is not harm in itself, and I also offer a preliminary discussion of some more general questions that this claim suggests about the relationships that hold among the concepts of risk, harm, interests, and rights.

It will be helpful to say something at the outset about the nature of risk. A risk is a chance or probability of a bad outcome. For present purposes, the bad outcomes in question will generally be harms to persons. The seriousness of a risk of harm clearly depends on both the probability that the relevant harm will occur and the extent of the loss that would be suffered if it were to occur. It therefore seems reasonable to define a risk of harm as the mathematical expectation of harm, i.e. as the product of the probability of harm and the magnitude of the loss that would occur if the risk materialized. The most important question that arises in the philosophical study of risk is not the analysis of the bad outcomes to which the concept applies, since it can clearly apply to almost any kind of bad outcome, but rather the appropriate analysis of the concept of probability. I have argued elsewhere that, from the point of view of the morality of risk imposition, probability is best understood by reference to the relative frequency theory of probability (Perry 1995: 327–29). A probability is, according to that theory, the relative frequency of a specified type of outcome within a reference class of entities, events, or actions that are, in some specified way, similar to one another.[1] To illustrate, the probability within the American population as a whole of getting a disease of a certain type within any given year might be .01 per cent. This means that, taking the entire American population over a year as the reference class, the disease in question occurs with a relative frequency of 1 in every 10,000 people. Notice that this is an *objective* probability in the sense that the relative frequency exists whether or not anyone knows about it or should know about it.[2]

There are, in addition to frequentist theories of probability, epistemic accounts of various kinds. According to the subjectivist or Bayesian family of theories,[3] a probability is the degree of subjective confidence or belief that a person possesses about the truth of a proposition. In the present context, the content of the propositions in question will always concern whether some state of affairs will or will not obtain in the future. Early subjectivists argued that this is the only possible understanding of epistemic probability, and indeed of probability generally (Savage 1954; de Finetti 1974). They maintained that relative frequencies do not have objective existence and that probability judgments can appropriately vary widely from person to person, constrained only by a requirement of coherence.[4] More moderate subjectivist accounts accord at least a practical or pragmatic role to relative frequencies,[5] and as a general matter there does not seem to be any reason why frequentist and subjectivist approaches to probability cannot peacefully coexist. No doubt both approaches have their moral uses.[6] But it is difficult to see how, as a matter of ordinary interpersonal morality, the idea that one person has *imposed* a risk of harm on another person – or, to use a different idiom, has *subjected* another to such a risk – could have any degree of moral significance unless the relevant concept of risk bore a systematic and more or less agreed-upon relationship to the physical world in which consequences, sometimes harmful in nature, follow from actions in ways that are at least partially predictable. More specifically, unless we assume, first, that probability judgments bear some relationship to relative frequencies in the real world, and, secondly, that there are intersubjectively valid methods of estimation and induction for making such judgments, it is not clear that we can even make sense of the claim that one person imposed a risk on another, as opposed to simply holding a belief with a certain degree of confidence. For purposes of this chapter I shall therefore make these assumptions, although I shall not attempt to justify them here. My reason for proceeding in this manner is that my concern is with the moral significance of risk imposition, and not with the concept of probability as such. I believe that these assumptions comprise a common starting-point, albeit usually an implicit one, for most moral philosophers and legal theorists who write about risk.

Bearing in mind the considerations of the preceding paragraph, I shall characterize epistemic probability simply as the estimation of objective probability, meaning the estimation of the relative frequency of some attribute within a specified reference class, rather than in the strict subjectivist sense of an individual's degree of confidence that some state of affairs obtains.[7] Thus the objective probability of getting a certain disease – that is, its relative frequency within a specified population – might be .01 per cent. But the epistemic probability of the disease – that is, our best *estimate* of that relative frequency – might be different. In fact it might be quite different, depending on the size of sample groups that have been studied, the number of studies that have been done, the sophistication of the statistical techniques employed, and so on.

Any estimation of the kind just described must obviously be made relative to (1) background knowledge and beliefs of a very general and pervasive kind about the nature of the physical world, (2) relevant evidence about the particular case at hand – for example, formal or informal evidence about relative frequencies within sample classes of various types – and (3) various assumptions, whether explicit or implicit, about the nature of inductive reasoning. Let me refer, in a deliberately rough and ready way, to any such comprehensive set of knowledge, beliefs and assumptions as an epistemic perspective. An epistemic perspective might involve, for example, advanced scientific knowledge in combination with a highly formalized understanding of statistical methods and induction. But the epistemic perspective of a particular agent, as it exists at a particular time and under some specified set of circumstances, will generally be far less sophisticated in character, and might well involve beliefs about the world, and implicit assumptions about the nature of induction, that are idiosyncratic, erroneous or both. It is also important to notice that it is possible to refer not just to the epistemic perspectives of actual persons, but also to constructed epistemic perspectives of different sorts. Consider, for example, the idealized perspective of a person who possesses all currently available scientific knowledge and who always accurately employs the most advanced statistical methods. There is also the constructed epistemic perspective of omniscience.[8] And there are, finally, various constructed epistemic perspectives in the legal and moral spheres. The notion of the reasonable person presents a familiar example from tort law: legal liability for the harmful consequences of risk-creating actions is determined not by looking to the actual knowledge and beliefs of the defendant, but rather to the knowledge and beliefs that would be held by a reasonable person in the defendant's situation. Moral judgments in everyday life that depend on what a person ought to have known or believed when performing potentially risky actions, as opposed to what he or she did in fact know or believe, implicitly presuppose an epistemic perspective which is similar to that of the reasonable person. For reasons that were given earlier, the moral assessment of risk imposition requires that there be some common, intersubjectively valid method for estimating relative frequencies. Reliance on epistemic perspectives such as that of the reasonable person obviously assumes that people generally have intuitive inductive capacities that, while no doubt less accurate than formal statistical techniques, are at least sufficiently accurate for the moral or legal ends at hand. This assumption may or may not be correct,[9] but it is a pervasive one in legal and moral life, and for present purposes I shall assume that it is true.

Risk is not harm

It has sometimes been claimed that when one person A acts in such a way as to subject another person B to the risk of, say, physical harm, the fact that B has been subjected to such a risk is itself a form of harm to B, and that this is so whether or not any physical harm ultimately occurs to B as a result of A's having performed the risky action. Such claims have, for example, often been made in the context of tort law as part of an argument for the conclusion that, at least under some circumstances, it is appropriate to compensate B, by means of an award of damages, simply for having been subject to risk.[10] There is, moreover, a growing number of cases, particularly in the medical malpractice area, in which legal liability has been predicated precisely on the claim that, as the result of negligence on the part of the defendant, the plaintiff suffered harm in the form of a lost or reduced chance of avoiding an adverse physical outcome.[11] In this section I wish to argue that risk as such cannot plausibly be construed as harm for purposes of compensation in tort law or, indeed, for any other purpose.[12] This is not to deny that there is some sense in which A's action of subjecting B to a risk sets back an interest of B. Not all setbacks to interests are harms, however, and the character of the interest which is set back just by virtue of A's having imposed a risk on B is not of a kind which can justify the conclusion that B has been harmed.

The basic argument demonstrating that risk is not harm concerns the well-known problem of multiple reference classes (Weatherford 1982: 165–78; Gillies 2000: 119–25). It is perhaps best presented by way of example. Suppose that A exposes B to a known dosage of some toxic substance S.[13] Suppose that, in general, 10 per cent of all persons who are exposed to S contract a certain disease D. It might seem to follow that the objective risk of B's contracting the disease as a result of having been exposed to S is also 10 per cent. But the matter is more complicated than this would suggest. The risk of 10 per cent has been defined with respect to a certain reference class, namely, members of the general population who have been exposed to the relevant dosage of S. Presumably there are physical factors that determine, among those who are exposed to S, who gets the disease and who does not. To keep the example simple, let me suppose that these factors are all physiological attributes of the persons exposed and not, say, facts about the manner in which the exposure occurred. Suppose that everyone who is exposed to S and who possesses physiological attributes X, Y and Z gets the disease, and that anyone who is exposed to S but does not possess all three attributes does not get it. Then there exists another reference class, consisting of persons who are exposed to S and who all possess attributes X, Y and Z, for which the relative frequency of the disease, and therefore the objective risk of getting it, is 100 per cent. There are, moreover, still other reference classes for which the relative frequency of D might well be somewhere between 10 per cent and 100 per cent. There exists, for example, a reference class consisting of persons who were all exposed to S and who all possess attribute X, but within which the attributes Y and Z are distributed in the same proportion as they are in the general population. For this particular reference class, the relative frequency of the disease might be, say, 25 per cent. There also exists a reference class consisting of persons who were all exposed to S and who all possess attributes X and Y, but within which the attribute Z is distributed in the same proportion as it is in the general population. The relative frequency of D within *this* reference class might be, say, 60 per cent. And there is also, of course, a reference class consisting of all persons exposed to S who do not possess any of X, Y or Z, and the relative frequency of D within this class is 0 per cent.

Suppose that B possesses all of the relevant attributes X, Y and Z. Then he belongs to the reference class for which the relative frequency of getting the disease is 100 per cent. He also belongs, however, to the reference class in which everyone possesses attribute X and in which the attributes Y and Z are distributed in the same proportion as they are in the general population. The relative frequency of getting the disease within this class is, we are supposing, 25 per cent. And B belongs as well to the reference class in which everyone possesses attributes X and Y and in which attribute Z is distributed in the same proportion as it is in the general population. For this class the relative frequency is different again; in the example, we are assuming it is 60 per cent. Should we say that the risk of getting the disease which is associated with A's act of exposing B to S is 10 per cent, 25 per cent, 60 per cent or 100 per cent? Notice that the problem here is not determining which reference class B *really* belongs to, because he is a member of all of them. Nor is the problem a matter of determining what, for any given reference class, the relative frequency of getting the disease *really* is, since we are assuming that, for each reference class, the associated statement of relative frequency is true; we are assuming, in other words, that we are dealing with objective rather than with epistemic probabilities. It is, on this assumption, a fact about the world that the relative frequency of getting the disease is, within the general population, 10 per cent. But it is also a fact about the world that, for a reference class in which every person possesses attribute X but in which factors Y and Z vary in the same proportion as they do within the general population, the relative frequency of the disease is 25 per cent. And it is, finally, a fact about the world that for a reference class in which every person possesses all three of the attributes X, Y and Z, the relative frequency of getting the disease is 100 per cent. B belongs to all of these reference classes, and to many more besides. This fact is true whether or not we know that he belongs to any of these reference classes, and it is also true whether or not we know what the relative frequency associated with any give reference class is. It is true, for that matter, even if we do not know that any of X, Y or Z is a factor that is causally relevant to the occurrence of the disease in someone who has been exposed to substance S.

It is of course true that, depending on our purpose and also on the state of our knowledge, we do speak of the risk of getting D that is associated with A's action of exposing B to S. For purposes of public health and disease prevention, for example, our concern might well be with the 10 per cent figure. And as a general matter, where we do not have any particular purpose in mind, our inclination is no doubt to say that the risk associated with A's action is the relative frequency of D within the narrowest causally relevant reference class that we happen to know about (or that someone knows about or should know about). Suppose, for example, that we know that attribute X is a causally relevant factor, but that we do not know that Y and Z are also causally relevant. Suppose further that we know that B possesses attribute X. Then we might well say, perfectly sensibly, that B's risk of getting the disease is 25 per cent. Our question, however, is whether or not B's risk of getting the disease is a harm in itself, or, alternatively, whether or not B has been harmed simply by reason of having been subject to a risk by A. It is surely very odd to claim that the 25 per cent risk is a harm in itself, given that our assessment of the risk would be quite different if the state of our knowledge were different. If we knew that X and Y are causally relevant factors but did not know that Z was such a factor, and if we also knew that B possesses both X and Y, then we would be led, again quite sensibly, to say that B's risk of getting the disease was 60 per cent. And if we were in possession of all the relevant facts concerning both B's physiology and the processes determining the causation of D, then we would say that the risk is 100 per cent. It is, surely, a very strange form of harm that varies in this way with our state of knowledge. To see the point more clearly, suppose that B possesses both of the attributes X and Y but does not possess attribute Z. If we knew that X and Y are causally relevant factors but did not know that Z was such a factor, and if we also knew that B possesses both X and Y, then we would again be led to say that B's risk of getting the disease was 60 per cent. Now, however, if we were in possession of all the relevant facts concerning both B's physiology and the processes determining the causation of D, then we would say that A had not subjected B to any risk at all, since the relative frequency of D within the narrowest causally relevant reference class that we know about is 0 per cent. It is, surely, a very strange form of harm whose very existence varies in this way with the state of our knowledge.

Notice that the difficulties associated with characterizing risk as harm cannot be avoided by saying, for example, that the risk that A has imposed on

B is uniquely defined by the relative frequency of harm that is associated with the narrowest causally relevant reference class containing B that exists, whether we know about that class or not. The reason that this will not do is that, at least in a deterministic universe, the relative frequency of harm that is associated with this reference class will presumably always be either 100 per cent or 0 per cent. If the relative frequency is 100 per cent then it is certain that B will suffer the physical harm in question and there does not appear to be any room for the idea that risk constitutes a separate form of harm; the notion of objective risk would become, in essence, synonymous with that of causing harm. If, however, the relative frequency of harm is 0 per cent, then we have no basis for saying that B was at risk in the first place, and we are again forced to conclude that there is no room for the idea that risk constitutes a separate form of harm. It is of course true that the universe we live in is indeterministic at the quantum level, and while there appears to be some reason for thinking that indeterminism might wash out of the system at the macroscopic level,[14] it is at least possible that this is not so. If indeterminism does exist at the level of the physical world that we are familiar with, then it is presumably true that there are some reference classes which cannot even in principle be partitioned, on the basis of causally relevant factors, to the point where the relative frequency of harm is always either 100 per cent or 0 per cent. If this were the case then the question of whether risk is ever harm in itself becomes much more complicated, in ways that I am not able to take up here.[15] For present purposes, I will limit myself to the following two observations. First, those who defend the thesis that risk is harm generally appear to have in mind estimations of relative frequency that are made on the basis of existing knowledge rather than relative frequencies that exist whether or not anyone knows about them, let alone relative frequencies that may reflect underlying indeterministic processes. The arguments of this section show that at least these versions of the risk-is-harm thesis are mistaken. Second, since both the law and everyday morality for the most part adopt an account of causation which is necessity-based rather than probabilistic in nature,[16] it is very arguable that, leaving aside issues of free will, both presuppose a deterministic rather than an indeterministic account of causation. If it in fact turns out to be the case that our everyday understanding of the natural world should be stochastic in character rather than deterministic, then the reworking of our moral and legal concepts that would be required goes far beyond the question of whether or not risk is a harm in itself.

I have argued so far that risk, at least as that notion is ordinarily understood in moral and legal contexts, cannot plausibly be regarded as harm in itself. In the final analysis risks are just relative frequencies, and relative frequencies are properties not of individuals but of classes of individuals; it is, however, individuals who suffer harm, not classes. As we have seen, the extent and indeed the very existence of the risk that one person can be said to have imposed on another is relative to the reference class with respect to which the relative frequency of harm is stated, and there is no unique or canonically correct way to specify the appropriate reference class. The only plausible candidate for such canonical status would be the narrowest causally relevant reference class that would in principle be specifiable in a world of perfect knowledge, and, at least in a deterministic universe, the relative frequency of harm within that class will always be 100 per cent or 0 per cent; either way, there is no basis for saying that risk is a form of harm in itself. In the world of imperfect knowledge in which we actually live we of course specify reference classes as best we can, based on the purposes we have in mind and the information that is available to us. But if risk is harm in itself then presumably it is harm regardless of what our current state of knowledge happens to be.

The argument that I have presented for the conclusion that risk is not harm does not, of course, entail that risk is not a useful or coherent concept, nor does it entail that the notion of one person *imposing* a risk of harm on another person is not a morally significant one. As was remarked earlier, we do quite sensibly tend to say, in the world of imperfect knowledge in which we live, that the risk associated with an action is the relative frequency of harm which is associated with the narrowest causally relevant reference class that someone knows about or ought to know about. The idea that an action increases the risk of harm to another would then mean something like the following. First, the relative frequency of harm within the narrowest epistemically accessible and causally relevant reference class into which the person at risk now falls is greater than it was before, and, second, if the relevant harm were to occur it would be physically caused by the risk-increasing action. Risk judgments of this kind are clearly of moral importance because they bear on such matters as how we are entitled to act towards others and when we must take responsibility for the consequences of our actions. It is, however, crucially important to emphasize the following three points: first, because such judgments are always made relative to what someone knows or ought to know, they are always made relative to some epistemic perspective; second, the epistemic perspective that is appropriate for different moral purposes can vary; and third, at least some of the factors that bear on the determination of which perspective is appropriate for a given moral purpose are, unavoidably, themselves moral considerations.

For some moral purposes – and no doubt for many non-moral purposes as well – the appropriate perspective might be that of someone who is possessed of all currently available scientific knowledge which is relevant to the assessment of the risk at hand. For other purposes, perhaps the appropriate perspective might be that of an omniscient impartial observer.[17] For many moral purposes, however, and perhaps for most, the appropriate epistemic perspective for determining what risk one person has imposed on another will be the perspective either of the actor himself/herself or of some idealized agent, such as a reasonable person, who is imagined to be in the actor's situation at the time of acting. Criminal law makes use sometimes of the one perspective and sometimes of the other – known, respectively, as the subjective and objective standards – in determining what knowledge should be attributed to a defendant charged with, say, criminal negligence. Tort law, for its part, almost always makes use of the objective standard of the reasonable person. Similarly, our everyday moral judgments of carelessness and non-legal negligence often make use of analogous objective standards that look to what the actor should reasonably have been aware of, or, perhaps, to what an idealized ordinary person would have been aware of. In order to decide which epistemic perspective to adopt in determining the extent of the risk that one person has imposed on another, it is, I think, quite clear that if our purpose is a moral one then we must look, in part, to moral considerations. Similarly, when we ask what level of knowledge should be attributed to the reasonable person and similar normative constructs, we are necessarily asking a moral question. It follows that the concept of risk imposition that we must use for moral purposes is itself a moralized notion. While the factual information about reference classes that is associated with a given epistemic perspective is obviously crucial in determining what risk someone did or did not impose on someone else, there is nonetheless no morally neutral concept of risk imposition which is made available to us simply as a matter of ordinary or scientific fact.

Risk, interests, and rights

Let me define a risky action as one that, when assessed from some morally appropriate epistemic perspective, gives rise to a morally significant risk of harm to another person. There is no need for present purposes to specify the appropriate epistemic perspective, nor is it necessary to say how substantial a risk must be in order to rise to the level of moral significance. In the preceding section I argued, in effect, that the risk associated with a risky action cannot plausibly be regarded as harm in itself. I did not argue, however, that risky actions cannot give rise to any harm at all (besides the potential harm which would lead one to say in the first place that the action was a risky one). Suppose, for example, that I am *aware* that someone else is subjecting me to a risk of physical harm. In that case, I might suffer severe fright or emotional distress. Or I might reasonably decide that I should not engage in some activity that I might otherwise have engaged in, or that I should no longer carry out some short- or long-term plan that I had in mind. For instance, if you have done something which increases the probability that I will get skin cancer, then I might decide that I should no longer spend time in the sun, and this decision might in turn reasonably lead me to cancel a plan to visit Tahiti. When I lose such options to live my life as I choose, I have suffered an interference with my autonomy (Raz 1986: 413).[18] A related possibility, if I am aware that someone else has subjected me to a risk of harm, is that I reasonably decide to take a certain course of action that I would not otherwise have taken, such as undergoing regular medical monitoring, and this puts me seriously out of pocket. Severe fright or emotional distress, interferences with autonomy and economic loss are all setbacks to interests which are sufficiently fundamental to well-being that the setbacks are in each case plausibly regarded as a forms of harm.[19] But the fact that I might suffer one or more of these harms as a result of knowing that you have imposed a risk on me is by no means the same thing as saying that risk is a harm in itself. If risk were a harm in itself then it would seem reasonable to think that it would be suffered whether or not one knew that one had been subjected to risk. Relatedly, harms of the kind just discussed do not *necessarily* flow from being subjected to risk or, for that matter, from being aware that one has been subjected to a risk. It is also important to bear in mind in this regard that so long as I believe that you have imposed a risk on me, I might suffer one of these forms of harm even if you have not, in fact, engaged in a risky activity. My mistaken belief might even be quite reasonable, since it is possible that the knowledge I bring to bear or ought to bring to bear in deciding whether or not I have been subjected to risk does not coincide with the appropriate epistemic perspective[20] – for example, the perspective of a reasonable person who was situated as you were when you acted – for determining whether or not your action was, morally speaking, indeed a risky one.[21]

In the preceding paragraph I argued that although certain harms may flow from being aware that one has been subjected to a risk, it does not follow that risk itself is a harm. We must now consider the possibility that risky action might give rise to harm which is grounded not in the knowledge or beliefs of the person who has been put at risk but rather in the knowledge, actual or constructive, of the person who is doing the risking. If the person engaging in the risky action knew or should have known that his action was risky, and if his action was accompanied by an intent to injure or was in some other way a particularly morally egregious one, then it is very plausible to think that the person who was subjected to the risk has, whether he knows about the risky action or not, suffered a harm in the form of a setback to his dignity. Kantians might argue that such acts fail to show adequate respect for the person put at risk (Railton 1985: 107), or that they give rise to a moral injury (Hampton 1992: 1671–685). Whether or not one takes a Kantian view of the matter, it is, as I say, quite plausible to think that actions that are sufficiently morally egregious interfere with a dignitary interest, that sometimes risky actions fall into this category and that such interferences are a form of harm. I have discussed this kind of harm elsewhere, and its analysis is not a straightforward matter (Perry 2003: 294–95). The harm consists of an interference with a distinct kind of dignitary interest, and at least in some cases it has a special relational character because, in those cases, it can only be caused by certain kinds of human action. None of this even begins to show, however, that risk is a harm in itself. An actor's knowledge, actual or constructive, that his action was risky can of course contribute to the moral egregiousness of his action, but this is a very different matter from saying that risk as such is harmful or that risky actions necessarily give rise to harm.

It might be objected, in response to my general claim that risk is not harm, that many people have a strong intuition that there *must* be a sense in which living with a risky situation is harmful, even if the affected person never knows about the risk and even if it never materializes. It seems to me that any such intuition is strongly and incorrectly influenced by the fact that risks of harm are, after all, risks of *harm*, and by the further fact that many risk-imposing activities are wrongful. The wrongfulness of an action does not, of course, necessarily make the action an inherently harmful one. Still, it will be helpful to follow this intuition to see where it leads. Suppose someone has buried a barrel of waste underneath my house, and that there is a 30 per cent chance that within the next ten years this barrel will corrode and leak an extremely toxic substance into the ground water. If such leakage occurs, it will pose, let us say, a 10 per cent risk of death to me, the resident of the house. Taking these two risks together, there is a 3 per cent risk that I might die as a result of having this noxious barrel stashed under my house, so surely it is obvious, it might be said, that I would prefer not to have to live with this state of affairs. Even if I do not know of the presence of the barrel, can we not say that if I *did* know, I would choose not to live with it there? Developing a suggestion along these lines, Claire Finkelstein has offered an affirmative answer to the question, 'Is the imposition of risk a harm to the person on whom it is inflicted?' (Finkelstein 2003: 965). She argues that there is a form of 'risk harm', which, although it is distinguishable from 'outcome harm' such as physical harm, is nonetheless a form of real harm. Risk harm, she argues, affects objective levels of welfare for the following reason:

> [I]t is clear from the fact that no normal, non-suicidal person would choose a higher rather than a lower chance of developing cancer that there is a perfectly commonsensical way in which being exposed to an increasing risk of developing cancer is a setback to a person's most fundamental interests.
>
> (Finkelstein 2003: 974)

While Finkelstein is not entirely clear about which concepts of welfare and fundamental interest she is employing, it is evident from her discussion that her understanding of welfare has a significant preferentialist component (Finkelstein 2003: 972), and she formulates her basic arguments in terms of what a normal person would choose or prefer. So far as *actual* preferences are concerned, however, Matthew Adler has pointed out that people can prefer or disprefer almost anything, so there would seem to be nothing in principle to prevent someone from preferring a risky to a non-risky state of affairs (Adler 2003: 1352). Since actual preferences about risk are a contingent matter, the existence of even a known risk does not, in and of itself, represent a welfare setback. Adler further points out that, in order to get around this and other difficulties, '[p]referentialists quite typically (and quite plausibly), stipulate that welfare-constitutive preferences must be *fully informed*', adding that once one has made this move it is natural to see a deep connection between the preferences of idealized agents and objective values of one kind or another; in this way, the possibly idiosyncratic character of the choices and preferences of particular persons tends to drop out of the picture (Adler 2003: 1352–354). The difficulty now, however, is that insofar as we are looking at the preferences that would be held by idealized, fully informed agents, the phenomenon of risk tends to disappear. A fully informed agent would be aware, for example, at least in a fully deterministic universe, that the 3 per cent risk that the toxic barrel will leak and cause death is simply the best estimate of relative frequency that can be made in our actual world of imperfect knowledge. Such an agent would, being possessed of complete information, realize that the relative frequency of death was in fact either 0 per cent or 100 per cent. If the relative frequency of harm were 100 per cent then it is certain that *physical* harm would occur, while if it were 0 per cent then it is certain that *no* physical harm would occur; in neither case does there seem to be conceptual room for the idea that risk constitutes a distinct form of harm in itself. The fully informed agent would no doubt be concerned to avoid the situation where the physical harm was certain to occur, but would be indifferent about avoiding the situation where such harm was certain not to occur. The 3 per cent risk that, according to Finkelstein, a normal, non-suicidal person would choose to avoid would simply not be a factor to be taken into account in the agent's decision-making process.

Finkelstein maintains that the existence of risk both affects objective levels of welfare and sets back a person's most fundamental interests. These two notions should, however, be distinguished more clearly than she distinguishes them. Suppose for a moment that I was mistaken in the preceding paragraph to downplay, on a properly developed preferentialist account of welfare, the relevance to welfare of actual preferences in general, and actual preferences about risk in particular. Even so, it requires a great deal more in the way of argument to show that a decrease in welfare which flows from the failure to satisfy a preference should be regarded as either a harm or as a setback to a fundamental interest. Suppose it is true that, if I happened to know about the noxious barrel in the example given earlier, I would prefer not to live with the risk that it poses. But there are *many* preferences that I either have now or would have under idealized conditions, and it is quite implausible to suppose that the failure to satisfy any and all of them represents not just a decrease in my welfare but a setback of a kind that is properly called harm. Perhaps I have a strong preference that the Bolshoi Ballet perform in Philadelphia next week, but it would be odd to say that I will be harmed if the Bolshoi fails to turn up. A preferentialist account of welfare does not, of course, have to accept that every preference is legitimate, but there does not seem to be anything unacceptable about this one. Finkelstein is not committed to saying that there is harm in every case in which a preference is not satisfied, and since her account of welfare is only partly preferentialist it is open to her to say that it is not in a person's fundamental interest to live with certain risks or to satisfy preferences for certain risky activities, or something along those lines. She would, however, have to provide an argument as to why this is the case. I cannot consider the matter further here, but I believe that any such argument will run into serious difficulties for the reasons discussed at length by Adler (Adler 2003: 1340–369).[22]

Harm is a relatively specific moral concept which requires that a person have suffered serious interference with one or more interests that are particularly important to human well-being, and which for that reason are appropriately designated as fundamental. Interests that can plausibly be thought to fall into this category include life, health, dignity, the physical integrity of the body, autonomy and freedom of movement, the interest in not experiencing severe pain, the interest in not experiencing severe mental or emotional distress, and certain kinds of property interest.[23] It is not a coincidence that this set of interests, or some very similar set, turns out to be of primary concern for both deontological approaches to morality and to theories of rights that are at least partly non-consequentialist in character. Nor is it a coincidence that these same interests also figure prominently among the interests that are protected by both criminal law and torts, which are the areas of law that are most plausibly thought to be non-consequentialist, or partly non-consequentialist, in their normative structure. If, relatedly, the account of welfare that is appropriate for consequentialist purposes has a preferentialist component, then neither criminal law nor tort law could be said to have the aim of preventing or rectifying reductions in welfare as such, as opposed to preventing or rectifying interferences with fundamental interests of the kind just mentioned.

I have suggested that there are certain aspects of human well-being which can be regarded as fundamental or core moral interests, and that setbacks to these interests, or at least sufficiently serious setbacks, constitute harm. In the second section of this chapter I argued that risk, by itself, is not harm, which should now be taken to mean that it does not constitute a setback to a fundamental or core interest of the kind I have just been discussing. Every harm is of course a setback to an interest, but I have not suggested, nor is it plausible to think, that all setbacks to interests are harms. Suppose I am right in thinking that the imposition of a risk does not, by itself, constitute a setback to my fundamental interests, and suppose further that I was correct in suggesting earlier that the imposition of a risk also does not set back my welfare more generally understood. Is it not the case, it might be asked, that there must still be *some* sense in which it is against my interests to live with the barrel of toxic waste under my house? I have argued elsewhere that the answer to this question is yes, because the very existence of a set of core interests necessarily gives rise to secondary interests of various kinds, and at least some of those interests will be second-order interests, meaning interests that I have in my interests (Perry 2003: 1307–309). To see that this is so, consider a type of case other than risking. Suppose you try to physically injure me but fail. To avoid unnecessary complications, assume that at no time was I aware of your attempt and that your action was not of a kind that interferes with my dignity. Your failed attempt thus does not set back any of my fundamental interests in life, bodily integrity, autonomy, and so on, and therefore cannot plausibly be thought to have caused me any harm. Even so, I wish to claim, it sets back a second-order interest I have that persons not even attempt to set back those first-order, fundamental interests. As it is with attempts, so it is with risk: I have a second-order interest that others not subject me to risk, meaning a second-order interest that they not engage in actions that are risky in the sense that was defined at the beginning of this section. And just as failed attempts do not necessarily cause me any harm, neither do actions that subject me to risks but that do not, in the event, lead to any injury.

I have argued at length in this chapter that risk is not a harm in itself, but of course it does not follow from this that risky actions cannot be wrongful in either a consequentialist or a non-consequentialist sense, nor does it follow that there cannot be a right not to be subject to a risk.[24] The question of whether or not there is ever a right not to be risked is a complex and controversial one, and I can only touch here on one or two aspects of the question.[25] First, assuming an interest theory of rights along the lines suggested by Joseph Raz and others,[26] what is the interest which a right against risk protects? I have suggested elsewhere that the relevant interest is a second-order interest of the kind that was just discussed (Perry 2003: 1307–309), but I do not think that anything of significance ultimately turns on whether or not that suggestion is correct. There is no reason to think that, on an interest theory of rights, the interest protected by a right need itself actually be set back by each and every action that violates the right. Assuming that my fundamental interests in life, dignity, bodily integrity, autonomy, and so on are sufficiently important to justify, say, a right that other persons not deliberately injure me, there is no reason in principle why those same interests cannot be sufficiently important to justify a right that others not attempt to injure me, or a right that they not subject me to certain risks. The truth of this statement is not affected by the fact that many attempts and most risky actions do not, in fact, cause any injury at all.

The most difficult question that arises for any account of a right against risking is the determination of which risks fall within the scope of the right and which do not (Nozick 1974: 74–5). This is too complex a topic to be adequately addressed here, but the discussion up to this point does at least suggest that one proposed solution to the problem will not work. David McCarthy has argued that we all have the right that other people not impose *any* risk of injury or death on us, however small in magnitude the risk might be (McCarthy 1997). He maintains (1) that many risky actions are permissible even though they infringe rights, because their benefits outweigh their costs; and (2) that while all rights-infringing risky actions in principle require compensation, one acceptable basis for meeting that requirement is a guarantee that the rights-holder will be compensated after the fact if the risk materializes and injury occurs. The account is a complex and ambitious one, but at its core is the straightforward Risk Thesis, which holds that we have a right not to be subject to any risk at all. While McCarthy says little about how the concept of risk is to be analysed, it is evident that he has in mind objective relative frequencies. He gives the example of my going for a drive in the country and thereby imposing a risk of death of one in a million on Jones, who lives near the road. McCarthy clearly assumes that there just *is* some determinate fact of the matter, which is independent of anyone's state of knowledge, as to what risk I have objectively imposed on Jones; he argues, for example, that one of the advantages of an after-the-fact compensation rule is it that it permits us to take moral account of even unknowable risks. The argument of the second section of this chapter shows, however, that there is no such determinate fact of the matter. Jones belongs, as a matter of objective fact, to indefinitely many reference classes which differ from one another with respect to how, exactly, the surrounding circumstances are characterized – was I simply 'driving', did I drive 'negligently', did I 'swerve', was I drunk, did the car have a perhaps unknown defect, how far was I from the edge of the road, how far was Jones from the edge of the road, was Jones drunk, and so on – and in each one the relative frequency of harm to Jones is different.

Can the Risk Thesis be saved by appealing to epistemic rather than to objective risk? Epistemic risk involves an estimation of objective risk that is offered from a specified epistemic perspective, and the specification of the appropriate perspective will, as we have seen, depend on moral considerations. As we have also seen, the most sensible epistemic perspective to adopt in cases of the kind being discussed is something like that of a reasonable person in the driver's situation. McCarthy, in defending the Risk Thesis, clearly assumes that such questions as when one person has imposed a risk on another and what the magnitude of the risk might be can in principle be answered in a morally neutral, fact-based way. Once it is conceded, however, that the very notion of risk imposition upon which the Risk Thesis depends involves appeal to moral considerations – that it is, in effect, itself a moral notion – what reason do we have for thinking that the line between risk impositions that violate rights and those that do not can be drawn in a way that does not also appeal to moral considerations? Perhaps the risks that violate rights are those which in some appropriate sense can be characterized as 'substantial', or those for which the mathematical expectation of harm exceeds a certain fixed level, or those for which the expected costs exceed the expected benefits. These are precisely the difficult questions which the Risk Thesis was meant to avoid, but which no plausible rights-based theory of risk imposition can, in the end, fail to address.

There is one final point to be noted about the Risk Thesis, which is that it presupposes a rather simplistic, unilaterally directed picture of risk imposition: one person acts and thereby unilaterally imposes risk on another person, who is to be regarded for these purposes as entirely passive. A parallel unilaterally directed picture of causation is implicit in the libertarian notion of a boundary-crossing defended by, among others, Robert Nozick (Nozick 1974: 54–87.) But just as the work of Ronald Coase has made clear that the notion of causing harm should be understood not unilaterally but in joint or reciprocal terms (Coase 1960) and that for that reason the libertarian notion of a boundary-crossing is seriously defective (Perry 1997),[27] so should we also reject the idea that an adequate theory of rights against risk can be based on a completely unilateral conception of risk imposition. For instance, if in the example given earlier Jones were closer to the road than he should be, then that might well affect both the appropriate moral characterization of any risk that I can be said to have imposed on him, as well as the determination of whether or not he had a right not to be subject to this risk. These are obviously complicated matters, and their further exploration must await another occasion.[28]

Notes

1 For helpful overviews of both relative frequency and subjectivist theories see Weatherford (1982), Gillies (2000).

2 The sense in which frequentist probabilities can be said to exist is affected by difficult technical and philosophical questions that I cannot take up here. These include, for example, the ontological implications of (1) including possible as opposed to actual entities within reference classes, and (2) formally defining a probability as the limit of a frequency within an infinite sequence. However these questions are to be resolved for purposes of the general relative frequency theory, I think it is reasonable to assume for present purposes and as a practical matter that most of the probabilities with which the morality of risk imposition is concerned, such as the probability that exposing someone to a toxic substance will cause him or her harm, are relative frequencies which are objective in the sense defined in the text. It is also important to bear in mind that there is another sense besides this one in which probabilities can be characterized as objective. I have in mind the probabilities which are associated with indeterministic causal processes, such as those which necessarily figure in the proper theoretical understanding of quantum mechanics. I will say a few words later about indeterminism and its possible effect on the analysis of risk that I offer in this chapter.

3 In addition to the overviews of subjectivism cited in note 1 supra, see also Howson and Urbach (1993).

4 The coherence requirement is that probability judgments should conform with the standard probability calculus.

5 Simon Blackburn, for example, while not conceding that we can have *knowledge* of objective probabilities, does nonetheless accept that there are pragmatic standards for assessing equally coherent probability judgments as better or worse. These standards 'involve a proper respect for frequencies, arising from a proper respect for induction' (Blackburn 1980: 195).

6 Matthew Adler argues, for example, that subjectivism offers the proper understanding of risk in the regulatory context (Adler 2005). Epistemic probability in either sense might be relevant to the determination of moral or criminal culpability. The nature of culpability is a topic related to, but obviously distinct from, the nature of risk imposition. If a person believes that her action creates a substantial risk of harm to someone else, then her state of mind would seem to be prima facie culpable even if the objective probability of harm is in fact low or non-existent. Perhaps it might be argued that such a person is prima facie culpable even if there is no such thing as objective probability, although the more plausible view would surely be

that, if objective probabilities do not exist, then any form of culpability which is based on the belief that one's action imposes risk on another person is a suspect and, possibly, an incoherent moral notion.

7 See Adler (2005: 1206–220) for a discussion of some problems with this characterization of epistemic risk.

8 There may in fact be an indefinitely large number of perspectives of omniscience, since there may well be an indefinitely large number of distinct ways of conceptualizing the world, but that is a complication that for present purposes we can ignore.

9 There is a large and sophisticated literature on the shortcomings of human reasoning about risk. See, for example, Sunstein (2005).

10 See, for example, King (1981), Wright (1985: 1814–816), Landes and Posner (1987: 263), Stapleton (1988), Goldberg and Zipursky (2002: 1651), Finkelstein (2003). For recent general discussions of the relevant case law in torts, see Goldberg and Zipursky (2002), Finkelstein (2003). I should note that the argument I will present that risk is not harm does not entirely rule out the possibility of legal compensation for risk imposition; it simply rules out the possibility of compensating for risk imposition on the grounds that it is a form of harm.

11 The idea that this kind of 'lost chance' is harm, and the idea that imposing an increased risk of harm is likewise harm, are morally and conceptually equivalent. For examples of cases in which such liability has been recognized, see *Falcon v. Memorial Hospital* (1990), 462 N.W. 2d 44 (S.C. Mich.), *Alberts v. Schultz* (1999), 975 P. 2d. 1279 (S.C. N.M). In England, liability for a lost or reduced chance has been explicitly denied by the House of Lords in *Hotson v. East Berkshire Area Health Authority* (1987), A.C. 750. The most sensible legal approach to lost chance would treat it as relevant to the determination of the appropriate standard of proof rather than as a form of harm in itself. See, e.g., *Beswick v. City of Philadelphia* (2001), 185 F. Supp. 2d 418 (E.D. Pa.).

12 I advanced an earlier version of this argument in Perry (1995). See also the helpful discussions in Porat and Stein (2001: 101–29) and Adler (2003: 1340–369).

13 I should note that my argument is, strictly speaking, limited to cases of risk imposition in which A increases what might be called the pure risk or chance that B will be harmed. In pure cases, B's person or physical condition is not necessarily causally altered in any way, although of course it might be. Pure cases of risk should be distinguished from cases in which B's physical state has definitely been altered by A's activity (Railton 1985: 94–5). Sometimes a physical alteration which does not affect a person's current state of health nonetheless has the effect of, say, increasing his physical vulnerability to future infection, and should therefore be treated as current harm; as Railton says, harm can be dispositional as well as manifest. The proper analysis of this kind of case is a complex matter which cannot be taken up here.

14 See Reichenbach (1933: 278), Weatherford (1982: 181), Howson and Urbach (1993: 341), Adler (2003: 1361–362).

15 For further discussion see Perry (1995: 336–37).

16 On the relationship between necessity and causation, see, e.g., Wright (1985).

17 The perspective of an omniscient impartial observer has been thought by many moral philosophers to be an important one. It is, however, interesting to observe that, when the world is viewed from this perspective, the phenomenon of risk tends to disappear. As was discussed earlier, if we had perfect information we would generally be led to conclude that either that physical harm was certain to occur or that it was certain not to occur. In neither case would we ordinarily have reason to speak of the *risk* that physical harm might occur.

18 Is the loss of an option that I do not know about an interference with autonomy? What about the loss of an option that, whether I know about it or not, I would not have exercised? These are difficult questions. John Oberdiek argues that in both cases the answer is yes (Oberdiek 2006).

19 Perry (2003: 1304–306). For an excellent general discussion of harm, see Raz (1986: 412–20).

20 It is worth pointing out that such cases show, among other things, that the appropriate epistemic perspective to adopt when morally assessing risky action is sometimes that of the person who has been put at risk rather than that of the person doing the risking. Whether a person's belief that he had been put at risk was reasonable or unreasonable might, for example, be relevant to determining whether or not he was entitled to compensation for emotional distress, economic loss, etc.

21 Adler argues that risk in the Bayesian or subjectivist sense, while harmless on its own, can be harmful as part of a 'larger psychological hybrid' such as fear, where fear is to be understood as having both propositional and affective components (Adler 2003: 1375). Adler summarizes his view as follows: 'The fear of premature death is harmful; fear essentially includes a cognitive component, namely uncertainty; and this cognitive component is realized, inter alia, by a state of probabilistic belief, i.e., by risk in the Bayesian sense' (2003: 1382). I have acknowledged in the text that fear can be a harm, and let me grant for present purposes that Adler's characterization of fear is correct. It seems uncontroversial that harms can contain states of belief as components, and since according to Adler a Bayesian risk just *is* such a state of belief, it follows trivially that risks as thus understood can be components of harm. But this is, at best, a very weak sense in which risks can be harms (more accurately, constitutive components of harms). As I argued in the first section, the interpersonal morality of risk *imposition*, in which one person subjects another to a risk of, say, physical harm, must be understood by reference to the relative frequency rather than the subjectivist sense of risk. This is not to deny, of course, that the subjectivist account of risk has its moral uses. Although I cannot discuss the point here, I do not think that the claim that the interpersonal morality of risk imposition must be understood in terms of relative frequencies is inconsistent with Adler's argument elsewhere that the decisions of regulatory agencies should be governed not by a notion of 'individualist' risk understood in the relative frequency sense, but rather by a notion of 'population risk' understood in the Bayesian sense (Adler 2005).

22 Adopting a broadly consequentialist perspective, Adler argues convincingly that risk, understood in the relative frequency sense, is not a harm in the sense of a setback to welfare, and this is so whether one construes welfare in terms of experience, preference, objective values, integration (meaning that the alleged welfare change must be sufficiently closely integrated with the subject's own life), or some combination of these possibilities.

23 These interests can only be defended as fundamental by reference to some general account of human well-being, and I am sympathetic to views that characterize well-being exclusively in terms of certain objective goods or values. See, e.g., Finnis (1980: 59–99), Parfit (1984: 499), Hurka (1993: 5), Adler (2003: 1353–354), Adler (2005: 1186–187). For present purposes, however, I am leaving open the possibility that, at least for consequentialist purposes, 'welfare' (perhaps to be distinguished from a non-consequentialist notion of 'well-being') might have a preferentialist as well as a substantive component.

24 Heidi Hurd suggests that it does follow that a right cannot be subject to a risk (Hurd 1996: 253, 267). I criticize her view in Perry (2001: 75–81).

25 For excellent discussions see Nozick (1974: 54–87), Railton (1985), McKerlie (1986), Thomson (1990), Coleman (1992), Oberdiek (2003), Oberdiek (2006).

26 See, e.g., Raz (1986: 166): '"X has a right" if and only if X can have a right and, other things being equal, an aspect of X's well-being (his interest) is a sufficient reason for holding some other person(s) to be under a duty.'
27 See also the helpful discussion of related issues in Fried (1998: Chs 2, 3).
28 I would like to thank Matthew Adler, Bill Ewald, Samantha Fisherman, Claire Finkelstein, Leo Katz, Tim Lewens, and Stephen Morse for very helpful comments and discussion.

References

Adler, M. (2003) 'Risk, death, and harm: the normative foundations of risk regulation', *Minnesota Law Review*, 87: 1293–445.
Adler, M. (2005) 'Against "individualist risk": a sympathetic critique of risk assessment', *University of Pennsylvania Law Review*, 153: 1121–50.
Blackburn, S. (1980) 'Opinions and chances', in D.H. Mellor (ed.) *Prospects for Pragmatism: essays in memory of F.P. Ramsey*, Cambridge: Cambridge University Press.
Coase, R.H. (1960) 'The problem of social cost', *Journal of Law and Economics*, 3: 1–44.
Coleman, J. L. (1992) *Risks and Wrongs*, Cambridge: Cambridge University Press.
de Finetti, B. (1974) *Theory of Probability: a critical introductory treatment*, vol. 1, London and New York: Wiley.
Finkelstein, C. (2003) 'Is risk a harm?', *University of Pennsylvania Law Review*, 151: 963–1001.
Finnis, J. (1980) *Natural Law and Natural Rights*, Oxford: Clarendon Press.
Fried, B.H. (1998) *The Progressive Assault on Laissez-Faire*, Cambridge, MA: Harvard University Press.
Gillies, D. (2000) *Philosophical Theories of Probability*, London and New York: Routledge.
Goldberg, J.C.P. and Zipursky, B. (2002) 'Unrealized torts', *University of Virginia Law Review*, 88: 1625–719.
Hampton, J. (1992) 'Correcting harms versus righting wrongs: the goal of retribution', *University of California Law Review*, 39: 1659–702.
Howson, C. and Urbach, P. (1993) *Scientific Reasoning: the Bayesian approach*, 2nd edn, Chicago: Open Court.
Hurd, H.M. (1996) 'The deontology of negligence', *Boston University Law Review*, 76: 249–72.
Hurka, T. (1993) *Perfectionism*, New York: Oxford University Press.
King, J.H. (1981) 'Causation, valuation and chance in personal injury torts involving preexisting conditions and future consequences', *Yale Law Journal*, 90: 1353–97.
Landes, W.M. and Posner, R.A. (1987) *The Economic Structure of Tort Law*, Cambridge, MA: Harvard University Press.
McCarthy, D. (1997) 'Rights, explanation, and risks', *Ethics*, 107: 205–25.
McKerlie, D. (1986) 'Rights and risk', *Canadian Journal of Philosophy*, 16: 239–51.
Nozick, R. (1974) *Anarchy, State, and Utopia*, New York: Basic Books.
Oberdiek, J. (2003) 'The moral significance of risking', unpublished thesis, University of Pennsylvania.
Oberdiek, J. (2006) 'Toward a right against risking', paper presented at the Rutgers University Institute for Law and Philosophy conference 'The Boundaries of Rights and Responsibilities', Philadelphia, May.
Parfit, D. (1984) *Reasons and Persons*, Oxford: Oxford University Press.

Perry, S. (1995) 'Risk, harm and responsibility', in D. Owen (ed.) *Philosophical Foundations of Tort Law*, Oxford: Clarendon Press.

Perry, S. (1997) 'Libertarianism, entitlement, and responsibility', *Philosophy and Public Affairs*, 26: 351–96.

Perry, S. (2001) 'Responsibility for outcomes, risk, and the law of torts', in G. Postema (ed.) *Philosophy and the Law of Torts*, Cambridge: Cambridge University Press.

Perry, S. (2003) 'Harm, history, and counterfactuals', *San Diego Law Review*, 40: 1283–313.

Porat, A., and Stein, A. (2001) *Tort Liability Under Uncertainty*, Oxford: Oxford University Press.

Railton, P. (1985) 'Locke, stock and peril: natural property rights, pollution, and risk', in M. Gibson (ed.) *To Breathe Freely: risk, consent, and air*, Totawa, NJ: Rowman and Allanheld Publishers.

Raz, J. (1986) *The Morality of Freedom*, Oxford: Clarendon Press.

Reichenbach, H. (1933) *Atom and Cosmos: the world of modern physics*, New York: Macmillan.

Savage, L.J. (1954) *The Foundation of Statistics*, New York: Wiley.

Stapleton, J. (1988) 'The gist of negligence, part 2', *Law Quarterly Review*, 104: 389–409.

Sunstein, C. (2005) *Risk and Reason: safety, law and the environment*, Cambridge: Cambridge University Press.

Thomson, J.J. (1990) *The Realm of Rights*, Cambridge, MA: Harvard, University Press

Weatherford, R. (1982) *Philosophical Foundations of Probability Theory*, London and Boston: Routledge and Kegan Paul.

Wright, R.W. (1985) 'Causation in tort law', *California Law Review*, 73: 1735–828.

INDEX

Related titles from Routledge

Ethics and the Limits of Philosophy
Bernard Williams

'Williams's discussions are much to be valued: his explicitness and argumentative ingenuity focus the issues more sharply, and at greater depth, than any comparable work I know One of the most interesting contributions of recent years, not only to ethics but to philosophy.'

John McDowell, Mind

'This is a superior book, glittering with intelligence and style.'

Thomas Nagel, Journal of Philosophy

'Remarkably lively and enjoyable... It is a very rich book, containing excellent descriptions of a variety of moral theories, and innumerable and often witty observations on topics encountered on the way.'

Philippa Foot, Times Literary Supplement

By the time of his death in 2003, Bernard Williams was one of the greatest philosophers of his generation. *Ethics and the Limits of Philosophy* is not only widely acknowledged to be his most important book, but also hailed a contemporary classic of moral philosophy.

Presenting a sustained critique of moral theory from Kant onwards, Williams reorients ethical theory towards 'truth, truthfulness and the meaning of an individual life'. He explores and reflects upon the most difficult problems in contemporary philosophy and identifies new ideas about central issues such as relativism, objectivity and the possibility of ethical knowledge.

This edition includes a new commentary on the text by A.W. Moore, St. Hugh's College, Oxford.

ISBN 10: 0-415-39984-X (hbk)
ISBN 10: 0-415-39985-8 (pbk)
ISBN 10: 0-203-94573-5 (ebk)

ISBN 13: 978-0-415-39984-5 (hbk)
ISBN 13: 978-0-415-39985-2 (pbk)
ISBN 13: 978-0-203-94573-5 (ebk)

Available at all good bookshops
For ordering and further information please visit:
www.routledge.com